# Keystone of 22 SAS

'Keystone': A central stone at the summit of an arch, locking the whole together.

# Keystone of 22 SAS

## The Life and Times of Lieutenant Colonel J M (Jock) Woodhouse MBE MC

Alan Hoe

Pen & Sword
**MILITARY**

First published in Great Britain in 2019 by
Pen & Sword Military
An imprint of
Pen & Sword Books Ltd
Yorkshire – Philadelphia

Copyright © Alan Hoe 2019

ISBN 978 1 52674 505 7

Printed and bound in the UK by TJ International Ltd,
Padstow, Cornwall.

Pen & Sword Books Limited incorporates the imprints of Atlas,
Archaeology, Aviation, Discovery, Family History, Fiction, History,
Maritime, Military, Military Classics, Politics, Select, Transport,
True Crime, Air World, Frontline Publishing, Leo Cooper, Remember
When, Seaforth Publishing, The Praetorian Press, Wharncliffe
Local History, Wharncliffe Transport, Wharncliffe True Crime
and White Owl.

For a complete list of Pen & Sword titles please contact

PEN & SWORD BOOKS LIMITED
47 Church Street, Barnsley, South Yorkshire, S70 2AS, England
E-mail: enquiries@pen-and-sword.co.uk
Website: www.pen-and-sword.co.uk

Or

PEN AND SWORD BOOKS
1950 Lawrence Rd, Havertown, PA 19083, USA
E-mail: Uspen-and-sword@casematepublishers.com
Website: www.penandswordbooks.com

*The Master of the Caravan*

But who are ye in rags and rotten shoes,
You dirty-bearded, blocking up the way?

*The Pilgrims*

We are the Pilgrims, master; we shall go
Always a little further; it may be
Beyond that last blue mountain barred with snow,
Across that angry or that glimmering sea,
White on a throne or guarded in a cave
There lives a prophet who can understand
Why men were born; but surely we are brave,
Who make the Golden Journey to Samarkand.

James Elroy Flecker, 1884–1915

# Contents

# Acknowledgements

This book has taken far too long to produce. Illness, among other things, caused many a false start in the early stages. It would not be possible to list all of the people I have interviewed over the years, sometimes for purposes other than this book, as I trawled for information from the Regimental Archives. At reunions and other more casual meetings I have informally talked to many people. My twenty-odd years in the SAS left me with many friends and acquaintances; some of them my peers and some of an earlier vintage. During those occasions it was quite likely that reminiscences would include tales of John Woodhouse. As word of the forthcoming book did the rounds I received many telephone calls and letters from veterans who had served with John. Sadly, since the time frame of writing has been so drawn out, many of those people have passed on to wherever we old soldiers go for our final rendezvous.

Of those who are no longer with us I would like to give belated thanks to the following: Colonel Sir David Stirling, Major Dare Newell, Sergeant 'Paddy' Finn, Warrant Officer Bill 'Lofty' Ross, Lieutenant Colonel Terry Hardy, General Sir Mike Wilkes, General Sir Johnny Watts, Brigadier Mike Wingate Gray, Sergeant Tim Holt, Major Tony Greville-Bell, Warrant Officer Bob Bennett, Warrant Officer Lawrence Smith, Warrant Officer Philip 'Gypsy' Smith, Warrant Officer Bob Turnbull, Lieutenant General Peter Walls, Major General Tony Deane-Drummond, Lieutenant Colonel Bob Walker-Brown, Major Mike Jones, Major General Dare Wilson and Lieutenant Colonel Joe Schofield. From all of those well-known warriors came warm recollections of John Woodhouse.

I owe very special thanks to Major General John Sutherell and Colonel the Viscount John Slim for their interest in the project and their wise counsel. Thanks also to General Sir Peter de la Billière, Vic Steyerman,

Mike Dillon, Major Stuart Perry, Major Donald Hobbs, Colonel John Waddy, Colonel Peter Walter, Colonel Ian Cartwright, Colonel Richard Lea and the many other ex-SAS soldiers who have passed on their tales (some of which I am sure are apocryphal).

Particular thanks must also go to members of John's family: his sister, Ann Sutton, for her warm recollections of early family life; his cousin, Mark Woodhouse, of the Hall and Woodhouse Brewery; and especially to John's son, Michael, for his support and kind permission to explore his father's documents and the family photograph albums. Of course there was also John Woodhouse himself, who chatted to me for many hours during the last few years of his life. I hope I have done him justice.

Unless otherwise stated, quotations are from John Woodhouse's personal memoirs and private papers or my own collection of notes and interview recordings.

All photographs displayed in the plate section are taken from and reproduced here with the kind permission of the Woodhouse family collection, apart from numbers 30, 32, 36, 38, 42 and 52, which are from my own collection.

# Foreword

## by The Rt Hon The Viscount Slim

I first met John Woodhouse in 1950 in Hong Kong when adjutant of my regiment. He was quietly impressive and factual with no embellishments. He was off to Kuala Lumpur to join the Malayan Scouts (SAS), then being formed by Mike Calvert, the wartime brigadier who had been a column commander in the Chindits, and he thought the challenge would interest me. The idea greatly appealed, but I knew I had to complete my present job; then I would volunteer. I liked John Woodhouse (or JW, as he was known).

A few months later, in North Korea just short of the Yalu River, John Sloane, our second-in-command and an outstanding soldier who had commanded a battalion in Burma, asked me if I knew anything about the Malayan Scouts (SAS). He had never heard of them but had just been ordered to leave immediately for Malaya to take command. I asked if he would let me join him. He said he would send for me once we had returned to Hong Kong. This he did, and on the train from Singapore to Kuala Lumpur, travelling to join the unit, I luckily found myself next to Dare Newell who had also volunteered. Dare was another wartime soldier who had served with the SOE (in Albania and Malaya).

It is sensible to write a biography of John Woodhouse as it contains some of the early history and formation of what was to become the post-Second World War Special Air Service Group (one regular and two territorial regiments). JW was in at the very beginning, made a major contribution throughout his service, and in the process gave up what could have been a successful normal regular military career. There is no doubt that his early meetings with Mike Calvert stimulated in him a new interest in the development of insurgency and terrorism throughout the world, and the need for a few special units to help combat these major new threats.

I applaud the author Alan Hoe, himself an excellent SAS officer with considerable service, who has spent a number of years and much devoted effort on what I believe is a successful biography. He has been most diligent in his research to get to the truth as far as possible.

In the early days of the Malayan Emergency there were more than whispers regarding the future of the Malayan Scouts (SAS) and the possibility that they would be disbanded when Malaya gained its independence. All of us with the regiment were working to ensure that this would not happen. We believed that a wider future was waiting for the SAS.

Calvert and Woodhouse worked well together and often discussed the future of the regiment. After Calvert had left there was a moment in the early years when Woodhouse, Newell and I were travelling together from Kuala Lumpur to Singapore on the night train. We sat up all night discussing the way ahead for the regiment. By the end of that journey we had decided on three main principles. Firstly, the SAS should be used only on tasks of strategic significance; secondly, we should be commanded at the very top level within the Ministry of Defence; and thirdly, we should be employed worldwide. We never deviated from this broad strategic vision, but we had to sell it!

Alan Hoe describes how JW and Dare Newell really masterminded progress. It was timely that JW, after his first years in Malaya, was returned to the UK and 21 SAS. This posting enabled him to get a real feel for what was needed and to mix with the old timers from the wartime SAS, particularly having long sessions with David Stirling and other retired senior wartime officers and men. This was also the time when, helped by Dare Newell on his own return to the UK, JW planned the Selection Course and got it up and running.

At this time there was some anti-SAS feeling here and there within the military which had to be overcome. This was achieved over time as our selection process, training and operations proved successful. We had to impress the authorities that we were worth keeping on the Army Order of Battle. The military at this time was heavily focused on the Russian threat and the British Army of the Rhine. We had to avoid being permanently locked into this commitment in Germany which a few senior commanders thought should be our only role.

The officers and men of the regiment were right behind JW and gave him every support. We were also gradually building up a rock-solid regiment of carefully selected officers and men who became very experienced internationally and served with us for many years. As commanding officer he led the regiment in an outstanding strategic and tactical manner. His time in command included the period of 'Confrontation' with Indonesia, where it was acknowledged that the SAS played a vital role in preventing the invasion of Malaysia and Brunei Darussalam. JW richly deserved an award on behalf of the regiment and this was made clear by Generals Walter Walker and George Lea. He had also accumulated unique and invaluable experience in counter-insurgency operations.

Alan Hoe aptly describes the disappointments JW unfairly suffered after command. There was no formal recognition; there appears to have been disagreement in the higher echelons that administered the Honours system. Then, on relinquishing command, JW was offered a derisory and entirely inappropriate appointment to what he described as the 'Senior Range Warden' of the British army's major training area in Germany. Sadly, but understandably, JW resigned from the army. An accomplished specialist in guerrilla and counter-terrorist warfare was lost to the army and defence. The officers and men of the regiment were more than a little miffed at his treatment.

David Stirling always publicly sang the praises of JW, as did other retired and serving senior officers. David, convinced that the reputation of the regiment was growing, recognized that this was largely due to JW.

JW had an interesting personality. He was very much a regular officer and could be a martinet, particularly concerning self-discipline or any slippage in the matter of tactics on the ground during training and operations. He ensured that the many different individual skills that all ranks had to learn were taken very seriously and our camp at Hereford resembled a university, with many different courses being undertaken by the colonel downwards. Successful selection was only the beginning of a long and thorough training period.

Underneath this somewhat stern exterior JW had a quiet sense of humour and, when off duty and in discussion, he had a sympathetic side. Every soldier mattered. He was to me a very great friend and I admired him immensely. We got on well together, enjoying some extremely good and positive debates. His favourite tipple was rum and Coca-Cola, which he could consume in large quantities and show no signs of wear and tear. He was kind enough to be godfather to my eldest son. Within the SAS we all acknowledge that he is owed a great debt of gratitude and this is given without reservation. I had the honour of speaking at his funeral and I could see genuine sadness in the very many people present. JW adored his wife and sons and always did his best for them; even in the middle of the jungle when we were together we would talk about our children (very quietly in whispers).

A small postscript: when Brigadier Michael Calvert fell on hard times both the Burma Star and SAS Associations got together to help him out. The brigadier was considered a wartime hero and we all felt that whatever had happened, he deserved care and treatment. For quite a number of years until his death we were able to do this. When I told JW, who had lost touch with the brigadier, he was very pleased.

SLIM
House of Lords, 2018

# Author's Personal Recollections

I first became aware of John Woodhouse and his awesome reputation when, in April 1960, following my SAS selection course and mentally celebrating my forthcoming 19th birthday, I arrived at the SAS base at Merebrook Barracks near Hanley Swan on the outskirts of Great Malvern in Worcestershire. Major John Woodhouse had been posted to 22 SAS Regiment as second-in-command to Lieutenant Colonel Tony Deane Drummond.

I had hitch-hiked from Worcester station and my ingress to the barracks was of a style quite alien to that which the Junior Leaders Regiment, Royal Corps of Signals and the rarefied atmosphere of the 23rd Royal Signals Training Regiment had prepared me for. The entrance to the soldier's home began at the end of a long straight walk from a minor road. An unoccupied sentry box dominated the open drop barrier that was situated at the public road junction and the entrance to the camp. A couple of ladies' 'business' phone numbers were scrawled on the interior walls of the roadside box; some ribald comments from possibly disappointed military clients were scratched alongside. One short notice proclaimed the availability and competitive rates of the Mahu Mahu Williams' taxi service (of course I didn't know who he was at that time).

Shouldering my various packs and kitbag, which contained all of the equipment that had been issued to me (and my scant civilian clothes), I walked down the straight road to the building that was obviously the guard room. From inside came the sounds of quite loud music and bursts of laughter. I knocked at the door and I was quickly confronted by a large, ginger-haired, unsteady sergeant with an unbuttoned battledress blouse. In answer to his snarled question I told him that I was joining the regiment. 'Good,' he said, 'you're on stag. Dump your kit in there, take that pick helve and get your arse out there and repel all comers.'

The next day, after stupidly wandering around the camp for much of the night, I learned about the guard commander and his little foibles of which I will say no more. My lonely arrival at the barracks was because, unlike the other men who had survived the same selection course, I had nowhere in particular to go on leave. It seemed uncomfortably senseless to hump all of my kit up to Yorkshire and back. Instead I homed in on the small signals troop which I had been told I would be joining. The then SQMS, Alan 'Big Steve' Stephenson, took me on strength and found me a billet. I spent the two weeks getting to know some of the troop and listening to tales of Malaya and Oman before joining the rest of the selection course at Abingdon for the parachute training. After completion of the parachute course (which I cannot claim to have enjoyed), I returned to the signals troop and began to understand, despite my qualifications, how little I really knew about being a 'field' signaller, but with tutors such as 'Chippy' Wood, 'Geordie' North, 'Taffy' Bartlett and 'Dad' Morgan I was soon brought up to scratch. The small troop was supporting both 'Sabre' squadrons and on occasions it was stretched.

Those two squadrons were staffed by soldiers who had passed the selection course and been deemed fit for operations. In April 1960 there were only two such squadrons in existence: 'A' and 'D' squadrons supported by a Headquarter Squadron which included the very small signals troop. During the evolution of the regiment in Malaya, John Woodhouse had commanded in turn all three of those Sabre squadrons ('B' Squadron having been disbanded when operations in Malaya ceased). Woodhouse was a tall, slightly stooped, quietly spoken, self-effacing man with a somewhat shy smile. He did not cut the sort of figure associated with his reputation. Many members of the two surviving squadrons were veterans of the Malayan Emergency and knew Woodhouse personally from those halcyon days. Obviously they held him in very high regard and they spoke of a man who was a rigid disciplinarian and as tough as any soldier in a regiment that was full of hard men, but some did say that he had a soft spot underneath his armour. Tales of his exploits, some probably apocryphal, have long since passed into SAS legend.

I later worked directly for John Woodhouse when, as the then commanding officer, he took half of 22 SAS Regiment to carry out joint exercises and training with the American Special Forces based at Fort

Bragg, North Carolina in July 1962. Being ex-Royal Corps of Signals I was obliged to serve with the signals troop of Headquarter Squadron whereas my ambitions lay elsewhere. Prior to one of the early exercises the word went out that the CO was looking for a volunteer to be his signaller. To great laughter from my peers in the troop, many of whom were veterans of the Malayan campaign, I became that volunteer. They told me that I would be on semi-starvation rations, get very little sleep and that in carrying the radio I would be in a state of permanent exhaustion as I tried to keep up with his demanding pace. They were almost right! He moved at a prodigious speed, carried very little food and insisted that I did the same. I was carrying not only the radio but also a basic medical pack. Haring after him left me little time to pause and check my navigation and on one occasion he suddenly stopped, thrust his map at me and asked where we were. I tentatively poked my finger towards the map in what I hoped would be roughly the correct position, only to have my hand batted aside. 'Your bloody finger covers a full map square. Use this.' He handed me a tiny twig. More by luck than judgement I was pretty close, but it taught me to keep a better eye on my position. I shudder now when I recall how I very cheekily retorted: 'If, sir, you would care to take either the medical pack or the radio that I'm carrying I may have a bit more energy with which to navigate.' A glower, belied by a slight shaking of his shoulders that was obviously caused by suppressed laughter, let me think that I was off the hook as he took the medical pack.

On another occasion I left my code book at base. I dreaded telling him, but as all radio traffic was encrypted I had no option. He exploded with anger and cursed me in a fashion that would have done justice to the most eloquent of Brigade of Guards drill sergeants and he threw away the mug of tea that he had made for me as I was setting up the radio. Mentally I knew that my days with the regiment were now numbered. To my great surprise, after an hour or two of sulky silence, John Woodhouse got out his brew kit, made some tea and gave it to me:

Consider that bollocking to be cancelled. I have thought this through and I believe that I, as the patrol commander, should have checked that you were fully equipped before we left base. We exercise realistically so that we may learn from our mistakes. As soon as we return to Fort Bragg the patrol commander's responsibility for those checks will be written into SOPs (Standard Operating Procedures which were a guide to soldiers' actions in the field). Remind me.

I didn't have to remind him.

We got on thereafter as well as a young trooper and a battle-hardened lieutenant colonel could in those days. I suppose that I could jokingly say that I got my baptism of fire on one of those exercises. In the hills of West Virginia we were walking through a melon field when the homesteader let loose at us with his shotgun. 'We're British soldiers,' called out my CO. 'I don't give a rat's ass what you are – get outta my God damned melon patch' came the response, followed by another blast of the shotgun.

At the end of the exercises the CO thanked me, commented that my signalling skills, my fitness and my navigation were OK and he asked me what I hoped to achieve in the SAS. I told him that my greatest desire at that moment was to shed the Royal Signals' mantle and serve in a Sabre squadron. He did not reply; he merely grunted but shortly after that I found myself in 'A' Squadron under the command of the remarkable Major Peter Walter. Walter, later lieutenant colonel, was an outstanding SAS operator. A veteran of the Malayan Scouts, he went on to be commissioned and earn three Military Crosses and become an MBE.

I served under John Woodhouse while he was the commanding officer throughout the active service campaigns in South Arabia, Radfan and Borneo, also on other more peaceful foreign fields, and witnessed, albeit sometimes by hearsay, much of the bureaucratic campaign in Whitehall. Throughout those years my respect for him continued to grow.

At various regimental reunions and due to my working with the SAS founder, Colonel Sir David Stirling, I came across John many times after our retirement from the army. The meetings were always interesting. For the last few years of his life he was confined to a nursing home in Dorchester quite close to my house in Poole. I became his 'librarian', finding appropriate books and visiting him as often as I could. I still took great care to be punctual! Over that period I slowly got to know the 'inner' Woodhouse. He was a man of infinite patience, the exception being that he could not tolerate lateness. His perception and far-sightedness into the future trends of terrorism and guerrilla warfare were acute and our chats were always stimulating. I learned from him the true extent of those formative operational years in Malaya and why the SAS had come to be such a dominant part of his life. He told me how his wartime experiences as a Battle Patrol commander had equipped him well for his future, especially with the embryonic Malayan Scouts. I also began to appreciate how much personal effort had gone into the 'Battles at Whitehall' to ensure a firm foundation for his regiment. I learned of his self-perceived inadequacies, his moments of pride and satisfaction, his aspirations, his disappointments and his concerns for the future. I also enjoyed the mild mental combat in which we engaged as he probed my own mind with questions on the future sources of terrorism with which the army may have to contend and our ability to face the reality. I saw a man who uncomplainingly accepted an unpleasant, debilitating and often painful illness with great stoicism. I visited him the day before he died when speech was very difficult and he made a great effort to thank me for the books and my visits! Imagine, John Woodhouse thanking ME!

In the weeks before his death we discussed a book about his life and in particular his time with Special Forces. He had very strong feelings on standards and strategies and though he knew that his input to the SAS had been significant he did not believe that it merited attention so many years after his retirement. After all, many other people had worked just as hard as he; why should he be different? I have to disagree with him on that statement. His efforts, at the cost of his career, were made during the infancy of the re-born regiment and without his ideas, persistence and leadership there would not have been such a solid base on which others could build and take forward. His actions and principles have stood the test of time and now – more than fifty years later – are still valid.

I have spoken to many people who served under John, soldiers of all ranks and from differing walks of life, and to a man they regarded him with enormous respect and fondness. Some of those who reached high rank in the army confess to having modelled themselves to some degree or other on John's actions and style of leadership. It was not for nothing that David Stirling, during his inauguration speech at the opening of the regiment's new home, Stirling Lines in Hereford, referred to Woodhouse:

I would like it to be recognised that I have five co-founders: Jock Lewes and Paddy Mayne of the original L Detachment; Georges Bergé who started the French SAS; Brian Franks who re-raised the SAS flag after the war and John Woodhouse who created the modern SAS during the Malayan Campaign by restoring to the Regiment its original philosophy.

John Woodhouse had an influence on my soldiering career that has not been matched by any other SAS officer and I was most keen to have his part in the establishment and continuance of the regiment properly recorded. It is a fact that during the Malayan Emergency SAS interests were represented to the War Office by a small cell in London spearheaded by Major Dare Newell, veteran of SOE, Force 136 and the Malayan Scouts (SAS). With Dare were other auspicious soldiers: Brian Franks, Hugh Gillies and Tom Burt. It was a common phrase in early SAS circles that 'If David Stirling was the Father of the SAS, then Dare Newell was the Godfather.' That small cell, which over the years expanded from RHQ SAS to become HQ of the SAS Directorate, played an enormous part in the survival of the SAS but an essential element of the team was missing until John Woodhouse reappeared on the scene.

The London HQ of the SAS was in prolonged negotiations with the War Office, but after the enforced retirement of Lieutenant Colonel Mike Calvert there seemed to be no voice of modern direct SAS soldiering experience to support, advise and brief the HQ. Until John Woodhouse's leadership, experience and far-sightedness were recognized (first by Calvert), there was no effective bridge between London and Malaya. Newell's own words were that the SAS needed a 'keystone'. John Woodhouse and I had long discussions about the book, but he eventually agreed subject to a few provisos. Indeed, he had actually started to write his own story (though not intended for publication), and I have used some of his manuscript in this work. What persuaded him, I asked, to continue his career with 22 SAS? Had he thought that it would lead him to senior rank? He hooted with laughter and told me to look again at the job he was offered when he left the SAS.

Throughout this book I have tried to mirror John's thoughts and feelings. By delving into his detailed letters, diaries and notes I believe I can show that his contribution to the development of the SAS was more than significant, it was unique. There are few books about the post-war SAS that do not mention John Woodhouse in highly complimentary terms.

Shortly before his death he reminded me of the occasion when he decided to host a party at one of the Hall & Woodhouse inns. His health was, by then, in the decline. He asked me to compile a list of all those officers who were in or had been in the regiment and had served in Malaya along with those who had been commissioned from the ranks. I was working in Colombia at the time and could not attend the party, but I will not forget the tears in his eyes when I handed him the list of those officers who had accepted the invitation; it was considerably longer than he had anticipated. He was amazed at the response and pleased to note that many of those who attended were ex-rankers and some had served in 'D' Squadron. At that party he proudly sported his 'D' Squadron tie. Before his death he left instructions that he was to be buried wearing that same tie.

# Prologue

Four sweat-soaked British soldiers weaved their way along a faint jungle track. They carried only small packs which were not heavy. Their faces were expressionless, but their attitude was alert as they moved slowly, virtually silently and purposefully. They were still fresh. The troop had split into four patrols and gone their separate ways only half an hour previously. They were keen to cover as much of the trail as they could before the daily rains came and washed away any possible enemy tracks. Occasionally the leading scout would halt the patrol by holding up his arm and showing his open palm, then he would listen for a moment or two. Each patrol member turned outward in alternate directions and the tail-end Charlie turned all the way round to watch the rear. Satisfied that all was well, the scout would beckon them forward to resume the patrol.

In the soft, diffused light of the jungle their dark green uniforms, which bore no badges of rank, merged well into the tangle of shrubs and creepers that grew in profusion from the damp jungle floor in their search for the sunlight. Above soared the straight bare trunks of giant trees occasionally creaking as they supported the load of a thick roof of luxuriant foliage and the host of jungle animals that made it their home. The occasional hoots of the gibbons seemed to mock the slow progress of the soldiers.

The men were soldiers of the Special Air Service Regiment (SAS). For five weeks they had been on similar patrols but had not even caught a glimpse of their elusive enemy. They knew that it was always like this: many weeks of searching for each few seconds of sudden action. This was just another day, with fifty more quite like it ahead of them before they could see a road again, meet other soldiers or drink a beer and lie in the sun. So it always was until something happened, something that made it different from other days. After a while in the jungle, senses that were barely used in normal barrack life became honed to an almost animal sharpness; the capabilities of sight, smell, hearing and pure instinct intensified with the passage of each day. Today the silence was broken only by the occasional soft scrape of leaf and twig against green canvas boot.

Suddenly the lead scout froze; so quick was his action that he stood momentarily immobile with one leg still in the air caught in the act of moving forward. He had heard a noise, indefinable but out of place within the natural sounds of the jungle; a noise so faint that he was only just conscious of it. His awareness heightened as he slowly lowered his foot and made a 'thumbs down' (enemy) hand signal to the men behind; he swung his arm to the left indicating the side of the track to which they should move. As one they silently melted into the vegetation and crouched down with weapons at the ready. Seconds later the whole patrol could hear the sounds, unmistakeably a file of men moving directly towards them. They gazed intently into the trees, hearing the continual soft brushing of leaves broken now and then by the slight crack of a crushed twig and a quiet murmuring of voices. Then the first source of the sound came into view. A small Chinese in yellowish khaki uniform. He was wearing a cotton cap with a red star above its peak. A rifle was slung over his shoulder and he was now staring directly at the SAS patrol in the fringe of the scrub.

In that split second of recognition he stopped and reached for his rifle. Too late. The lead scout raised his own rifle and fired even as the butt touched his shoulder. From behind the SAS scout the tall patrol commander moved onto the track and fired two shots down the track in the direction of the enemy. The terrorist, a look of surprise frozen on his face, folded up untidily and fell dead on the track. A lot happened in the next few seconds: the patrol leaped into new positions where they had an all-round view and could also gain some protection from tree trunks. The terrorist platoon, for that is what it was, had fallen to the ground at the first shot. Now a stream of orders and exhortations in Chinese drove them forward and they quickly opened a ragged but heavy barrage of fire into the area occupied by the British.

The British patrol leader (Sergeant Bill 'Lofty' Ross) had to think fast. There was no time to worry about the heavy odds they faced. He could withdraw fast with little or no risk. If he did that the enemy would recover the rifle and ammunition from the body of their fallen comrade and also any useful documents he may be carrying. Such an action was not in the nature of Bill Ross. He was not going to let that happen! The enemy were obviously keen to recover the body as the heavy fire continued. Ross turned to the trooper on his right: 'Go back to where we left Stainforth's patrol. Lead him back here and come in behind them. Tell him to attack from there.' He pointed towards the enemy's right and rear. 'You stay with that patrol, we'll hang on here. You got that?'

'Yes, Sarge. I've got it.' The trooper slipped away, lost to sight and sound within 15 yards. Every trooper in the SAS carried a map and compass and knew how to use them. Without that skill a man could be irrevocably lost in a few minutes. In deep jungle he might then be lucky to avoid a lingering death from starvation or an enemy bullet.

Now it was the enemy commander's turn to think. He faced a dilemma. By using his superior numbers he could probably overwhelm the SAS patrol, but with the British showing no sign of panic this might be expensive in men. Dead terrorists were not easily replaceable, even by raw recruits. The creeping encirclement now in progress was slow and difficult to control. He knew the SAS patrols were usually small but they seemed to be everywhere. Perhaps even now another one, attracted by the sounds of the fire-fight, was making haste to join the battle. His men did not have great amounts of ammunition but immediate withdrawal would be an admission of defeat by a smaller enemy and result in a loss of face that could not be entertained. He decided to stay longer, slowly closing his men around the patrol.

The members of the SAS patrol knew that they were in a tight corner but they were in it as a corporate unit, not as three individuals. They were very conscious that they were SAS. It had not been easy to join this regiment, nor had it been a piece of cake to stay in it. They were proud too of their squadron. 'D' Squadron was a hard squadron; nothing but the best ever satisfied John Woodhouse, the squadron commander. He would expect them to exploit this contact with the enemy to the full. It was those things allied to thorough training that were going to see them through now.

The minutes lengthened. A further two advancing terrorists were shot and fell back wounded. The patrol listened, watchful and determined, to the enemy about them. The Chinese terrorists showed a marked reluctance to move any closer in spite of a further blast of orders from their commander. Instead they contented themselves by firing off a few more shots.

A new burst of firing was heard some distance from the enemy's right flank, followed by more urgently shouted orders in Chinese. Corporal George Stainforth's patrol had arrived. The terrorists speedily disappeared in several directions. Unluckily Stainforth had met an enemy section far off to one flank. Their shots had given warning of his approach to the rest of the enemy.

Immediately the SAS patrols went into pursuit. Dark bloodstains on the leaves showed where the enemy had begun his retreat. However, with their usual practised skill in evasion, the tracks soon broke into two, then four or five in a confusing criss-crossing pattern that was very difficult to follow. The action was over but the hunt went on. The skies darkened and the daily rain came suddenly to add to the difficulties of tracking. Later Bill Ross was to be awarded the Military Medal for his actions that day.

It was December 1956. Throughout Malaya deep in the jungle a few hundred soldiers of the SAS regiment were scattered in similar patrols. The deep jungle was home to the aborigine tribes, the refuge of the Communist terrorists and the hunting ground of the SAS.

In 1950 there had been sporadic forays by government forces into the jungle fringes, but the deep jungle had remained under Communist control with at least 20,000 aborigines doing their master's bidding.

Eight years later all but a few score of aborigines had deserted the Communists. In vast areas where Communist bands of 100 men and more had once roamed, there was now not a single large unit left. Only in the north a few broken remnants remained, living a hand-to-mouth existence.

Victory in Malaya was won by many people: by civilians manning the rubber plantations and other businesses; civilian administrators who carried on in the face of extreme intimidation (3,000 of them were murdered); by the police who won the confidence of a terrorized people; and by soldiers of many races and regiments who hunted down the enemy. The emergency in Malaya encompassed and depended upon those involved in the normal running of government remaining stable and resolute. Some 2,000 men of the army, police and home guards lost their lives. One of many leaders stands supreme Field Marshal Sir Gerald Templar. 'He gave us our morale back,' said one civilian. He spoke not only for his fellow planters, but for everyone in Malaya.

Victory in the deep jungle was, however, the onerous task given to the Special Air Service regiment. It was not accomplished without mishap. Communist terrorism posed new problems for the British army and none harder than in the interior jungles of Malaya. New ideas and new methods were necessary.

The Special Air Service regiment conceived, formed and led by David Stirling in 1941 to raid behind the German Afrika Korps lines in North Africa was disbanded after the war ended in 1945. In 1947 a Territorial Army SAS regiment was raised and in 1950 the regular army formed a Special Service unit in Malaya. This is the story of how that unit, after a stormy and unpromising beginning, grew over the next decade and a half into a force unique in its character, secretive in its operations and unequalled in cost-effectiveness. It is a story seen through the eyes of Lieutenant Colonel John Woodhouse who, after beginning his army career shortly after the start of the Second World War, was almost continually involved in the development of the Special Air Service from 1950 until 1965. A story that moves from Malaya into Borneo, Arabia and Africa.

In 1963 ex-members of the SAS, on their own initiative and in spite of attempts to stop them, went into the Yemen to provide medical assistance to the victims of Egyptian bombing and to support the resistance of the loyal tribes to the Egyptian occupation. In 1965 Mr John Woodhouse also went to the Yemen to step up the scale of operations. Those who were behind this unparalleled action saw it as an essential step to assist the British army, including SAS units, then heavily engaged around Aden. At that time it was the only occasion that members or ex-members of the British SAS had cohesively engaged themselves as mercenaries and the primary motive was the simple one of patriotism.

This book aims to show how vital the experience, energy and wisdom of John Woodhouse were in the rebirth and development of the SAS of which he was so very proud. The work covers in some detail John Woodhouse's time in Malaya because this was the period during which his views on the values and future of the SAS were formulated and solidified as he experimented with equipment, tactics, selection, training and techniques. Contributing to his ideas and philosophies were arguments and discussions with many of the remarkable officers and men he met. Shared experiences and long debates created an eclectic circuit of ideas; nothing was too minor to be discarded without serious debate. Some of these characters were to be with him for much of his active service career and beyond.

*Chapter 1*

# The Early Years

John Michael 'Jock' Woodhouse was born at 40 Horton Court, Kensington, London on 29 September 1922. The name 'Jock' was unofficial; it was both a family custom and a way of distinguishing him from another John Woodhouse (a cousin). Although he used 'Jock' in signing off his wartime letters to his father, it was not used outside the family until after he retired from the army. At that time his mother, Stella, was living in Kensington with her aunt because her husband, Charles Hall Woodhouse, then a captain in the Dorset Regiment, was serving in Khartoum.

John's father was born in 1891 and was educated at Malvern College and Magdalene College, Cambridge. He was commissioned into the Dorset Regiment in 1913 at a time when it was serving in Ireland. In August 1914 the Dorsets went to France where Charles Woodhouse commanded the machine-gun platoon. He was awarded the newly-instituted Military Cross for his bravery and leadership during the Battle of Mons. Shortly after that he was taken prisoner and during the four years of his captivity he developed a lifelong hatred and distrust of the German nation.

In 1919 he took part in the abortive operations in North Russia. Later he was to command the 2nd Battalion of the Dorset Regiment in Palestine (1936–37) where he was appointed an OBE. During the Second World War he commanded the 211th Infantry Brigade in Plymouth (1940–41) before he was medically downgraded after a hernia operation. He retired from the army in 1944 and went to help his uncle to run the family brewery at Ansty in Dorset. An austere and reserved man (though with a good sense of humour), Charles Woodhouse was an excellent botanist, public-spirited and generous. He was a man of high morals and greatly respected by the local community. He later became colonel of the Dorset Regiment, a deputy lord lieutenant of Dorset, president of the County Museum, a Justice of the Peace and he was chairman of the Hall and Woodhouse family brewery from 1952 until his death in 1962. His interest in botany is preserved even today in the well-planned and healthy wooded areas of the Higher Melcombe estate.

Stella Woodhouse was born in South Africa in 1897, the only daughter of Lieutenant Colonel C.E. Fairlie of the Natal Mounted Police. She came to England in 1908 and during the Great War she was a member of the First Aid Nursing Yeomanry (FANY) working as a driver at the War Office. Her marriage to Charles Woodhouse was happy at first but their affection slowly withered over the years until in the 1930s it died, although they stayed together as good friends.

His father and mother's service to the military and the fact that many of Charles Woodhouse's friends and relatives still served in the army and visited the family frequently stirred an early desire in young John Woodhouse to also serve. As a child he saw little of his father, although he knew that this did not signify a lack of affection for either him or his sister, Ann, who was three years his junior. It was simply not the custom of his age and class to outwardly show feelings. Though John recognized the Military Cross and the OBE that his father had earned, he could not persuade him to talk about the Great War except to condemn the Germans in general. John's love and respect for his father never wavered throughout both of their lives. Charles Woodhouse made it clear that he expected his son to go to Cambridge University and John set his sights on a career in the Diplomatic Corps. His mother, Stella, made the majority of school visits in her 1930 Morris Oxford car; if Charles did accompany her on some special occasions it was because she had pressed him to do so. John had a fascination for history, which never left him, and most of the school visits, when afternoon outings were allowed, were spent touring round old churches and castles. He was not a pushy child and being small for his age he did not excel at sports, though his passion for cricket was enough for him to captain the Second XI at preparatory school in Seaford (batting at number eleven).

In 1936 he passed the common entrance exam and was enrolled at Malvern College where illness was to mar his progress for two consecutive Lent terms; on one occasion he was seriously ill with pneumonia following a bout of measles. At Malvern he discovered that he was a competent cross-country runner and he also began to further develop his strong interest in military matters which prompted him to become an unfashionably enthusiastic member of the Officers' Training Corps (OTC), reaching the rank of sergeant. Holidays from Malvern were spent in the married quarters high on the cliffs of Dover from which base he was able to pursue his cricket interest by watching as many as possible of the Kent matches. For the last year of his time at Malvern (1939), the school was moved to Blenheim Palace which was most exciting for a boy with a passion for history. Lessons were held in the forecourt, but the boys slept in the state rooms where the old tapestries and paintings were still on the walls. An avid reader since the age of 9, John became a great fan of the novels of G.A. Henty with their mixture of military and historical settings. He was intensely patriotic and proud of the British Empire but thought very little of what he perceived as weak British government. He joined the 'Right Book Club' which published works sympathetic to the Fascist countries of Germany and Italy. With the naivety of youth he greatly admired what he saw as the exhilarating national enthusiasm of the Nazi state, contrasting that with the lack of martial spirit among his own peers. He was very careful to keep those opinions to himself, knowing how controversial they were at that time.

The outbreak of war and the presence in the grounds of Blenheim of part of a Canadian Division all helped to create a tense and exciting atmosphere. During this period Charles Woodhouse bought Higher Melcombe. That house, which is still in the family, then became home during holidays. It was there in August 1940 that John took up his first military duties. At the age of 17 he was given command of the twelve-man Melcombe Section of the Local Defence Volunteers (LDV), later to be renamed the Home Guard. Some of the section had Great War experience but there was no rancour as in those days it was normal for the 'Squire's son' to be given early responsibilities. There were no clearly defined duties and a sentry was mounted every night to await the 'invasion'. John slept in his own room above the front door of the house, while the rest of the section stayed in a wheeled, wooden shepherd's hut. Occasionally a German bomber would fly overhead on a mission unknown.

On 7 September 1940, John Woodhouse learned his first military lesson. He was not on duty but the rattle of gravel against his window woke him and he heard the voice of one of his men urging him to 'Wake up – the invasion is on!' He became highly excited and totally disorganized as he scrabbled around for his denim uniform and the Canadian Ross rifle with its twenty rounds of ammunition, dropping things on the floor as he fumbled around. His father was home that night and came into the bedroom. 'Calm down! Calm down and just think of what you need.' This quelled the lad's excitement and he absorbed the lesson – 'Think before you act' – it was rarely to be forgotten. The platoon assembly-point was at the Folly Inn some 2 miles away and John took his section to report to the platoon commander, Farmer Gould, whose son was to be killed later in the RAF flying over Germany. The night was still and cold but it was no surprise to learn that it was a false alarm. John was deeply disappointed.

In December 1940 he failed the entrance exam to Cambridge University and this left him free to go to the Dorchester recruiting office where, on 13 March 1941, he enlisted into the Dorset Regiment: 5733825 Private Woodhouse, aged 18, was going to war. In fact he had advanced his age to 19 for the records in order that he could enlist as a regular soldier.

*Chapter 2*

# The Second World War: Britain and North Africa

The 'Squire's son' took the culture shock of 1940s' barrack life in his stride. He was kitted out at the impressive Victorian keep (now the Dorset Regiment museum) in Dorchester and marched to the nearby hutted camp at Poundbury. He joined his platoon which had already benefited from several weeks training but he soon caught up, even though his comrades were all at least two years older than him. Some of the senior NCOs had served in the Dorset Regiment with either his father or his cousin L.J. Woodhouse. They remained strict, fair and impartial to all. Officers were visible but only as observers of training. The recruits were kept on the go from 7.00 am to 5.00 pm and the evenings were occupied in cleaning boots and equipment, cookhouse fatigues or guard duties. Life was spartan. Thirty men slept in one room on wooden boards laid on low trestles. On this there would be a straw–filled mattress and four blankets that could be augmented by the greatcoat on cold nights. There were no sheets. They slept in their shirts and underwear. Once a week they would be marched to the showers for a lukewarm clean-up. The lavatories were equipped with cut sheets of newspaper. The food was basic but good and the recruits stayed very healthy. On 14 shillings a week there was no high life in Dorchester. Most of their pay went on tea and food, but there was usually enough for one night out in the town where beer was one shilling per pint and the cheapest seats in the cinema were three pence.

John was lucky in that his father's car was parked in a local garage and he was able to use it to drive to Higher Melcombe whenever he could wangle a weekend pass. Driving licence: what's that?! In July, with basic training behind him, he volunteered for the Commandos. He was curtly told by his CO, Lieutenant Colonel G.P. Thwaites, who knew both John and his father: 'The Commandos are not for you. They are looking for coal heavers and the like, you are too young. You must listen to my advice. Your father is a fine soldier but he has one failing. He never listens to advice.' Though this was said in a kindly enough way, any criticism of his father was certain to annoy the young Woodhouse and he was forced into a surly acceptance that his application would not be processed. He had an enormous respect and love for his father both as a man and a soldier and he never feared asking for advice from him right up until his death.

John did well in training; he had initiative and intelligence and a number of his kinfolk had served in the Dorset Regiment so it was not a surprise that he should be marked out as a potential officer. He was promoted to lance corporal and went before the Officer Selection Board in September 1941. After two attempts he passed the board. In those days selection seemed to him to be based on a verbal interview that centred on education, social status, sporting interests and so on; military ambitions or patriotic reasons for volunteering to serve were simply not mentioned. Woodhouse thought, perhaps with some justification, that he was being vetted more for his potential behaviour in the officers' mess than on the battlefield.

In January 1942 he was posted to Barmouth to join 164 Officer Cadet Training Unit (OCTU). Those cadets in his intake were a mixed bag. Some, like him, had come from the ranks of a variety of regiments and corps and others had arrived directly from university. Reflecting on his early days in the army, John later said:

> I enjoyed my life in the ranks and learned an important lesson. The officers that we liked and respected were those who took an interest in us as individuals, were concerned with our welfare and were good instructors. We disliked intensely those who were aloof. Perhaps though, my time at that level which had not required any great display of initiative had, to my mind at least, blunted my confidence and I dreaded being appointed cadet platoon leader. Cadet appointments changed weekly. I usually escaped that responsibility though I was a cadet section leader. I looked and indeed was young for my age but I passed. In fact most of us did. My report said '… immature but has guts…'

An excerpt from John's memoirs gives a flavour of the times:

On 6th June 1942 I was commissioned as a Second Lieutenant in the South Wales Borderers. My father met me at the London railway station. He was not pleased that I was in the SWB and I was greatly impressed that within a day I was re-badged as a Dorset Regiment officer. After one week of leave at Higher Melcombe, I reported for duty with 5th Battalion, Dorset Regiment then stationed at Walmer in Kent. I was the OC of 15 Platoon of C Company. The Battalion, along with the 4th Dorsets, was a pre-war TA Battalion, not yet having been in action. C Company officers, under Major Harry Jesty had a company Officers' Mess in a seafront house. My platoon defended Walmer Castle; the shingle beach was heavily wired and had oil pipelines for flame defences; on very clear days the German-occupied French coast could be seen.

In August 1942, shortly before the Dieppe raid, the 43rd Wessex Division, of which we formed a part, was put on a higher state of alert. Only officers were to be informed of this. I was foolish enough to pass this on to my platoon sergeant – in confidence of course! The news flashed around the Sergeant's Mess and 'young Woodhouse' was quickly fingered as the source. I was then severely reprimanded and learned my lesson for the rest of my service. Further trouble came along during a night exercise when the lanyard attached to my pistol broke in a wood. The loss of a weapon was a Court Martial offence. After a very anxious few days the Quartermaster 'fixed' the loss in ways known only to himself and I was quietly rearmed.

The days passed quickly but not quickly enough for young Woodhouse who, with the impatience of youth, was keen to get into the fray. When he heard that many junior officers were being sent from the 43rd Division to replace battle casualties in the 78th Division (then fighting in Tunisia), he and four others from the 5th Dorsets volunteered for overseas service. After Christmas at home Woodhouse found himself, on 6 January, embarking on the liner *Empress of India* for an uneventful journey to Algiers. After docking on 20 January it was not until 19 February that he was despatched to join the 1st Battalion, East Surreys which was holding several miles of the battlefront to the south of Medjez el Bab. He was designated platoon commander of 10 Platoon of B Company under the command of Major Toby Taylor. The company was dug in among the low hills bordering the Goubellat Plain with the German army approximately 2 miles to their front. Looking younger than his 20 years (he could easily have passed for 17), he stood out from the men in his platoon who by now considered themselves veteran soldiers after two months of action. He was nervous and conscious of his inexperience and he made the mistake of suggesting to his platoon sergeant that the men might benefit from some local training; not unnaturally this idea was greeted with some derision. Later that evening he heard, as he was no doubt meant to, remarks such as 'Fucking school kids being sent to us now!' Initially those comments disturbed him and he found it difficult to face up to the NCOs when he did his twice-daily rounds of the platoon position. He forced himself to adopt an unconcerned air and he constantly questioned his men about their lives and hopes. The younger soldiers responded well but some of the older ones answered in monosyllabic terms. This only served to make him more determined to put on a good show.

About 1,000 yards to the front of B Company's position was a small rocky pimple about 150ft high. On this hill, nick-named Fort McGregor, the whole of D Company was dug in and encircled by barbed-wire defences. The feature was too far away for any fire support from B Company to be effective and it was completely surrounded by German paratroopers. Just before dawn, Woodhouse began to get a first-class view of the German army in action. The assault began with heavy small-arms fire and explosions as the Germans began their advance. The tracer rounds criss-crossing the position added an almost theatrical quality to the impotent observers. Time and time again the Germans were beaten back by the spirited defence. Both sides were taking very heavy casualties. Woodhouse had viewed the scene with some trepidation and he could only imagine what was happening to the soldiers on either side of the conflict. Constantly running through his mind was the thought that if he were to die then he must do so bravely.

Eventually the Germans succeeded in taking the hill and B Company had a grandstand view of the apparent destruction of their comrades. Several sorties were made by vehicle to try to rescue survivors and for the rest of the day Fort McGregor was mercilessly subjected to barrages by the 7.2in guns and 25-pounders of the British artillery battery deployed alongside B Company and, despite the range, both light and heavy machine guns joined the fray. As night and darkness fell the barrages ceased and an uncanny silence reigned. The observers could see no lights on the hill and Woodhouse was ordered to take a patrol of six men and find out if the Germans were still on the position.

Inwardly quaking, the young Woodhouse set out on his first patrol into probably occupied enemy territory. He took the patrol formation straight from the textbook: one soldier in front to act as 'leading scout', followed by himself and the five remaining men in file. With soldiers as good as those of the German army it was reckoned that the only way to find out if they were still there was to proceed to the objective until either being challenged or shot at. As the patrol neared the hill in the eerie silence, the scout slowed to a nervous halt and Woodhouse decided that it was up to him to display some leadership. Heart in mouth, cocked pistol in hand, with finger on the trigger, he moved forward alone, mentally rehearsing one of the German phrases he had memorized: 'Don't shoot.' He started instinctively as he saw a German soldier not 5 yards in front of him. His finger tightened nervously and he fired before he aimed the weapon. A second later and he realized that the soldier was dead and had been propped against a rock to look like a sentry. He felt an instant change in himself and his nervousness disappeared. The shot had been heard by the patrol and later the platoon sergeant told him that they thought he had been killed. Moving forward again he realized that the Germans had abandoned the position and he fired a green flare from his Verey pistol to inform the battalion. Aware of the danger of booby traps, the patrol found a relatively secure spot to await daylight.

Dawn arrived to light up one of the bloodiest scenes that Woodhouse was ever to witness. Now reinforced by the rest of his platoon he began to explore the hill. About forty German paratroopers' corpses were mixed up with the casualties of D Company. One German body still had a cigar clamped between its teeth. Two German officers laid out behind a trench had been booby-trapped. Fortunately an alert soldier spotted this and the explosive devices were dismantled. British and German corpses, some whole and some blown apart, lay everywhere and Woodhouse, who having been attached to D Company during training in Scotland, recognized many of the faces. Fighting back the nausea, he forced himself not to let his gaze linger too long on the already swelling bodies and the thickening swarms of flies and rats that seemed to come from nowhere. He breathed through his mouth to try to lessen the foul stench of death. Though sickened by the carnage, he kept his feelings under control as he organized defensive positions while continuing the search.

A dugout produced three German soldiers who were eager to surrender. They were stood with their backs against the wall of a disused quarry and nervously listened to the soldiers who were shouting out 'Kill the bastards!' The Germans did not know it but they were quite safe while in the hands of Woodhouse. Only three wounded Surreys had survived the barrage and they were in a state of shock when they were located. Inspired by the Nazi propaganda, the German soldiers had shown fanatical courage during an assault that cost them at least as many lives as the defenders who had fought to the end. They had been left with far too few soldiers to successfully defend Fort McGregor and Woodhouse wondered at the lunacy of such a savage battle that had achieved absolutely nothing except the deaths of well over 100 men.

The personal effect on the young Woodhouse was outwardly minimal as he contained his revulsion, but his ability to cope with the early exposure to front-line danger affected his platoon differently. They recognized that their commander was a courageous man and he was now fully accepted as their leader. There was no more cold-shouldering as he did his nightly rounds of the defences and he was welcomed into the conversations of his men. He took quiet satisfaction from the change of attitude from 'Fucking school kid' to respected young officer. He enjoyed his chats and so did his men – there was no pomposity in their young subaltern – he was genuinely interested in them and a mutual respect was quickly formed. He was, therefore, bitterly disappointed when he was sent on an anti-tank gun course and put in charge of the six 6-pounder guns. The guns were spread over a 3-mile line and he had to use a motor cycle to visit his teams. Life was relatively comfortable in his new role and he messed with the other officers at the battalion HQ where he dined at a table with proper plates replacing the mess tin and slit trenches he was used to. Nonetheless he yearned to be back with his old platoon. On 12 March he received his first letter from home since he had departed in December. March was the end of the rainy season and as the thunderstorms gradually ceased the soldiers got the news that the 78th Division was going to spearhead a new offensive.

In the early hours of 7 April 1943 the anti-tank platoon was ready to move as the 450 guns of the division commenced a barrage on the German positions in the hills north of Medjez. The East Surreys led the advance against the crack Austrian mountain troops and they were soon taking casualties. Woodhouse's old friend, Dick Watkins, who had taken over command of 10 Platoon, was killed soon after the advance started. Later that day, while chatting to his CO, Lieutenant Colonel Bill Wilberforce, Woodhouse saw his chance. There was clearly no role for the anti-tank platoon and he asked Wilberforce if he could resume command of 10 Platoon. Permission was granted and he raced through the mud to join his old comrades. They had been somewhat shocked at their casualties and Woodhouse was warmly welcomed back. Exuding (if not feeling) confidence and showing his great delight at being reunited, he soon had morale back to its former high level.

The days of 8, 9 and 10 April saw the advance, against light opposition, continuing northwards. Actions were brief and one-sided and about fifty German prisoners were taken. During a lull in operations Woodhouse wrote home. In a letter dated 11 April, he remarked on the quality of the food: 'The rations are excellent. Breakfast: sausages, biscuits, margarine and jam. Lunch: salmon, biscuits and tea. Dinner: steak and kidney pudding, treacle duff and tea. Daily chocolate ration and a rum issue at dawn.' The respite from battle, however, was to be brief.

On the night of 13/14 April the battalion began an attack on a formidable German position on Djebel Mahdouma which rose steeply to about 1,250ft above the valley that formed the attack start line. As the troops massed on the line they were shelled vigorously by the German artillery, causing confusion among the mules that were being used to bring up supplies. The British artillery began a creeping barrage in steps of 100 yards. With bayonets fixed, the troops kept as close to their own falling shells as possible. Woodhouse was leading his platoon when one shell dropped short and he was thrown to the ground and concussed. Temporarily deafened, staggering and with his head ringing, he somehow managed to stay ahead of his platoon as they neared the German positions. Though it was not in the textbook, he ordered his 2in mortar team to fire smoke at the enemy. This unusual tactic had the effect of distracting the Germans and as the battalion closed in, the enemy either fled or surrendered.

By dawn the hill was secured and the troops dug in for the anticipated counter-attack. A few men were wounded by the constant shelling and inaccurate small-arms fire and Woodhouse detected the soldiers' nervousness. He countered this by having them count and recount ammunition, digging deeper and fixing bayonets. The whole time he walked between sections of soldiers, showing complete unconcern at the odd shells and bullets that came his way. Everyone calmed down and prepared for the coming battle. Much to their surprise, the counter-attack never came. Battle casualties had reduced 10 Platoon from twenty-eight men to fourteen but morale was reasonably high, in part due to the fact that they drew rations for twenty-two men which were also augmented by Norwegian sardines captured from the Germans. As will be seen later in the book, sardines became a favourite food of Woodhouse. The battalion took advantage of a few days' rest to recover from the rigours of battle, but on 20 April they were withdrawn to an assembly area in preparation for a major attack on the key position of Longstop Hill (Djebel el Ahmera) which lay to the north-east of Medjez.

On 22 April 1943, Woodhouse, who had been suffering weakness, dizziness and fainting spells, was sent by ambulance to the field hospital where sandfly fever was diagnosed and quickly cured, in his opinion by twelve hours' sleep in a comfortable bed. He was ordered by the doctor to go by train to Algiers for further treatment. Seeing that argument was useless, Woodhouse accepted the lift to the railway station. As soon as his escort had driven off he turned about face and hitchhiked back to the front line. When he failed to appear at the terminus he was posted as Absent Without Leave which could be a court-martial offence. By the time the paperwork was complete (25 April), he was back with the 1st East Surreys where he found to his chagrin that he had missed the bloody opening assault on Longstop Hill during which his batman, Private Rodwell, had been killed after stepping on a mine. Rodwell's death saddened him; he had liked the young soldier who always had a ready smile and a willing attitude.

On 5 May the battalion was resting in the flat fields north of the main road between Medjez and Tunis. They knew that the final assault to take Tunis was imminent and took the time to write their letters home. Woodhouse, for the first time, was convinced that he would be killed in the coming battle. His letter to his father ended: 'Thinking always of England and at last realise what a great country it is.'

As it turned out the men of the battalion were virtually spectators at the final offensive. As they advanced across the open ground in extended line, squadrons of British bombers roared overhead and regiments of tanks thundered towards a collapsing resistance. On 8 May the army marched into Tunis to loud cheers from the citizens. Proud and excited by their victory, the troops of the East Surreys moved through Tunis to La Goulette where they were to stay for three days living in seaside villas. While his platoon was moving to a Tunis suburb Woodhouse accepted the surrender of the German C-in-C's (von Arnim) driver. He was a young officer with six years' service and an Iron Cross awarded for taking six English prisoners in France in 1940.

Recalling those years in a post-war conversation, Woodhouse said:

We did not hate the German soldiers. Certainly in North Africa we experienced what I believe has been described as the 'Clean War'. I cannot recall any stories of atrocities. We knew and understood the lives of our opponents which in many cases were the mirror images of our own. We had heard from soldiers that had been released that they had been treated well. In the aftermath of the North Africa campaign I was briefly involved in civil affairs in Tunis as I spoke enough French to cope with everyday situations. The Germans had handed over Jewish property to the Arabs and the Jews were asking us to return it. Though I felt sorry for the Jews (the Germans treated them like swine) I felt that they were being very selfish in their priorities. We were, after all, in a state of war.

Around this time, a disillusioned Lieutenant John Woodhouse began to question his earlier decision to make the army his career. In a letter written on 10 June to his father he wrote:

The army is <u>out</u> as a career. I can name officers who proved incapable of leading men into action as opposed to out of action..... soldiers have to serve under these 'do nothings'. I was most happy when with my platoon. I considered applying to join the Army Air Corps but withdrew when I heard that the 'runaway' who was coming here had been shifted to another company.

Many years later Woodhouse found it difficult to remember the strength of his feelings at that time. He did, however, recall his pleasure at being able to wear his Dorset Regiment forage cap at all times:

I, like others, was intensely proud of being a Dorset and so, of course, were the East Surrey Regiment officers proud of their regiment. The regimental system was, and still should be, a source of strength to the British army. It certainly had a downside when one was posted to another regiment. I found the ceremonial duties irksome and I was no doubt a 'difficult' young 20 year old, probably over confident after a successful three months in action as a platoon commander. A friend of my father, the CO of 105 Light AA Regiment in Tunisia, wrote him a letter on 24th July in which he said: 'Woodhouse is a real acquisition to the Regiment. He is doing exceptionally well and is one of my best platoon commanders....I think he is a young man who is clearly going to "get on" in the service.' These were kind comments but a little premature.

# Chapter 3

# Sicily

In late June the East Surreys moved to the coast near Hammamet where they were to stay until 23 July 1943. On that day they embarked in landing ships for an uneventful crossing to Sicily where they disembarked onto a beach near Syracuse. From there, by lorry and foot, they progressed to the centre of the island. The overall plan was to head to Adrano after first taking out the German positions at Centuripe. On 30 July, after having taken over as spearhead for the 78th Division, they prepared for a night attack on the enemy-held area of Catenanuova.

In night attacks it was usual to mark the start line with white tape so that platoons could begin the advance together in line. On this occasion the artillery support guns fired by mistake on this line. This created a lot of confusion but, luckily, very few casualties. During the advance 10 Platoon came face to face with the enemy through a cactus hedge. One German paratrooper immediately surrendered but the rest ran back and in the dark 10 Platoon's small-arms fire was ineffective. As dawn broke the advance continued up a steep hill into heavy machine-gun fire. Sergeant Hawkins, who was only a couple of feet to the left of Woodhouse, was shot through the head. Heavy fire from their own Vickers machine guns tore over their heads, bringing down twigs and olives. When the firing stopped all appeared to be quiet and Woodhouse walked slowly forward alone but covered by his platoon. The Germans of the 3rd Parachute Regiment had vacated their position.

On 1 August the East Surreys had a grandstand view of 38 Irish Brigade of the 78th Division advance in daylight to take the hilltop town of Centuripe. With British artillery shells bursting on the enemy-held hills, the Irish Regiment, in scattered lines and blobs, pressed on across the valley in front of the Surreys. That night it was the turn of the East Surreys to attack the German-held cemetery on the top of a narrow ridge. They were obliged to advance up a track bordered by stone terraces that were impossible for heavily-laden troops to manoeuvre through at night. 'A' Company's initial assault failed and a gaggle of troops came stampeding back down the track. As Woodhouse recalled:

> Panic was in the air, it was almost tangible – it was contagious. I felt a great urge to join the fleeing crowd; it was quickly suppressed. I shouted for 10 Platoon to hold fast. This was the only time I ever witnessed panic and it was a shocking experience. The running troops were stopped further down the hill and they quickly recovered. We hung on below Centuripe all day of the 2nd August and this was the only day I can remember when we got no food. The QM staff had given us great service through three intensive campaigns.

On the next night both the town and cemetery were finally captured in heavy fighting by 38 Brigade. The advance continued in very hot dry weather towards the towering volcano of Etna. At dawn on 7 August, B Company, behind a heavy artillery barrage, advanced from orange groves uphill towards the town of Adrano which lay on the road encircling Mount Etna. As he stumbled across the hot lava rocks, Woodhouse, feeling very vulnerable after the death of Sergeant Hawkins, wondered when the enemy would open fire; there was precious little cover to be taken. At the edge of the town it became obvious that the Germans had pulled out when the artillery barrage had indicated a major attack. From Adrano the brigade advanced along the Etna encircling road towards Bronte; companies and battalions took it in turns to lead the advance. Off the road the ground was mostly lava which was baking hot in the August sun; the heat penetrated the boots and the soles of the feet became very uncomfortable. The Germans left behind them small rear guards with machine guns and mortars which forced the attackers to move higher and higher up the slopes of Etna. No. 10 Platoon luckily escaped casualties. On 8 August the battalion attacked and took Bronte. During that attack they encountered for the first time the dreaded German multi-barrelled mortar (the *Nebelwerfer*) which resulted in a number of casualties.

At Adrano and Bronte, Woodhouse witnessed at first hand the full horror of war as it affected civilians. This was a population with hardly any men between the ages of 20 and 40. They had suffered horrifying casualties and death from the bombing and shelling. Mutilated corpses lay in the rubbish. Men wept; women screamed; children stared uncomprehendingly. The battalion gave away as much food and medical supplies as they could spare. As individuals the soldiers quickly learned to switch off their emotional sympathy, not from callous disregard but from the necessity of continuing to fight the war and the impossible enormity of civilian suffering. With many casualties from the 'S' mines, the advance continued to Randazzo where on 17 August they were informed that the Germans had completed their evacuation of the island.

The battalion was billeted in the small north coast town of Gioiosa Marea and it was here that Woodhouse received some good news from his CO, Harry Smith. Smith told him that the 78th Division had ordered every battalion to form a 'Battle Patrol'. These were to consist of a lieutenant, a sergeant, a corporal, lance corporal and twelve privates; sixteen men in all. The objective was to raise the standard of patrolling. Smith had selected Woodhouse to command the patrol. The call for volunteers was quickly answered. The patrol members were well-armed with the heavy Thompson machine gun (aka Tommy gun), but Woodhouse opted for the lighter, simpler German Schmeisser machine pistol. He was absolutely delighted with his new role, not the least because the Battle Patrol was given its own separate billets which he was able to share with his men.

The Italian surrender was announced at a battalion concert party on 7 September. Woodhouse was very disappointed that the prospect of leading his Battle Patrol into action seemed to have slipped away. Everyone else appeared delighted that the war in Italy was over. Within two days it became obvious that the Germans had other ideas!

*Chapter 4*

# Italy

On 22 September 1943 the battalion embarked at Milazzo on the north coast in Royal Navy minesweepers to be landed at the Italian naval base at Taranto. To the battle-weary soldiers it seemed odd to see hundreds of Italian sailors still in uniform wandering freely around the streets. They had so recently been the enemy. The battalion moved north to Bari by train and from there, by truck and foot, to Serracapriola. On his 21st birthday Woodhouse marched exactly 21 miles. On being told to report to the CO that night, he was delighted to be given a dram of whisky to celebrate his coming of age. He was also given the news that the battalion had been ordered to advance to the town of Larino, some miles inland from the small port of Termoli which was the division's objective. No-one knew if the Germans were still present in that area.

On 3 October the Battle Patrol set off at dawn, ahead of the battalion in the direction of Larino. Their orders were to find out where the Germans were. Woodhouse had been told to be careful as he may meet soldiers from the Canadian army which was 'somewhere over on the left flank'. By midday the patrol had covered some 15 miles and was close to Larino. The countryside consisted of low rolling hills peppered with occasional farmhouses and olive groves.

Woodhouse moved into a small deserted house on a slight hill. He posted a sentry to observe a possible approach along a small stream. When the sentry reported the sighting of a single man, Woodhouse looked and saw that he was wearing a khaki drill shirt similar to both British and Canadian armies. Disastrously he concluded that he was 'one of ours' and took no further action. The soldier in khaki drill stopped and as he did so Woodhouse spotted a platoon or more of German soldiers running through an olive grove with the obvious intention of getting behind the house. Instantly he shouted 'Run for it!' and did so himself.

He did not wait to see if his Battle Patrol members followed him. They did not! With the exception of Sergeant Bunting, they stayed put. They were surrounded by the Germans and, seeing no choice but death or surrender, they opted for the latter. Having lost Sergeant Bunting in his headlong flight, Woodhouse slowly returned to the scene of the disaster, hoping against hope to find some of his soldiers. All was silent and he despondently headed back to the battalion lines to report the loss of his patrol. In a later interview Woodhouse said that he thought that there was no mention of the incident in the East Surrey's regimental history but Bryn Evans, the author of *With the East Surreys in Tunisia, Sicily and Italy 1942–1945*, states that a version of the patrol was mentioned in the *Surrey Comet* of 12 August 1944.

From any point of view the patrol had been a disaster. Fifteen of the battalion's most experienced soldiers had been lost! Woodhouse was forced to contemplate the catastrophic mistakes he had made. He felt inordinately guilty. Various lessons now became ingrained in his mind. From that point on he vowed to take all possible precautions against all possible eventualities, make sure that there was always an emergency RV (rendezvous) known to every man and never to become over-confident.

Possibly to shock Woodhouse out of his obvious depression, his CO ordered him to take a section from the Carrier Platoon on a daylight foot patrol to see if a ridge in front of the battalion position was occupied by the enemy. The patrol advanced well spread out and they quickly came under fire. Running back they experienced the familiar 'crack' of bullets passing close to their heads. Two men were hit but survived. This episode ended daylight patrolling.

The Battle Patrol was re-formed on 16 October, much to the delight of Woodhouse. Understandably there was hardly a rush to volunteer and Woodhouse was forced to wonder if his last disastrous battle patrol had caused the soldiers to lose confidence in him and his sense of guilt returned. However, he need not have worried on that score and he soon had his full complement of men. All the 78th Division Battle Patrols were authorized to wear the divisional sign (a yellow battle-axe on a black background) over their left breast pockets, while all other soldiers wore it on the upper sleeves of their battledress. This distinction was a source of pride to the men who, with a little push from their OC it must be said, now considered themselves as 'an elite'. As the division slogged its way across river defences the Battle Patrols went out, always by night, on a series of reconnaissance and fighting patrols. They now tended (at Woodhouse's suggestion) to operate in patrols of four men when more than one reconnaissance was required. Training and practice had made these men much more effective than patrols made up by the rifle companies. Not all of the patrols were routine reconnaissance. An Italian ex-officer of the Alpini (Italian mountain warfare troops), Doctor Guido Fano, had joined the battalion as an interpreter and his information led to one of the more bizarre excursions into the night. Woodhouse was ordered to take his patrol, along with Fano, to a hut within the German lines to meet a Scotswoman who had information for the battalion intelligence cell. It must have been exceptionally difficult to concentrate while half expecting to be rudely interrupted by German soldiers!

By 10 November the East Surreys were at Paglieta on the south side of the River Sangro. It was from here that Woodhouse, with the assistance of Guido Fano, led his full-strength Battle Patrol on an 8-mile foray through the German front to the rail station at Piazzano. The objective was to take a prisoner. The patrol moved cautiously across an open field to a small cluster of houses that probably contained sections of the enemy. After a period of silent observation they crossed a ditch and waited close to the wall of the house. Without a sound a German soldier appeared on a path leading to the house. The terrified soldier remained silent as he was grabbed by a couple of the patrol members. The prisoner was taken off in the direction of the planned withdrawal route and the remainder of the patrol placed captured German explosive charges to the windows of the house and one armoured car parked outside. When the charges were detonated there was considerable, but inaccurate, small-arms fire from a number of the houses. During the escape march, and despite still wearing his greatcoat, the prisoner kept up with the rapid pace of the patrol; they covered the 8-mile journey back to Paglieta in just over three hours, returning at around 0400 hours. At first the prisoner was sullen and silent. Later it came out that he was a lance corporal in the Defence Company HQ of 16 Panzer Division. When asked what he thought about the war, he said: 'It is not entirely clear at the moment.'

There had been no casualties in the Battle Patrol and for his leadership Woodhouse was awarded the Military Cross; Corporal Wood was awarded the Military Medal. The Military Cross citation reads:

On the night of 13/14th November 1943, Lieutenant J.M. WOODHOUSE, who commands the Battle Patrol, led a small raiding party to PIAZZANO station (Map sheet ATESSA 147/2 344918). Guided by two friendly Italians this party attacked with explosives and grenades a number of houses known to be occupied as sleeping quarters by tank crews of 16 Panzer Division, which had been located two nights previously in this area. Thanks to the bold planning and leadership of Lieutenant Woodhouse the enemy was taken completely by surprise. Casualties were inflicted on the enemy whilst one prisoner, identified as belonging to the defence company of 16 Panzer Division, was captured and brought back to our lines. Lieutenant Woodhouse brought the whole of his raiding party back to our lines without loss on completion of this successful operation.

This officer has constantly distinguished himself since he has been with the Battalion, both as a platoon commander and a patrol leader. His personal courage and coolness in action are a wonderful example to his men. He has previously had his name submitted for mention in dispatches.

Unlike the carefree approach that led to the disaster at Larino, Woodhouse now planned his patrols in meticulous detail and, whenever possible, rehearsed his men.

Paglieta had suffered only minimal damage and, with an eye to his mother's morale, Woodhouse described a typical day in a letter dated 12 November:

I have my old 10 Platoon billeted with me, a bed with sheets.....
in the morning I read the weekly Times, I have copies up until 25th September.....write, walk around the town, make a plan for a patrol, read the Divisional Intelligence Summary. Have a drink with English speaking Italians…Lunch of roast veal, potatoes and peas, apple fritter and tea. An afternoon walk, perhaps a short sleep and then buy eggs and apples. Then visit the B Company commander

and talk shop and personalities. Dinner of roast chicken, chips, cabbage, flap jacks, jam and bread and tea. That is the sort of day I have here.....some nights, of course, there is work to be done.

All Woodhouse's letters home, particularly those to his mother, were cheerful and optimistic. Those to his father were a little different:

My dear Dad,

I suppose I have done thirty or more operational jobs since I landed in Africa, and have developed a technique and almost a sixth sense about the business. It is the only part of war that appeals to me as truly an art. Strategy is presumably an art to a certain degree, but tactics seem to me to be very stereotyped, and attack and defence is just a matter of will and weapon power.

I have a bed and slept right through the night of 10/11th, first full night for some weeks.

After seeing one or two places in Italy and Sicily, I doubt if air attack can do any more than they are doing to help us win. Close support by medium bombers has devastating results as we saw at Massicault and to a lesser degree out here and in Sicily.

Ever your loving son, Jock

The battle for the 78th Division to break the German Winter Line along the River Sangro began on 20 November and went on for nine days before the Germans were finally dislodged. The Surreys were on the extreme flank, next to the river mouth and the sea. During this time Woodhouse, who was in command of both 10 Platoon and the Battle Patrol, led several reconnaissance operations up to the German trenches in constant fear of the mines from which the battalion suffered many casualties. He led all of his patrols from the front. In the dark it was difficult to direct a leading scout and in any event he had decided that his own eyes and ears were his best protection. That decision further increased his standing with his soldiers and they openly boasted to other platoons about their leader's prowess; when he became aware of that Woodhouse was secretly pleased at the confirmation of his leadership ability.

After the Sangro battle on 4 December the division was withdrawn to the area of Campobasso for a rest. The 1st East Surreys were billeted in

Frosolone with B Company being housed in the Law Courts complete with electric lights and other luxuries. From 10 to 14 December, Woodhouse was on leave and staying at the Officers' Club in Naples where he met an old family friend, Brigadier Harold Matthews. Matthews was familiar with Naples and, knowing Woodhouse's passion for history, took him on a two–hour tour of Pompeii set below a smoking Mount Vesuvius. He found it strangely unreal that he should be a tourist in this ancient scenario while the war raged on not very far away. All too soon the rest period was over and the battalion was back in the front line by 17 December. This time their positions, in three small villages around Capracotta, overlooked the River Sangro. While settling in to the new habitat, Woodhouse bought three sheep for 10 Platoon at an equivalent cost of about £2. In early January the snows came, and to the envy of other soldiers, the Battle Patrol was handsomely kitted out with string vests, windproof jackets, fleecy white jackets, oiled socks and boots with ski fittings.

From 18 to 20 January 1944 Woodhouse led his Battle Patrol across the Sangro, which was little more than a stream at that point, into a village behind the German outposts. Though the village had been almost destroyed there were still Italians living in it. By day the patrol hid on the upper floor of an ancient house. Woodhouse, with an old civilian coat over his uniform, made a reconnaissance. He made contact with some locals and explained that he wanted a prisoner. He was told the German soldiers often came into the village to see what they could scrounge. After returning to his hiding place he did not have to wait long before a local man told him that there were two German soldiers in a particular house. He despatched a four-man patrol under command of Private Frank Gage to surprise the Germans. This they did and Gage, in German, told them to put their hands up. One did so immediately but the other chose to try to flee; he was shot in the stomach. The wounded soldier was carried back to the house and was given morphine. As he died he was heard to murmur 'Mutti' (Mother). This made Woodhouse very sad but the death was ignored by the other men. The prisoner was 20 years old and a member of the 5th (Austrian) Mountain Division. He confidently predicted that Germany, which was building a new Luftwaffe, would win the war. They would begin by pushing the Russians back to Moscow in 1944.

On his return to base Woodhouse was called by his CO to meet the 8th Army commander, General Sir Oliver Leese, who was on a visit to the 1st East Surreys with the GOC of the 78th Division. The general was immaculately dressed, Woodhouse less so! He congratulated Woodhouse on his successes with the Battle Patrol and wished him well.

On 22 February the 1st East Surreys were put under command of the New Zealand Division near Cassino opposite the strong German front at San Angelo on the River Rapido. In January the Americans had already mounted a determined assault on the German positions and had been bloodily repulsed. The debris of that defeat was scattered all around, including rubber assault boats. The malevolent eye of the ruined monastery at Monte Cassino looked down on the Allied positions. Woodhouse was ordered to make a series of patrols to try to find a crossing point on the Rapido. On a very dark night he took a patrol with an American assault boat to a point where the river deviated about 100 yards or so from the German outposts. The river was about 20 yards wide and obviously very deep. They launched the boat with some difficulty and were straight away swept downstream by the very fast current. Eventually they managed to make it to the other bank which was fortunately clear of German troops. This place may have made for a feasible crossing, but in order to confirm that, Woodhouse had to observe it by day to assess the German movements.

On 29 February, Woodhouse took Private Dickinson and another soldier to a point in front of the battalion lines. With great caution they belly-crawled to one side of a ruined barn from where they could look down onto the flood plain and the German positions on and close to the Sangro. Dickinson, Tommy gun in hand, was lying next to Woodhouse and the third soldier maintained a watch to the right flank. Suddenly, from a house round the corner from the barn came the instruction, in English, 'Hands up.' Two German soldiers appeared, one with a Schmeisser and the other with a pistol. Woodhouse was paralysed with shock but Dickinson was not. Rolling onto his back, he squeezed off a burst from his Thompson. The German fired at the same time as he leaped back behind the wall. Woodhouse gave the order to run for cover. Returning in force some hours later they discovered that the Germans had also run, leaving behind a Luger pistol with the hand grip shattered by Dickinson's bullets. The owner's hand must also have been damaged.

When Woodhouse reported back to his CO on 1 March it must have been obvious that he was shaken up because he was told that he needed a rest, was instructed to join D Company right away and take command of 16 Platoon. Soon after that the Battle Patrol was disbanded. Sergeant Bunting and the rest of the men returned to their various companies. Woodhouse was very disappointed but in truth the sheer density of the German front left little, if any, scope for the Battle Patrols to penetrate their defences. The OC of D Company, Major Enoch Harvey, was a well-respected regular officer from the Royal Berkshire Regiment and he had been told by Lieutenant Colonel Smith that he did not want Woodhouse to be sent on patrols for a while.

Harvey asked permission, on 2 March 1944, to send out a night patrol. He knew that Woodhouse knew the ground in front of his position and he wanted to see it for himself. Woodhouse remembered the patrol vividly:

We set out with Pte James as leading scout, then me followed by Harvey and two Privates (Moody and Hart). We went for 300 yards along a track to a T-junction. Harvey had given me command of the patrol. James, the lead scout, stopped just before reaching the T-junction. I crawled up beside him and he told me that he had heard men talking at the junction. I waited and listened. I hardly knew James having been in the company only two days. After listening longer I decided that we must go on and take our chances. We went one by one to the right at the junction. We went about 500 yards and came out of the olive grove onto the flat flood plain of the River Rapido opposite San Angelo. I pointed out various landmarks and other features to Harvey which he noted down. Around midnight we returned to the T-junction which we had to pass through as there were mines on each side. We were going very slowly as I was still mindful of James' warning even though no enemy action had resulted on the way out. We were about 100 yards away from the junction when the Germans fired about a dozen mortar bombs around it. I whispered to Harvey that there could not be any enemy there or they would not have mortared the position. We resumed our move. As we reached the T there was a long burst of firing from about six Germans and two or three hand grenades were thrown. These struck Harvey and James but, apart from a minor shrapnel fragment in my leg, I was all right. The Germans had been in ambush not more than three or four yards from the track. Pte Moody and another soldier behind me were not caught up in the firing and had dived for cover. My Schmeisser was later found by the battalion with a round jammed in it. I have no memory of firing and believe that I fell flat when the firing started. A German stuck his gun in my back but instead of pulling the trigger shouted a word or two which made it very clear that they wanted me as a prisoner.

Had Major Harvey listened to Lieutenant Colonel Smith's instruction regarding his wishes for the near-exhausted Woodhouse to be rested for a few days, the quite unnecessary patrol, under his command, would probably never have used the T-junction as a crossing-point. An alert Woodhouse would have investigated Private James' report of an overheard conversation and would almost certainly have spotted the ambush.

*Chapter 5*

# For You the War is Over

Woodhouse and the wounded James had fallen into the hands of 15 Panzer Grenadier Division. The six Germans relieved them of their weapons and ammunition pouches before taking them back to a boat crossing-point over the Rapido and they were passed back from Company HQ to Battalion HQ where they were given coffee and cigarettes. Somehow James made it and Woodhouse was given an assurance that his wounds would be properly treated. He believed that. He was escorted across the track to what was obviously an officers' mess and during the short walk he realized that he still had a grenade in his pocket. Assuming that a proper search must soon be made, he managed to slip it into what appeared to be a potted plant container. He was kept on his feet and constantly moved around in what was, he supposed, a plan to make him even more tired.

At the Battalion HQ, in a well-furnished dugout, Woodhouse was greeted by a tall, fair-haired 'Leutnant' who spoke some English. Major Harvey's wallet was produced with his identity given away by his visiting cards and, more seriously, a letter from the 11th Infantry Battalion to him in the 1st East Surreys. It was strictly against orders to carry personal details and papers on patrol. Having ditched the grenade before he was searched, Woodhouse had only had eight cigarettes, some matches, a handkerchief, a pencil, an unused notebook and about 400 lira in his pockets. He also had an escape map which was not found. When the German asked what regiment he was in he stayed silent. He laughed and said: 'This one's certainly an Englishman', which made Woodhouse think that the Germans were as yet unaware of the presence of the US army.

The first formal interrogation took place at 0100 hours on 4 March; Woodhouse, who had not slept since 2 March, was desperately tired. He limited himself to giving only number, rank and name. The interrogator was polite but threatening; he had already identified the 1st East Surreys from Harvey's wallet and he soon lost interest in trying to extract more information.

After the war ended Woodhouse found out that a German patrol had been ambushed in the same area and the patrol commander had a diary in which he had written that they had killed the CO (Harvey) and his adjutant (Woodhouse) on 3 March.

Woodhouse was moved, with a fellow prisoner, Pioneer Corps officer Jock Crichton, to a house on the Ceprano road where they were confined for four days. From there they were taken to Fiuggi to join a group of recaptured PoWs in the Grand Hotel.

Hunger began as the rations were reduced. Breakfast was two slices of bread and ersatz coffee, lunch a half litre of barley soup, and a supper of four slices of bread and margarine. The hunger, inactivity and a fevered imagination threw Woodhouse into the depths of dark depression. Would he get back into the war again? He desperately wanted to. On 13 March the group was moved to 'Cinema City' just south of Rome. Here further interrogation took place: 'The interrogation was a shouting and bullying performance. The dregs of armies tend to collect in base units and I guess that the Wehrmacht was no exception.'

On 21 March the prisoners were moved to Laterina and put aboard trains. Forty-four soldiers were sealed into each carriage and twenty-three officers and six German guards into the next one. In this manner they crossed the German frontier at the Brenner Pass and moved along to their destination of Moosburg to the north-east of Munich. Many of the prisoners fainted from hunger and the severe cold, but that night (23 March) they were each issued with a Red Cross parcel.

Stalag VII-A at the village of Moosburg was a vast hutted camp with Russian and French prisoners as well as British, though the British officers were segregated from the other nationalities. A corner of the hut was partitioned off to provide accommodation for about a dozen British soldiers who acted as orderlies for some 200 officer prisoners. Escape was paramount in the minds of most of the prisoners and Woodhouse joined a team of eight tunnellers. The tunnel was begun under the bunk of one of the orderlies. The soil was very sandy and there was a constant need to shore up the walls and roof of the tunnel; bed boards were used for this task. The team estimated that they needed to excavate for about 30 yards to get under the perimeter fence. There was a revetted slit trench halfway to the wire and by passing close to this and boring sideways they were able to get a crude air supply.

On 6 June Woodhouse was digging at the face of the tunnel when he heard a loud cheer. The word was passed down that the Allies had landed in Normandy. He carried on digging.

Woodhouse's mettle was tested to a very high degree. He was absolutely terrified of being buried alive in a tunnel collapse and each session at the face left him weak, shaking and mentally exhausted. It was hot, sweaty work and the grains from the sandy soil seemed to find their way into every orifice. The air was heavy with particles and the urge to cough was great but to cough once may well have led to a spasm which could lead to an even greater inhalation of the dust with very unpleasant results. He was not alone in those fears but it was a great relief to him when it was calculated that the tunnel had passed under the perimeter. Celebrations were short-lived! The tunnel had been constructed too close to one of the large poles from which the fence wire was suspended and it had begun to lean over. The Germans spotted it and were quickly on the scene with soldiers and dogs. The active tunnellers just managed to get out in time. One sad result of the escape attempt was the loss of a very unusual but most enjoyable privilege. For some time small groups of officers had been allowed out of the camp, under guard, to go for local walks.

Huge fleets of high-flying American bombers could often be seen and Woodhouse would fantasize about the fact that the lucky crew would be back in Blighty in a few hours.

On 23 August all the British officers were herded into cattle trucks and began the transfer to Brunswick. During the journey they could hear the noise of aircraft which was soon joined by the crack of the German flak. Through the ventilation slot Woodhouse could see the aircraft and he watched sadly as one burst into flames and plummeted to earth. He no longer felt jealous of the crews. On 25 August the convoy reached Oflag 79 at Brunswick. The camp had been hit by American bombers a few days earlier and three PoWs had been killed and a further thirty-seven wounded.

Oflag 79 had been a Luftwaffe barracks and was built to a high standard: it held 2,000 British officers and 150 soldiers in quite comfortable quarters. The eight barrack blocks were surrounded by high wire fences and nine watch towers. Woodhouse was accommodated in a small room with eleven other officers. He recalled:

> Air raids were frequent and apart from the one in which the PoWs were killed it was not uncommon for the occasional small bomb or incendiary device to be dropped into the compound. In November a very heavy night raid by the RAF destroyed Brunswick. We shivered in the cellars where the shock waves from the blasts were continuous.
>
> The currency in the camp was cigarettes together with the food parcels from the Red Cross. Just before Christmas the parcels stopped coming as the German transport system began to collapse. From that point on a typical day's food would be potato soup for breakfast and a pint of barley soup with a couple of slices of bread and margarine for supper. We really missed those Red Cross parcels!

It was in Brunswick that Woodhouse met Eric Newby who had also been awarded the MC while serving with the Black Watch (he then transferred to the SBS). He later became famous as a writer and traveller and will be known to many for his authorship of the book *A Short Walk in the Hindu Kush*. They were kindred spirits and the friendship lasted for the rest of their lives. On 12 April 1945 at 0900 hours, a cheer went up. The Americans had arrived in the form of the 125th US Cavalry Regiment. It took only about two weeks before Woodhouse and Newby returned to London by train via Brussels and Tilbury. They celebrated in true style with lunch at the Savoy Hotel before it was time to travel onward to join their respective families.

## Chapter 6

# And Where to Now?

Charles Hall Woodhouse, now the Managing Director of the Hall and Woodhouse family brewery in Blandford Forum, was very keen that his son should join him in the business. John was enjoying rural Dorset again and taking long walks, often with Eric Newby who had a common interest in history and they explored Dorset's many connections to the Roman occupation. During those walks he was appraising his situation. He had not yet decided whether he wanted to stay in the army now that hostilities were over. He had enjoyed his five years in the military but he had to accept that he had a somewhat false picture: he had been on active service and, therefore, not subjected to any of the ceremonial bullshit that he detested. What would a peacetime army be like? The operational aspects of army life were what appealed to him but how much of that would there be? He enjoyed the company of soldiers but surely the further up the promotional ladder he climbed, the greater would become the gap between him and the men he commanded. On those extensive country walks he was still looking at the ground like a soldier; assessing defensive positions or considering how a hill might best be attacked. Certainly he would earn more if he joined the brewery – army pay was not generous – but his financial needs, at least for the time being, were not great. His sense of duty to the family business tugged at him but there was no real affinity with brewing. In July 1945 he decided to attend an officers' assessment centre for two days at Oxshot. That consolidated his thinking and he decided to stay in the army for at least the foreseeable future. The decision opened the way for his two younger Woodhouse cousins, Edward and John, to go into the brewery.

It was during this brief interlude of rest and recuperation that Woodhouse wrote a short and honest note in his diary, which he titled 'Reflections on my War. 19 Feb 1943 – 3 Mar 1944':

The German soldiers had an unshakable belief in their superiority over all other nations and armies. They had been led to believe that war was glorious and Hitler, their Fuhrer, was invincible. The 'Wehrmacht' was very well led, better equipped and by 1943 more battle experienced than we were. We did not believe in the glory of war. Unlike the Germans we were not fighting to enlarge our empire. We fought with skill and bravery through pride in our Regiments just to finish the job and go home.

I was often fearful but it always mattered greatly to me that I should be well regarded and respected by the soldiers I commanded. This helped in overcoming fear. However, I was generally cautious, weighing the odds carefully. As a platoon commander one is almost always in attack or defence – part of a large force with limited opportunity for independent action. 78th Infantry Division ordered the formation of a Battle Patrol. I was appointed to command it – the other ranks were all volunteers. I was under command for operations of the Battalion CO. We would discuss operations and the plan was largely left to me. This was much to my liking being very different from the heavily supervised platoon commander's lives!

Now back with his beloved Dorset Regiment he was posted to the Infantry Training Centre at Norwich. His task was training 18-year-old recruits who had been conscripted to join the Norfolk or Dorset regiments. It was not long before his cavalier attitude to set rules and regulations got him into trouble. While training the soldiers in grenade-throwing, one failed to detonate. The regulation time to wait before approaching a dud grenade was ten minutes. He waited only two minutes, and as he approached the grenade he distinctly heard the 'pop' as the four-second fuse ignited. He managed to cover 2 or 3 yards and threw himself to the ground just before the explosion. Two or three small fragments of shrapnel landed in his right shoulder. On return to barracks he sought out the doctor Captain Jimmy Logan DSO (he had fought at Arnhem). Logan agreed not to report the incident and patched up the trivial wounds. Unfortunately Woodhouse forgot the lesson he should have learned after he told his sergeant the news in Kent before embarking for Africa. He told his mother in a letter. It happened that the CO, Colonel

Hewick, was an old friend of his parents and his mother, not knowing that he had not reported the incident, told the CO how shocked she was that her son had survived the war only to be wounded in training! Both Logan and Woodhouse had reprimands put on their record sheets.

Although he was given quite a lot of scope in devising interesting exercises, Woodhouse was beginning to get bored. When he saw that volunteers were being sought to learn Russian at Cambridge University he was quick to go forward. Heavily exaggerating his contacts with Russian soldiers while he was a PoW, he managed to get a place on the course. Along with sixty other men of all ranks from the army and the RAF he joined the School of Slavonic Studies under Liza Hill. They were comfortably accommodated in the requisitioned Bull Hotel and in September 1946 Woodhouse passed the course in the lowest grade of interpreter.

On the successful completion of the Russian course he was posted to Germany where he joined the Control Commission to act as interpreter between Russian and British teams. Mainly the work consisted of visiting German industrial sites to value what plant had survived the war. The Russians were entitled to reparation to a fixed total remuneration in deutschmarks and they sought to value the plant at low rates while the German management wanted a higher value. The British, of course, inevitably opted for compromise. Woodhouse liked the company of the Russians and was amused that when they used the telephone to obtain instructions from their headquarters in Potsdam, the lack of trust dictated that always two of them would use the kiosk together.

Most of the sites inspected were vast affairs on the Ruhr and when that job was completed in September 1947, Woodhouse was transferred to the Anglo-Soviet Border Commission in Lübbecke. The work was mostly dealing with minor border incidents and tracking down and arresting deserters. There were some occasions like the Russian October Revolution Day (7 November) which were quite memorable for the vast consumption of fiery vodka and Cossack dancing. A short time later he was switched to HQ Rhine Army in Bad Oeynhausen as a GSO3 to Colonel Richardson, then Head of Army Intelligence.

In Lübbecke Woodhouse met Helen, an Estonian refugee and a beautiful woman to boot. She was in her early twenties, working as a

Russian interpreter with the British Military Mission. His self-confessed shyness when coupled with his natural charm and politeness made him more attractive to women than he imagined. Despite the scarcity of social events, he and Helen developed a very close friendship and spent many off-duty hours together. The relationship, warm though it was, lasted only for the few months of his tenure with the mission. They shared confidences together and good-humouredly discussed their personal feelings and joked about some of their co-workers. Much of their leisure time was spent just walking and chatting; he was as interested in the situation in Estonia as she was in questioning him about life in the West. They corresponded for a while afterwards but the relationship inevitably cooled with the lack of physical contact. He often wondered what had become of Helen and some years later he tried but failed to establish contact again.

In the meantime Helen revealingly wrote:

Dear John,
Many thanks for your letter which I received yesterday.

I am glad you made such a good start on your new, or old, job including turkeys and Christmas puddings and children's parties and 'twisting' till 2.30 am. Jolly good effort!

On Christmas Eve I was all alone in our house and felt a bit glum. Still, there is nothing like being all alone with a clever and understanding person. Maurice went to some German party. On Christmas Day I was on duty paying visits to Dr. Schultz & Co. and similar charming people, loaded with presents. On the whole I have been very good. They say that virtue is lack of opportunity.

We passed the New Year in a perfectly sober state due to the fact that we only had a bottle of whiskey the Mission sent us. So we were very sober (the old tale about the virtue again). In the first hour of the New Year I had a huge portion of (you are wrong if you think it was turkey) sauerkraut and fried potatoes. Smashing grub!!

On New Year's Day the opportunity came in the shape of a Flight Lieutenant who took me to a party with a bunch of friends. We had a most wonderful time rolling champagne bottles over the dance floor and dancing 'Hey Barba-riba' (I remember the tune we often heard on the radio, which you hated!). Entirely my idea of spending the night – as a bishop once said to an actress.

Thank goodness that the holidays are over. 'Tano' spent them enjoying a worm treatment. Poor creature was as sick as a dog. Again he thought he was dying all over the place. He is in perfect shape now, healthy, clean and full of pep.

Apropos I just finished the Saint book you disapproved of. I personally think it is a most delightful piece of literature as far as language is concerned. The Saint is a most fascinating piece of humanity. If you enjoy the American slang you should enjoy the Saint's way of speaking even if you don't like his type of character, which, I agree, is a bit fictitious. Anyway I nearly died laughing, maybe because I am not English and this kind of humour is new to me and seems rather out of the ordinary.

Oh, I forgot to a) bawl you out and b) to thank you for those 'couple of cigarettes' you left for me. I hope you have not been absent minded again.

And now comes something which does not fit into the mood of my letter at all, but I have to say it. I should have said it before you left but never had the courage. I was afraid you might misunderstand me. I want to thank you for everything you did and meant to me. Please, don't think I'm sentimental. I am just very grateful to you, and, as there is no better way, I've got to try and express it in words. I often wondered whether you ever realised how much you helped me to keep my balance. You may not be interested in it, you have your own life, interests and ambitions. I don't want you to laugh at me, but it's not just a 'couple of cigarettes', it is more. I am terribly sorry if I ever interfered with your personal matters by getting personal myself. But you were of a great help to me all the same. Meeting people like you, John, strengthens my good opinions of the mankind.

Please, if you write to me don't make any comments on what I have just said. There is nothing much you can say anyway. I wish you the best of luck and success.

Yours very sincerely,
Helen

Around 90 per cent of the work was downright boring for a fit and adventurous 25-year-old officer. There were hours of clerical work logging the movements of Soviet army divisions, checking vehicle registrations and reading excerpts of intercepted German correspondence. At that time there were interesting rumours that the Russians had formed a Communist German army from PoWs but they remained just that: rumours. The senior interpreter-cum-interrogator was Alex Philipson, a Tsarist officer in the British army. The most prominent defector during Woodhouse's tenure was Colonel Tokrev of the Soviet Air Force who had been responsible for jet aircraft engine development. Life was getting depressing again:

> Only once did I get to Berlin to negotiate the defection of a Russian Major. We met in the British Zone and I got precious little information out of him. I think he was a plant but now we'll never know.
>
> While in that job I took up gliding at a former Luftwaffe club. There I met Hanna Reitch who had been Hitler's personal pilot. She spoke quite openly about her wartime role of which she remained very proud. She was the only German I met who had the courage still to proclaim loyalty to the Nazis.

The year 1948 found Captain Woodhouse in Austria happily enjoying life as the second-in-command of a company in the 1st Battalion, the Dorset Regiment. The Dorsets were based in Völkermarkt to the east of Klagenfurt but for six weeks in the spring and again in autumn the battalion moved to the Meidling Barracks in Vienna. Here Woodhouse developed a taste for opera that never left him. He loved the grandeur of it all and usually managed a weekly visit. His father, then colonel of the Dorset Regiment, travelled to Vienna to present the 1939–45 Second World War medals to those entitled; this, of course, included his son which made it a unique occasion.

This was a happy period during which he raised and trained the battalion ski team in the Kanzel Mountains near Klagenfurt. He was already an accomplished skier due to family holidays in Austria. He came third in the British Army Ski Championships in 1949. Apart from the skiing, there was little by way of a social life as the British tended to stay distant from the Austrians. All good things come to an end and in the summer of 1949 he was called back to the intelligence world and more demanding duties.

## Chapter 7

# Working for a Genius

On his return to England Woodhouse was ordered to report to Major General Geoffrey Evans in the War Office. Not knowing that military personnel did not wear uniform in that august environment he was embarrassingly conspicuous. A rotund and genial figure, Evans had been a successful divisional commander in Burma; in contrast his GSO1, Lieutenant Colonel Lewis Pugh, was a thin, trim and neat officer with no apparent sense of humour.

Between them the pair explained that a new 40th Infantry Division was to be formed which together with a Commando Brigade was to be based in Hong Kong. In 1949 the Communist Army under Mao Tse-tung was sweeping the Chinese National Government from the country. The Communists were expected to reach the borders of the British colony by the end of 1949. Would they stop? The 40th Division would be there to halt the advance and show Chairman Mao that he would have a war on his hands if he carried on. Woodhouse was to join the Divisional Intelligence Cell. He relished the prospect of working in the Far East.

At the end of July an advance party from Divisional HQ took off from the Solent in a Sunderland flying boat heading for Hong Kong. Flying only by day at a height of about 10,000ft, it was scheduled to make five night stops at Sicily, Alexandria, Bahrain, Calcutta and Bangkok. Even minor upsets such as the general being paired off to share a room with his batman did not impair the pleasure of the trip. Below the upper deck was a bar with downward-facing windows and the aircraft was flying low enough to allow grand views of the North African desert battlefields and those of India, Burma and Indo-China. An engine failure granted the passengers a pleasant three days' break in Calcutta. On arrival in Hong Kong the advance party was found a base in Sekong in the south-west corner of the New Territories.

The work was interesting. The requirement was to produce the Divisional Intelligence Summaries, meet newspaper correspondents, site observation posts on the Chinese frontier and join General Evans and the C-in-C General Frank Festing on the occasional days off. In October Woodhouse flew a number of sorties in an Auster spotter aircraft expecting at any moment to sight long columns of the People's Liberation Army (PLA). He flew several miles across the frontier without incident, then one day several black shell bursts appeared below the aircraft. The PLA had arrived and the Auster beat a hasty retreat.

Military life in Hong Kong with its huge garrison settled down, but in Malaya a Communist terrorist uprising was in full swing. Brigadier Michael 'Mad Mike' Calvert, a former Chindit Brigade Commander in Burma with General Orde Wingate, and later, as commander of the SAS Brigade in which position he took the salute at the disbandment parade. Having reverted to the peacetime rank of major, and as the incumbent GSO2 Intelligence, he had been summoned to Malaya to advise the C-in-C on how to deal with the rebellion. Of Michael Calvert, Woodhouse was later to say: 'As soon as I met him I knew he had that spark of genius that a soldier's lucky to see at close quarters even once in his career.'

As a result of his study of the situation in Malaya, Calvert made a number of suggestions which included a very persuasive proposal that a 'Special Force' should be formed. This force would be trained to operate for prolonged periods in the deep jungle, befriend the aboriginal tribes, cut off the enemy's supply and communication lines, and hunt down and destroy the Communist terrorists in their bases. The plan was immediately approved and Calvert was promoted to lieutenant colonel, put in command and granted the authority to call for volunteers to join the Malayan Scouts. He returned to Hong Kong to begin his search for suitable officers.

The possibility of active service very much appealed to John Woodhouse and, having already met Calvert as part of his intelligence duties, he was quick to volunteer. He was interviewed by Calvert who immediately spotted the potential in this already battle-hardened officer and accepted him on the spot. Woodhouse had applied assuming that his request to be assigned to a squadron would be honoured. Calvert had seemed to agree to that wish, and he was deeply disappointed when his posting became official and he was nominated as the Malayan Scouts Intelligence Officer.

John Woodhouse's personal memoirs record the details and emotions of his journey to take up his duties with the Malayan Scouts. He flew from Hong Kong on 19 August 1950:

Half an hour after I landed at Singapore airport I was still waiting for the driver I had been told to expect to meet me. I wondered if perhaps his absence was part of a deliberate plan by Lieutenant Colonel Mike Calvert, CO of the Scouts, to see if I was the sort of officer who would then sit and wait and do nothing. This worried me a lot because, not knowing where to go, I **was** just sitting, waiting and doing nothing! Several Jeeps drove up the straight approach road to Kallang airport. Each time my hopes rose only to sink again in increasing anxiety when I saw they were not for me. At last, as one Jeep approached, hope grew into certainty and relief. Hunched over the wheel was the familiar big figure of 'Willie' Wilson, Adjutant of the Malayan Scouts whom I had met in Hong Kong the year before. In the relief of his arrival I readily forgave him for being late.

But – anxiety soon returned. Willie was a keen horseman and seemed to drive the Jeep as perhaps he rode to hounds! We went straight at everyone and everything for as long as possible. Once in the streets of Singapore city our progress was made in a series of violent rushes brought to sudden halts. I tried to listen intently as Willie told me that fifty men and eight officers had arrived in the first fortnight of August and that more were expected by the end of this month. I was distracted from Willie's monologue by pyjama-clad Chinese men and women who skipped across our path so late that it seemed at least one must die before we left the swarming streets. In Hong Kong a police inspector had told me that the Chinese did this purposely so that any evil spirits which may be dogging their footsteps would be run over. Well – that seemed a good enough reason.

We were waved through the Customs Control point as we crossed the causeway onto mainland Malaya and we were soon leaving the small town of Johore Baharu. An immediate and significant change came over the road. The traffic changed from a turbulent torrent to a thin trickle. Most of even this was military. Scout cars manned by unsmiling Gurkhas escorted columns of three-ton trucks filled with pale-skinned young British soldiers. They drove as fast as they could. Our Jeep no longer seemed alien as it had in the civilian streets.

With assumed nonchalance I said to Willie, 'Are there any bandits near here?' That was a question I had wanted to ask for some time.

'Not here old boy, but there's stacks of them further up the road. The train gets shot up almost every night. The night train to Kuala Lumpur is really quite something.' Willie chuckled.

'Doesn't sound like much fun being shot up like that.'

'Wait till you go up on the night train – it's more like a night club.'

I digested all this slowly and, looking at the carbine next to Willie, said 'I suppose I should be armed?'

'Fix you up when we get to Tampoi, don't worry.'

This seemed to be sensible advice and there was plainly no alternative. At a road junction close to the sea Willie slowed down and between the sea and the road, under some scattered palm trees, I saw a small group of British soldiers drying themselves vigorously. We stopped and got out and Willie asked if the CO was still there. He was told that Calvert had departed a few minutes earlier, leaving an instruction that Willie and the new officer should go to see him immediately. While Willie chatted to the men I noticed that most of them looked at me with a gaze both curious and critical. New officers are naturally the object of some speculation and never more so than in this unit where we expected to serve together in a rough and dangerous life. I knew they would reserve their opinion of me until I had shown what I could do. All in all it gave me an agreeable feeling of challenge reminding me of a hill in Tunisia when I joined the East Surreys as a 20-year-old Lieutenant. There was among them, in their conversations with Willie Wilson, none of the timidity and nervousness shown by many young soldiers when speaking to officers. They were confident, vigorous and cheerful.

Leaving the swimmers, they drove on to Tampoi where a bare institutional building, once a lunatic asylum and in 1950 the home of the Far East

Training Centre, then housed the Malayan Scouts. The training centre instructed newly-arrived officers and soldiers in jungle-fighting on conventional lines, a job it did with efficiency and notable success. The Scouts must have been a severe trial to the training staff during the eight weeks they lived there.

Wilson took him to the officers' tent lines. As the intelligence officer of the unit he was lucky enough to have one to himself. It was large but gloomy inside. Two white sheets on the bed were shrouded by a low, dark green mosquito net. A little wooden chair stood unevenly on the yellowing grass beside the bed. A chest of drawers leaning dangerously forward completed the furnishings except for a paraffin lamp and a piece of string stretched between the two tent poles. He put his suitcase on the chest of drawers and caught it again just before it slid off. The floor was better. Wilson showed him the open air taps and sluices with their tin bowls which was the communal washing place. The soldiers' tents were on the other side. Willie told him that he would give him a half hour to sort himself out and then he would take him to see the colonel.

While Woodhouse was unpacking and awaiting the summons from Calvert, his mind was occupied with thoughts of the coming meeting. He had met him a couple of times in Hong Kong where he had been interviewed along with thirty or so other volunteers in June 1950.

When he had joined the army in 1941 he had, as a private and lance corporal, followed the advice 'Never volunteer for anything'. However, later in the war and then commissioned, he started looking for a wider experience than could be found in one regiment. By 1950 he had spent two years learning Russian and working as an interpreter, one very happy year with the Dorsets in Austria and two years on intelligence duties. In the summer of 1950, just before the Korean War, Hong Kong was becoming very dull for Woodhouse. The Communists had arrived at the border in October 1949 and just stayed there quietly. Into this situation – like the key to a mysterious new door – had come the invitation (circulated to all) to join the Malayan Scouts and fight in the deep jungles of that country. Woodhouse volunteered because he thirsted for action, he was anxious to get away from the stultifying intelligence duties, he was curious to see Malaya, and he was very keen to serve under Mike Calvert whose name and face had become known throughout the post-war army as a result of his exploits when commanding a Chindit Brigade under Orde Wingate in Burma.

He recognized Calvert as a man of exceptional bravery and endowed with a vivid imagination that allowed him to continue to produce original ideas and concepts. After his Chindit days he had commanded the Special Air Service Brigade which was then operating quietly and most effectively behind the German fronts in Europe. With the return to peace and the disbandment of the SAS Brigade it was found that some unorthodox soldiers were difficult to employ and at the Staff College Calvert's original solutions to the problems set by the Directing Staff were not always appreciated. At any rate his time there was followed by a dull posting to the Trieste Garrison staff, but in 1949 Calvert, a brigadier in 1944 but then a major, was sent to Hong Kong.

Early in 1950 the rebellion by the Malayan Communist Party had become a serious threat to the economy of the country. Reinforcements, including the Royal Marine Commando Brigade and 26 Gurkha Brigade had been sent from Hong Kong. However, it was ideas that were in short supply and they were needed just as much as troops. With that in mind, General Sir John Harding, C–in–C of the Far East Land Forces and well aware of Calvert's success in the jungle of Burma, sent for him to get his advice on the conduct of operations against the Communists. From those ideas arose the Malayan Scouts, SAS Regiment with the now Lieutenant Colonel Mike Calvert in command.

Woodhouse was very nervous as he waited to be called for. He was also a bit resentful that Calvert had brought him to Malaya to become the Unit Intelligence Officer when he had specifically said during his interview that he was volunteering on the understanding that he would command soldiers in the jungle. Nonetheless, he felt that his service with the Scouts would be the beginning of an exciting and instructive period; it should certainly never be dull. As Calvert's Intelligence Officer he surmised that he would probably have some difficult times, but who cared for difficulties when they came from a military genius!

'John. The Colonel wants to see you now. Next tent.'

## Chapter 8

# 'A building site is muddy and rough'

The meeting that followed was to change Woodhouse's perspective on soldiering for the rest of his service.

'Sit down, Woodhouse. Have a drink.' A command, not an invitation. Mike Calvert, a big man, was sitting. His legs were squared to the front and his hands rested on the arms of the wickerwork chair. He wore a thoughtful expression on his heavy, square face and his eyes locked steadily onto Woodhouse:

> You have a big job here, a very important one. General Evans spoke very well of you in Hong Kong; I went very carefully into your record before I selected you. I shall expect a lot from you. Have you read the report that I made to General Sir John Harding?

Calvert, good psychologist that he was, probably knew full well that his opening sentences had already disarmed the resentment that he rightly suspected Woodhouse harboured at becoming the Intelligence Officer. Woodhouse had not read the report and Calvert told him to get a copy from Willie Wilson. He then went on to give a succinct appraisal of the situation in Malaya as he saw it. Woodhouse realized what Calvert had learned a long time ago: that it was better to meet a new officer over a drink and chat rather than the possibly stultifying atmosphere of an office.

The enemy being faced had their roots in the Malayan Communist Party. Early in 1942 as the Japanese advanced on Singapore, the British came to terms with the still outlawed Communist Party. Hurried efforts were made by a few British officers to train some volunteers from the party in guerrilla warfare to fight against the Japanese. During the Japanese occupation, mainly under Communist leadership, these guerrilla bands multiplied. In 1944 several British officers and wireless operators were successfully inserted into the country by air or submarine to join

Freddy Spencer Chapman who alone survived of the British left behind in 1942. His book *The Jungle is Neutral* provides an excellent backdrop to the political and military situation during those years. These men had the task, in different parts of the country, of assisting in the arming and training of the guerrillas. Those guerrillas were mostly Chinese. The Malays hated the Japanese and hoped for a British return. However, 100 years of peace under British protection had not fitted them for the hard life of guerrilla warfare. With some notable exceptions they remained understandably quiescent. The Chinese, however, made it clear that they were fighting the Japanese not to restore the defeated British, but in order to set up a Communist state independent of them. In 1945 the Japanese surrendered a few weeks before British forces were due to invade Malaya.

The Communists had agreed, under pressure from the British, to withhold their attacks on the Japanese communications until the day before the landing. Consequently very few offensive operations were ever undertaken by them. Though many were well trained, they lacked practical war experience and this was to prove fortunate for the British army three years later when the Communist rebellion began in earnest.

In 1945 the Communists realized that in the face of the strong British force that landed in the country after the Japanese surrender nothing could be gained by military means. Accordingly they concentrated on the political struggle. In particular they aimed to secure control of the trade unions. By early 1948 they had made considerable progress with the strategy but as in Indonesia years later, 'advice' from the outside persuaded them to strike too soon. It was clear to the police that the Communists were about to attempt to seize power, probably during a general strike. The British government, rightly reluctant to proscribe a political party and arrest its leaders, hesitated. In June that year in the state of Perak, three European planters were murdered and police action to arrest the Communist Party leaders came just too late; most of them fled to the jungle to join the many others who had been in the rain forests since 1942 befriending the aborigines.

In Calvert's opinion the Communists had begun their fight by biting off more than they could chew. They had tried to set up a liberated area but failed. The probably quite accurate estimate of numbers put the Communists at about 5,000 armed men in the jungle with an inestimable number of sympathizers outside in the towns and villages. Many of those supporters worked on the rubber plantations. The majority of the armed force was reckoned to be near the jungle fringes but many were living deep inside, near or with the aborigines.

The aborigines were completely under Communist control. They did everything for their Chinese masters: they grew food, hunted for meat, provided guides when necessary and reported on the movements of the security forces. The Communists treated them well and that was a problem in Calvert's view. Fixing Woodhouse with an intent stare, he said:

Now – what we must do is to win over the Sakai. Win them over and the bandits are lost. The Sakai are their eyes and ears – they must become ours. Win the Sakai battle and we win the war. It's just like Monty in Europe insisting on winning the air battle first; we out here must win the Sakai battle first. The Malays fiddle them right, left and centre. They take their produce and give them next to nothing for it. On the whole the Communists seem to give them a straight deal. This will not be an easy battle. To get to know about the Sakai you must go and see Yorkie Bjorkman at Kampong Aur. He's running a first class show there. He really knows the local Sakai and he's got several Communist kills to his credit. With a good intelligence network the battle is half won. Yes. You can learn a lot from Yorkie. He's a man with personality, guts and imagination. He's got thirty Malay police there and he controls the jungle for miles around – controls the jungle. Do you see?

Calvert was at pains to mention that the term 'Sakai' had become common in usage but it was actually a derogatory term as the literal translation from Malay was 'slave'.

Woodhouse well remembered the question being fired at him and hoped his reply was the right one: 'Yes. We set up places like Kampong Aur all over the deep jungle and do the same thing.'

'That's it, Woodhouse, you're getting into my mind; you must always be in my mind. That way you'll always be on the right lines.' He was grinning widely and Woodhouse gained a comforting feeling of pride, but Calvert suddenly frowned and gazed into space above John's head.

'Sins of commission I can forgive, sins of omission – never. There are far too many officers afraid to make a decision, looking for the rules before they do a bloody thing.' Fixing his eyes back on Woodhouse, he continued:

An officer who never makes a mistake is not doing anything, he's useless – but don't make the same mistake twice. We've got to get a move on with our training. People want to see results from us. They put a lot of faith in us. There isn't time to do a 'Monty'. We can't afford to wait until everything is ready before we begin operations. I know you wanted to go on operations but you and Willie and chaps like you who got into the last war must let the chaps who missed it have a chance.

I could have picked up twenty officers like you with war service but that isn't in the best interests of the army. The more young officers, chaps who joined since the war, the more experience they get now the better for the army. I want you to be quite clear what I want from you. You must get around the country and see people; get them to talk to you and then get their ideas. I'll put you on to the chaps worth seeing and Willie can fix up your movements. There are too many officers who put their preconceived ideas into practice. There is not enough thinking out there. They are so stereotyped and moulded by the service that they are incapable of change. These sweeps through the jungle fringes with whole companies of infantry are quite, quite useless. They usually return to base and say, 'There are no enemy in the area.' What they mean is that they made so much fucking noise that the enemy always saw them first and quietly disappeared.

There are no manuals or battle drills to tell us the answer. We have got to find the answer ourselves. A new sort of war requires us to find a new sort of counter war. How long do you think this war will last?

Woodhouse had not thought about that at all, but said that with his present scant knowledge it could take two years. Calvert's response was snappy.

'It will take five years at the very least and it will only be done in that time frame if everyone in this country gets down to it.' Noting Woodhouse's surprise, Calvert carried on:

What you don't realise yet is what hunting men in the Malayan jungle is like. Imagine England, all of it except a strip about thirty miles wide in the west, covered in jungle. In jungle you can see a man, indistinctly, if he's moving at perhaps as much as twenty-five yards. If he's not moving you probably won't see him unless you tread on him. If he's armed you won't get that far anyway. Imagine one road up the clear strip running from Southampton to Carlisle and about four winding roads crossing the country from east to west. Hide five thousand men in it in hundreds of small groups all adept at concealing themselves. Put twenty groups, each of a thousand men, very few of them knowing the jungle, and many hating it, along the roads. In each group of a thousand a third are busy looking after the other two-thirds and can't do anything else. Tell the rest to go into the jungle and find the others, not only find them but kill them too. Get the idea?

Woodhouse did get the idea!

Now, Woodhouse, you'll have heard that there have been complaints about a certain lack of discipline amongst the men we have so far recruited. Some of those complaints may be justified but remember that this is a building site and building sites are muddy and rough in the early stages of construction. I'll see you in the Mess shortly and we'll meet the Sergeants later. Don't worry, John, work hard and you'll do. Get in my mind, stay in it and we'll get on all right.

Woodhouse later wondered whether the first-time usage of his Christian name was a sign of tentative acceptance. Before going to the mess he got a thumbnail sketch of what Calvert's report comprised. In that report, which went directly to Sir Harold Briggs, the first Director of Operations, Calvert had recommended that the police should stop sending patrols into the jungle and concentrate on the protection of civilians in the villages and plantations along the jungle fringes. Special Branch should be expanded. It was, he wrote, essential to move the isolated Chinese, known as squatters, into new villages where they could be protected. This would be a tremendous undertaking that would involve hundreds of thousands of people. The army should concentrate on setting ambushes near the jungle edge to intercept the Communists as they came out for food or for offensive forays. Once these things were under way, he recommended that the main military effort should begin in Johore in South Malaya with the aim of clearing the country methodically from south to north. If these proposals were put into practice, then and only then should a special force be formed to operate for long periods in the deep jungle. The special force operations would be complementary to those of the infantry on the jungle fringes.

In an interview many, many years later John Woodhouse reflected on the brilliance of 'Mad' Mike Calvert:

He dominated all of us. None of us in experience, prestige, personality, even age, came anywhere near him. In consequence he was a very lonely man. He greatly admired Australians, seeing in them a resurgence of the old pioneering spirit of Britain. He really believed in the British Commonwealth. His faith and enthusiasm was infectious and exhilarating. Ideas flowed from him in a way which I had never heard from anyone else in the army. He predicted to me that we would have to stay in the jungle for months at a time and if I found that difficult to believe then I should remember that the CTs had been living in deep jungle for six years! Up to that point in my life Calvert was the most impressive, free-thinking strategist I had ever met. He was known in the Army as 'Mad Mike' but that was not an indication of foolhardiness – it was because he was simply a larger than life character. His personality and powers of argument forced you to be on your toes, widen your thought processes and look at a problem from all angles. I don't know about 'being in his mind' but he set my mind on fire and propelled me on a course of different thinking. At that moment in time I was probably more excited than I had ever been and the future seemed to be full of fascinating promise.

Interestingly, this appreciation of Calvert was to cause John Woodhouse to study 'The Master' from many different perspectives which would eventually lead to recognition of some of his weaknesses.

# Chapter 9

# 'You're in my mind, Woodhouse'

The next morning Woodhouse was rudely awakened by shouts from Willie Wilson. Jerking himself upright, he instantly regretted that he had drunk so much in the Warrant Officers' and Sergeants' Mess the night before. He rubbed his eyes and noted the time: five minutes to six. Wilson told him to get into his PT kit and draw a rifle from the armoury. Woodhouse had heard from his brother officers that Calvert's methods of training were to say the least unorthodox and he was full of trepidation. Along with his rifle he was told to draw ten rounds of ammunition. He and Wilson then trotted over to where an impatient Calvert was already stamping his foot.

The introduction to his first parade in the regiment, suffering as he was from lack of sleep and a hangover, was a rude one. In a half-circle facing Calvert the session began with rifle exercises. This form of self-torture (commonly known among the soldiers as 'pokey drill') was agonizing to the wrists and forearms which was caused by holding the rifle at arm's length, in improbable positions and hopelessly unbalanced. The aim, of course, was to strengthen the wrist and arm muscles. As his rifle sagged in his arms which were behaving like wilting plants, Woodhouse wondered how many colonels in the army paraded and drilled with their regiments at that time of the morning. Not many, and he fervently wished that Calvert didn't!

Next they ran over an assault course and into ragged scrub on the fringe of the rain forest. Woodhouse just had time to be violently sick before snap shooting practice began. While walking along a broad jungle track Calvert would suddenly drop to his knees and shout an order: 'Fallen tree, half right, one round, fire.' This would continue at a smart pace until the ten rounds of ammunition had been expended. The sound of other squads doing the same thing was nerve-wracking, especially as bullets could occasionally be heard whistling overhead. Then it was a run back to the camp for a wash and shave. This PT was done daily, the only variation being the mornings when they were issued with grenades instead of rifles. Woodhouse was never sure which he hated more. With grenades there was no proper grenade range. The grassy land between the clumps of jungle was intersected by monsoon rain drains. These were about a foot deep with another foot of banked earth above them. They were very narrow, but lying flat along them the body could be hidden. On grenade mornings they ran alongside the drains. Suddenly they would be stopped, leap for cover into the drain and hurl a grenade. They grew very good at taking cover quickly and amazingly no-one was ever hurt.

Later in the morning individual training in stalking one another was given in a realistic and uncomfortable way. In a patch of scrub ground perhaps a couple of hundred yards or so wide, two soldiers were armed with air rifles. They also wore fencing masks to protect their face and eyes. Starting from opposite sides of the scrub they had to worm their way to a central point and try to shoot their rival before being shot by him. The pellets, striking exposed flesh, were painful. It was, therefore, not surprising that there was a great deal of effort by the participants to get their shot in first. There was a rapid improvement in everyone's fieldcraft.

Woodhouse was not to suffer many of Calvert's early morning PT sessions as it inspired him to get his programme of visits organized quickly and soon he left the atmosphere of boyish enthusiasm that prevailed in Tampoi. However, before he departed there was an incident that aroused considerable controversy within the small community of the Scouts. Being on active service in Malaya it was permissible to use military transport to go to the city for recreation. One evening three officers including the doctor, Matt Forster, went, with a soldier driving the Jeep, into Singapore. They told the soldier to meet them at midnight at the Military Police car park where the Jeep had been left. At thirty minutes past midnight the soldier had still not returned so the officers drove the Jeep back without him.

The soldier reported this on his return and Mike Calvert sent for the officers. Their case was that the soldier, since he was late, deserved punishment and therefore they were not wrong to leave him. Calvert frowned as they spoke:

'Now listen to me,' he said, fixing them with a stern gaze and emphasizing his words. 'You must realise that it is your job to look after your soldiers at all times. Not just in barracks but at all times. When they have done something wrong then, more than at any other time, you must look after their interests. You have no idea, simply no idea, how to command men. The doctor perhaps has not much experience but you two should know.' He glared angrily at the two troop commanders. 'You could have punished him for being late back here, here where no-one else would have known about it.'

Attempts at remonstrating by the officers were cut short. The colonel decreed that the officers concerned would do the guard on the camp that night in place of the soldiers.

The news was greeted with superficial amusement by the soldiers. In fact, however, they were sharply divided over the propriety of the action and there was a good deal of sympathy for the officers.

Woodhouse thought that the startling and palpably unfair punishment achieved what Mike Calvert wanted but – paradoxically – it did not enhance his standing in the eyes of the soldiers. None of his officers ever forgot again what they had been told many times in lectures: your soldiers' interests always come first, however inconvenient it may be to you. Calvert never repeated this punishment.

The tour of visits that Woodhouse had organized was extensive, but only two of them made lasting impressions on him. The reasons were that in the main the people he had talked to did not have any practical experience of fighting the CTs. It was also a fact that his own lack of experience made it almost impossible to assess the value of other people's opinions.

Early in September 1950 he went to Majedec Barracks near Johore Baharu. That was the headquarters of the 26th Gurkha Infantry Brigade that was under command of Brigadier L.H.O. Pugh who had been Woodhouse's GSO1 in Hong Kong. The brigade on its arrival in Malaya a few months earlier had quickly made a name for itself. The Intelligence Officer was Frank King, later to become General Sir Frank King and a good friend to the SAS. From King he got a clearer picture of the fighting methods of the elusive enemy as he described numerous small-scale actions which the brigade had fought with the bandits. This briefing brought home to Woodhouse that tremendous patience would be required in this war. Literally thousands of hours might be spent before a soldier so much as saw one of the enemy. Each hour, he imagined, could mean an exhausting struggle through tangled masses of creepers, many barbed and sharp. He also was made to realize that most of the successes won by the British troops were based on police information. That was the picture forming in his mind.

Two weeks later he went to Majedec Barracks again. This time he was driven down to a rifle range where three light Auster aircraft were parked. This was the day that he was going to see deep jungle for the first time and meet one of the few men at that time who knew much about it: Bjorkmann (alias Yorkie). The pilot of the Auster was a captain in the Royal Artillery and as he showed Woodhouse the destination, Kampong Aur, on the map he said that Aur was a police post with a dodgy landing strip and confirmed that Yorkie was 'A bloody good bloke'. He was keen to get airborne as he had another task for that afternoon. He had some crates of beer on board and surmised that if they crash-landed then they would not be thirsty. The full length of the runway was needed for take-off.

Shortly the jungle filled the view in all directions and the potential difficulties of navigation impressed themselves on the newcomer's mind. The trees which varied in colour from dark to light green were, in many cases, festooned with creepers with full bright flowers striving to catch the sun. Woodhouse, who had learned to fly in Hong Kong, took a keen interest in the view and also the instrument panel. He was shocked and felt a little nausea when he saw that the oil-pressure gauge needle had swung silently round to zero. As he was about to mention it, the pilot calmly stated: 'Oil pressure gone. Sorry. Have to return to JB. We'll climb as we go. We should be there in half an hour. There's a good chance we'll make it as we've got plenty of height and there are bags of clearings right ahead of us.'

Woodhouse's eyes flickered between the altimeter rising steadily and the oil-pressure gauge grimly stuck on zero. He then studied the ground below, noting with relief the first clearing. He was glad that he had brought a rifle, compass and full jungle kit. He was confident that if they got down in one piece they would get out. He had an interesting thought that it would be a novel way to go into the jungle for the first time and he almost hoped that it would happen. He changed his mind quickly when he got a closer look at the first clearing and saw that it was littered with lethal-looking tree stumps. The engine, however, maintained a steady roar and they landed without incident. The fault was quickly diagnosed – a broken gauge – there had been no actual loss of pressure. An hour later and they were airborne again with the clouds already building up for the almost daily rainfall. The pilot had to descend lower than he wanted in order to follow the Sungei Rompin which flowed past Kampong Aur. Woodhouse recalled this, his first landing in jungle:

I had by now lost what little idea I'd had of our position. I was definitely afraid in this stormy scene as we were at least fifty miles from any known human habitation. We were thrown about violently in our frail little single-engine aircraft. I felt a tremendous admiration for the pilots who flew those aircraft over the jungle day after day.

Very suddenly the river came into sight, we crossed it and I saw in a quick flash a row of thatched bashas (a term used to describe any sort of accommodation) along the west bank. We turned steeply now only scant feet above the trees and I saw a narrow grass strip on the opposite bank to the bashas. On one side it was lined by the jungle with two-hundred-foot high trees. On the other side it dropped thirty feet or so down a cliff into the swirling deep waters of the Sungei Rompin. We levelled off, a treetop loomed out of the rain and flashed by us on the right, the engine was cut back and we dropped swiftly on to the grass strip, landing with only a slight jolt. The pilot took off as soon as I, my kit and the beer could be disentangled from the plane. The rain had stopped and I saw a short, blue-eyed man striding towards me.

I took an instant liking to Yorkie who was of a diminishing breed that one half expected to meet in those days at the far-flung outposts of the Empire. He had served with great distinction on special operations behind the German front in Yugoslavia. He was a much-decorated soldier who, of course, never mentioned that and probably never wore his medals. He was short, self-confident and slightly aggressive in his bearing. He respected men for what they did and their rank did not impress him at all, neither did it inhibit his speech which had an Elizabethan robustness. As the Police Commander of Kampong Aur he controlled thirty Malay policemen. He ruled with a rod of iron but I noticed that he could joke with them and I also saw that they had a smile in their eyes when they chatted with him. Very quickly I recognised an outstanding leader and I looked forward to his briefings. His official job was to collect and collate information and do what he could with his small force to disrupt the bandits' local organisation. He had killed about six of them without loss at the time of my visit.

After a very good evening meal, a chicken curry of gargantuan proportions, I expected that we would turn to work. But Yorkie was not in the mood and perhaps wanted to find out what sort of chap I was as I do not give much away at first acquaintance. Living at Aur for three months at a time was probably a good way of saving money but it was a lonely life for Yorkie so we talked and drank beer and whisky. We discussed Malaya and the folly of war in such a lovely country; the prospects of mining, iron ore and timber; the little-known aborigines; Chinese customs and some of the leading characters in military and police hierarchies. The night was still and clear and we sat in chairs on an earthen path overlooking the river and the airstrip. The air smelled of damp earth and a sense of peace prevailed. It was quite late when we retired.

After breakfast the next morning Yorkie took Woodhouse to his office. The papers on his desk were jumbled, but it was a sure hand that reached under a pile and pulled out a marked map. The markings were tracks and terrorist camps which he and his men had found. Kampong Aur was surrounded by them, each camp marked with the date on which it had been discovered. Most had held only three or four men and all were now abandoned but others, well hidden, were known to be in the area.

The report also listed several aborigines who had reported the presence of terrorists together with such details as they remembered, or cared to pass on. The CTs sometimes bought food from the aborigines but were careful not to let them know the exact location of their camps.

'This is just the area for your boys,' Yorkie spoke earnestly, looking hard at Woodhouse with his fists clenched over the map. 'You can see they are obviously using the area as a base to build up food stocks and to serve as a safe retreat whenever things get too hot near the jungle edge. I personally am convinced from what the abos say that there is a big camp somewhere on the Sungei Sekin. I'd bet my bottom dollar on it.'

Woodhouse was impressed by Yorkie's conviction and convinced that he was not talking just for effect. Yorkie went on: 'Tell Mike Calvert about it. Tell him I'll do anything he wants me to do now or later. I know this is an op worth doing and the Deputy Chief Police Officer, Mansfield, agrees. Don't listen to any other stupid bastard who tells you there is nothing here.'

Woodhouse told Yorkie that he was sold on the idea and that he would pass it all on to Calvert. He said that in his estimation it would be two or three months before the men were trained up to a suitable standard. Yorkie did not like that statement and he somewhat grumpily left Woodhouse to read through old reports to try to get a better feel for the problem.

As he read the reports and studied the marked map, Woodhouse began to shape his ideas on how the Malayan Scouts should operate. First of all would be the collection and collation of strands of information from the aborigines, captured documents and from other patrols that might suggest the CTs' presence. Perhaps air reconnaissance might also produce some intelligence. Then, once a squadron was committed to an area, it would start from a central base, perhaps Kampong Aur. Each of the four troops in the squadron would probe outward, like the spread fingers of a hand, twisting through the jungle searching for signs of the CTs. Each troop would field four patrols of three men and these in turn would branch off from the troop base and meet up again three or four days later to report their findings. With each troop there would be a wireless and trained operator to report information to the RHQ at Dusan Tua. Calvert would want a European police lieutenant with each troop to speak with the aborigines and eventually organize them into a network of informers. Inevitably some troops would draw a blank but as soon as news of the enemy was reported back by one troop, others from the blank areas would move to join it as fast as possible. The troops would be periodically resupplied by air.

Woodhouse clearly remembered Calvert telling his officers one night in the mess that the Scouts must get to feel that the jungle was their home and that they would only abandon it for short periods of leave. They would stay in the jungle for at least three months at a time. It would take some weeks to locate the enemy and the pressure of the hunt would have to be maintained if the CT were to be defeated. This was logical because sometimes it would take a week or more just to reach the area of operations so obviously it was not economical to stay in the jungle for anything less than three months. A myth, which sadly was supported by the Royal Army Medical Corps, had grown up among the British army in Malaya that it was inadvisable (if not impossible) for British soldiers to stay in the jungle longer than three weeks at any one time. Clearly in deep jungle if the Scouts were to wrest control of the aborigines away from the enemy they would have to stay there until the enemy were killed or gave up. All Woodhouse's theorizing at that time gave understanding and credence to one of Calvert's statements: 'I want long-distance runners in this regiment, not sprinters.'

Putting his notes aside, Woodhouse went to find Yorkie to ask if he could go out for the rest of the day to see for himself what the jungle was like. Yorkie pointed out a track on the map and told him that he could get there and back the same day. The track had not been checked for some three weeks. He gave him a corporal and five policemen as escorts. Some notes from Woodhouse's personal log book are very interesting as they record some mixed emotions:

We started out, six policemen and myself, in a boat with an outboard motor. The river above Kampong Aur opened out growing broader and slower. The jungle leaned over high banks trailing fingers of some exotic green creeper into the muddy water. It was impossible to see inside its umbrageous depths. Every time we curved round a bend a new vista came into sight, some longer, some shorter but each like the last, with the same broad central avenue of muddy water with its two fringes of vast primeval jungle.

Occasionally a startled bird shrieked away but otherwise apart from the buzzing motor there was a heavy silence. I became acutely

conscious that we were plainly visible and audible – at the mercy of
any terrorist who happened to be near the river bank.

When we finally ran silently into the bank, having cut the engine,
I was relieved to jump ashore. The police corporal led the way and
I followed him. For a few hundred yards we went through a partly
cleared stretch of forest and then we were into primary jungle. Both
its silence and its immensity impressed me. The giant trunks of
trees stretched straight and unbroken for two hundred feet or more
towards an invisible sky. Occasional small holes in the tree canopy
glittered with the light of the glaring sun above it. But down on the
damp leaf-carpeted floor the light was dull. The floor itself sprouted
innumerable saplings, trailing thorns and bushes, so intertwined
and dense that I could see for only ten or twenty yards.

There was time to wonder. Within a few minutes I was running
with sweat, my hands already torn and scratched. I did not succeed
in spotting all the thorny creepers which clawed at me as I passed – I
just blundered through them. At first I detached the thorns with care
as a man will release himself when his trousers hook in barbed wire,
but after an hour or so I began to tear myself free, feeling a sullen
fury surge within me each time I was hooked. At last, near noon, we
stopped. The corporal pointed dramatically: 'Jalan – track,' he said.

I looked hard – I had seldom felt so cheated. This miserable
overgrown little path – for this we had sweated and struggled for
three hours. Speechless, I looked with bitter envy at the unruffled
policemen. I drank my water. The corporal lit a cigarette. I was
about to tell him to put it out but suddenly felt conscious of my
own inadequacy and decided not to do so. Then I was thoroughly
ashamed of my weakness, angry with everything. The journey back
was a nightmare. I began to think the corporal must be lost but my
compass kept telling me we were going the right way. In six hours
we covered a total distance of three miles. Yorkie later told me that
this was normal for good primary jungle away from any track. It was
on this day that I fully realised the immensity of the task in front of
us. These jungles stretched for roughly five hundred miles and there
were about eight thousand terrorists hiding in them, nearly all well
if lightly armed.

That little trip into the jungle opened Woodhouse's eyes to the basic aspects of training and the lessons that he and others would have to learn. He had had a small taste of the potential problems of navigation and the difficulties of concentrating when dripping with sweat that burned the eyeballs. He had doubted the police corporal's chosen route back to the boat but now realized that the corporal was probably backtracking using tell-tale signs that he himself simply could not detect. Great patience would be required to counter the annoying, clinging creepers and thorns and the clumps of bamboo that were sometimes simply too enormous to circumnavigate. On his day trek he was not even carrying a noticeable burden. What would it be like with ten or more days of rations and basic equipment weighing him down?

Soon afterwards he was back with Mike Calvert in Tampoi. Talking to him in the officers' mess he enthused over what he had seen in Kampong Aur. He told him:

> If we start posts like Aur we can win control of the area around. I am quite sure of it, sir. One day we shall have a whole series of posts like Aur up and down the country wherever there are aborigines and in the end there will be no place, however remote, which will be safe for the communists.

The colonel chuckled and called out to the other officers: 'Here, come and listen to John, he's in my mind you see; you're in my mind, John.' The colonel was delighted; the other officers were more sceptical.

At the end of August 1950 the colonel decided to take John Woodhouse with him by night train to Kuala Lumpur to visit Army HQ. They were due to leave camp at six in the evening. The driver was late and Calvert, already in a bad temper, became fiercely abusive to everyone in sight. The others managed to disappear one by one so Woodhouse bore the brunt of his rage:

> 'Why the hell didn't you see the driver was here on time?'
> 'I'm sorry, sir, I didn't know you wanted me to check up on him.'
>   'You bloody infantry officers are all the same. You never know and you never do anything unless you have it in writing. You didn't know – you didn't know – well why the bloody hell don't you bugger off and find out now.'

The driver eventually appeared and the journey to Johor Baharu was conducted in a strained silence. Once inside the sleeping carriage, Calvert began to unpack and asked Woodhouse how many grenades he had packed. Once again he exploded with anger when told that Woodhouse had not packed any grenades. 'For God's sake, John, you always pack grenades on the night train. It's the ideal weapon at night when the train gets shot up.' As they moved to the bar Calvert's temper evaporated quickly.

The bar on the night train was a famous one in those years. As the lights were extinguished when the train rattled through scrub and jungle, a candle would be lit as the occupants settled down with their drinks, listening with half an ear for the smack of terrorist bullets. The situation gave the bar a spice unique in Malaya. Nearly all the clientele were army officers, seldom above the rank of major, and planters. Senior officers, civil servants and business executives usually chose to travel by air which was a pleasant journey as well as safe, and took only a couple of hours instead of twelve. Planters and officers tended, in most bars, to keep in their respective groups, but on the night train conversations were easily opened with complete strangers.

Once the lights were switched off the Chinese barman sat on the floor. He would stand up only when drinks were called for. When the train was fired on it would come to a stop and a platoon of soldiers stood by to follow up the enemy withdrawal. In most cases little damage was done to either the train or the terrorists. In the bar soldier and civilian vied with one another as to who could show the most indifference when the shooting started.

On this occasion, Woodhouse's first experience of the night train, he and Calvert had gone to bed before the shooting started. As the train ground to a shuddering halt Calvert, clutching a carbine and bemoaning Woodhouse's negligence in omitting to bring grenades, went rapidly in his pyjamas to the open door of the carriage. Woodhouse followed more circumspectly and peered out into the blackness. He had the same uncomfortable naked feeling that he had experienced on the boat at Kampong Aur. Calvert seemed about to leap from the door to follow the enemy, but Woodhouse managed to dissuade him by telling him that the escort was about to board the train again. Calvert's last words before he went to sleep were 'If only you'd brought the bloody grenades.'

In later chats another SAS officer, apart from John Woodhouse, told the author how stimulating the journeys on the night train could be. Captain John Slim, as a veteran of Korea and the Malayan campaign, remarked on the sheer delight of the free-flowing conversations about the SAS and its future. At the time no-one suspected that the threat of disbandment would one day face the regiment. Before the end of the Malayan campaign Dare Newell, a squadron commander in the SAS who had wartime service in Albania with the SOE and with Force 136 in Malaya behind him, would become a key figure based in London bearing the brunt of the military and political battles as the SAS fought to preserve its future. John Slim, an SAS troop commander in Malaya who later commanded a squadron and then 22 SAS Regiment and currently serves as patron of the SAS Association said of those train journeys:

> They could be almost electrifying. The ideas bounced back and forth at great speed. We drank a little because it was a long journey and this only helped the flow of conjecture. There was no thought of disbandment initially – we thought just of the present and discussed SOPs, regimental characters and our last operation.
>
> But later our thoughts and discussions would turn to the future. I can quite clearly remember an occasion when Dare and I sat up all night in John Woodhouse's cabin on the southbound night train and the ideas were flowing thick and fast. The question of the future of the SAS came up – it was raised by John. We came to certain conclusions, each of which was reached by prompts from John. We concluded that the SAS must continue and that three conditions should prevail if the Regiment was to remain effective; (a) the Regiment should only be used on strategically significant operations; (b) the Regiment should not be commanded by local divisional commanders but must be under direct command of the CIGS; (c) the Regiment should be trained and organised to operate on a worldwide basis under any geographical conditions. Remember that this was before any of us really got to know David Stirling. Through energetic discussion and argument his concepts for the Regiment came naturally to us. Later on return to base we sat and talked with

other officers and told them that what we had determined as the way ahead was what we had to sell in order to stave off disbandment. For me, most certainly, it was the start of a love affair in that I wanted nothing more than the SAS.

## Chapter 10

# Tactics Put to the Test

On 29 September 1950 (Woodhouse's 28th birthday) the regiment moved into their new camp at Dusan Tua. This was to become the operational HQ as well as the regiment's base camp. Early in October 'A' Squadron were to complete their training by spending six to eight weeks in the jungle north-east of Ipoh. This was an area where terrorists were known to be and the squadron was hoping for the first kill.

'A' Squadron was not going to be alone. RHQ, including the second-in-command, John Harrington, the signals officer, Wilf Batty and Woodhouse with some of the intelligence section were to go in with them. The colonel himself would command and direct the training and his first orders were that the squadron would move through the bordering rubber estates by night. He aimed to have his men into the jungle by first light before their presence could be reported by civilian agents or terrorist lookouts.

Apart from his painful experience at Kampong Aur Woodhouse had no practical experience and so he went to chat with Mike Pearson who commanded 2 Troop. Pearson showed him what he needed and into his small green pack went a mess tin, spoon, four days' rations, solid fuel, socks, cigarettes, matches (in tins), rifle oil and cleaning kit, water sterilizing tablets, candles, anti-malaria pills, torch and batteries and three small luminous balls which were supposed to be put next to grenades and weapons at night so that they could be picked up instantly. This was another of Calvert's brainwaves but they proved to be superfluous, except as the basis of some crude soldierly humour. Rolled inside a waterproof poncho cape which hung from straps underneath the pack went pullover, PT shorts, more socks and a parachute strip. The latter were all for sleeping in at night. The parachute material, though light in weight, was warm enough up to an altitude of about 2,000ft. Clothes worn in the day were always soaked in rain as well as sweat and impossible to sleep in. Some men carried a pair of hockey boots to wear at night; replacements for the sodden jungle boots in case of a need to stand to during the night. On his body he had a field dressing, maps and compass, a carbine and ammunition, water bottle and a grenade. Everything carried was waterproofed as well as possible using plastic bags. A heavy sharp machete 18in long hung in a sheath from his belt.

In addition to those personal items he carried a vast aerial photograph, spare maps, pins, message pads, cipher pads and other paraphernalia associated with the job of Intelligence Officer. Perhaps his biggest folly was to pack an enormous torch which could be placed over a map so the map appeared magnified through an illuminated glass. He was perturbed when he found that he could only lift the pack onto his back with great difficulty; even more perturbed when he remembered that Calvert had estimated that the initial march would take one night and two days. He took a little heart from noting that other men seemed to have similar problems.

About this time a matter arose that has plagued Special Forces ever since. The regimental base began to endure a number of visits from the press, both local and international. Calvert did his best to emphasize that the unit was certainly not going to bring spectacular or quick results. However, special units have a fascination for the public that makes it difficult to avoid them being over-publicized. This has two bad effects. It attracts the wrong type of volunteer (as well as the best) and, more seriously, it can arouse jealousy in other more conventional units. Goodwill and help are essential to special units, whether they are newly-formed or well-established. The publicity can lead to swollen heads among a few of the soldiers and in Malaya the bad behaviour of the few was quickly seized upon to brand all members of the regiment as an ill-disciplined rabble. Amusingly, the day before 'A' Squadron was launched on the training operation, a press correspondent arrived who plainly had no experience of the services and little of Malaya. He was told that the next day would see the regiment moving into the jungle in search of the enemy. Very solemnly he asked 'Tonight I suppose all the officers will assemble for a Last Supper?' and from that point on 'The Last Supper' was the name given to the often hilarious parties that were held before going back to the jungle.

On 10 October a convoy of 3-ton trucks transported the men to the area of Tanjung Rambutan. After leaving the trucks the eighty men moved into single file and began the trek through the rubber estates. They made little sound. Woodhouse was in the middle of the line leading the RHQ section. The colonel chose to be up in the front. They passed a Marine Commando encampment. The road soon ended and became a footpath. A Marine sentry in the trees murmured 'Good luck mate.' Once past him they knew they were out on their own and Woodhouse felt a tingle of excitement knowing that at last they were starting to do their job: the hunting down of CTs.

He was soon brought back to reality. In order to see the man in front in the pitch darkness under the trees, they had tied their luminous balls or open compasses to the back of their packs so that they showed a tiny glow of light.

As any soldier knows, single files stumbling through the dark means that towards the back of the column men are either standing waiting while those in front surmount any obstacle, or they are rushing to catch up when they in turn have crossed the hurdle. Also in Malaya there are many 'fireflies' which appear with a glow like that of a lighted cigarette end or the luminosity of a compass. Before long the column was broken when a man followed the light of a firefly for a few yards instead of a compass. This happened several times. After two hours of stumbling through the dark the whole force came to a soggy halt in a grassy swamp between the rubber and the jungle. Further progress at night was plainly impossible. For another two hours they slept fitfully in damp and crestfallen huddles wherever they could find a spot that was not under water.

At dawn they could see the line of the jungle edge several hundred feet above them. They were going into hills that were rising steeply to heights of over 5,000ft, though the climbs on this first day would be rather less than half of that. They continued to move throughout the day slowly and laboriously in single file. Mike Calvert was determined to get his men in together to the site of an old terrorist camp he had visited early in the year. From there they would train, gradually patrolling further away and living on stores that would be air-dropped in sufficient quantity to last six weeks.

They reached a suitable spot for a night stop and Woodhouse made only a very basic shelter. A soldier appeared with a message from Mike Calvert to report to him at once. The colonel was displeased that so far their wireless had failed to get through to Dusan Tua 150 miles away. They had tried and tested radios that were powered by pedal generators. These were pedalled by one man who sat on a bicycle-style seat on a tripod, but the effort was similar to that required of a cyclist going hard up a very steep hill. The men took it in turns and cursed at the physical effort required after a hard day's march. At that time all their signals were sent in cipher which was slow and laborious to code and decode. The colonel wrote signals that were graphic and emphatic, but not concise. He told Woodhouse to see that the signals got through and not to go back until he could tell him that all had been sent. He spent the next three hours hopping between his own basha and the signaller who was with his officer about 50 yards away. Finally the weary signaller finished. The colonel grunted a 'Well done' when he reported and he felt that somehow it had been worthwhile.

The next day after several hours slogging along, a message came back to Woodhouse saying that contact had been lost with the front of the column. Plainly it was up to him to lead the tail half of 'A' Squadron on to the planned destination. Fortunately he had carefully studied his map and knew roughly his position. In jungle the words 'map reading' are nonsense. The art of movement is a form of dead-reckoning navigation. It is not possible to look at an expanse of country and find its counterpart on the map. So here they navigated. Indeed when there was no track to follow it became possible, with experience, to pick the best route by detecting faint animal trails or spotting 20 yards ahead which bushes and creepers were the least dense. Using the compass to see that they were roughly headed in the right direction, they forced their way on by what seemed to be the easiest going, for example following a long spur climbing up to a big ridge.

(On this operation Woodhouse concentrated on improving his jungle navigation. In the blank spaces on the maps he would draw faint pencil lines to indicate the probability of river routes and where spurs to high ridges may occur. He carried an aneroid barometer, which was not only useful in areas where the heights of hills may be marked on the maps but also invaluable in his tracings to fill in the blank spots.)

When he next stopped the column, after an hour's march, he had to make a guess as to how far they could have gone. With a little practice this became easy; hardly ever did they manage more than 1 mile an hour and this was only possible on good tracks. So by watching his compass at frequent intervals he could tell the direction the spur was taking them; by guessing the speed he had a fair idea of how far in that direction they had travelled. With this crude fix of his position completed, he studied the map and recalled the ground they had walked over. By comparing what ground they had covered with what the map showed (or didn't show), it was then possible to get a nearly accurate fix of position. Never did he travel on a compass bearing – that would have been quite impossible – so the easiest physical route would be chosen and the compass was used to establish the general direction of travel. Judging the distance travelled was a matter of experience in which Woodhouse soon became expert.

On this, his second day in the jungle, he was untrained and far from confident. Urgent necessity forced him to use his head, and the thought of the colonel's fury if he failed as well as his probable pleasure if he succeeded made him decide to go forward instead of waiting for Calvert to come back. They met the colonel to his relief in the late afternoon. He was a little disappointed that what he considered a rather skilled piece of navigation, especially for his first attempt, was taken completely for granted by Calvert when he spoke: 'Ah, John, glad to see you. Get your men back in to proper position. I want to move on to the base camp site at once. Get moving.' Woodhouse soon discovered why Calvert was impatient to move: he had made a small error in his own navigation. If he had not, they should probably have missed him. Nonetheless the lack of praise had an effect on him; why the hell should he be congratulated for being an able officer? It was a lesson that he carried with him, sometimes to the detriment of his leadership principles. If a soldier, regardless of rank, excels in some way then his commander should at least show some appreciation.

That night a base camp was established. Under the torrential rain, which was almost a daily occurrence each afternoon, two man bashas were erected. The construction of a 'jungle' bed and efficient shelter were skills that Woodhouse had yet to learn but there was good-natured assistance from men who had experience and he was a fast learner. He shared his position with the signaller and encoded Calvert's often long-winded messages. All of this was done in the dark by spluttering candlelight. Crude candle-holders were fashioned from cutting down the side of empty food cans and inserting the candle onto the base. The inside of the can gave a degree of light amplification and reflection along with protection from draughts.

The base camp that Calvert had selected was ideal for a number of reasons. It had been used by about thirty CTs and it was skilfully sited. Woodhouse later said that it was, without doubt, the best CT camp site that he ever saw in Malaya. That alone demonstrated to 'A' Squadron that the CTs were jungle-wise and tactically competent. The camp was on a small steeply-sided conical hill which rose off a spur that was itself an offshoot of a main ridge. A tiny stream trickled less than 30 yards below the camp. The lower side of the hill dropped 700ft in 500 yards. The approach to the hill from the ridge above was also steep. There were signs that *punjis* had been used. These were sharpened bamboo stakes pushed into the ground and angled to the likely approach routes of the enemy and sometimes the points were smeared with dung in the hope of setting up an infection in the hapless soldier who happened to get speared. The camp offered as much visibility as the jungle allowed and it was a first-class defensive position.

During this operation a parachute resupply drop was taken. Finding a more or less clear area, the co-ordinates were sent to base. There was visual and voice contact with the aircraft which dropped the parachutes from a height of about 300ft. A smoky fire was used to give the aircraft pilot the wind direction and a 'recorder' marked on a sketch map the approximate points where each parachute landed. Collecting the stores afterwards and carrying the heavy loads back to the base camp was brutally hard work, made palatable only by the thought of the fresh food and rum ration in the packs.

Most of the soldiers in the squadron would have been half-expecting an attack by the Chinese, even if it was confined to firing into the camp from a safe distance. The army in Malaya insisted on sentries being posted by day and night in every camp. On the whole Mike Calvert agreed with this philosophy in large camps but he taught the Malayan Scouts that with a strength of one officer and about twelve soldiers who would in any case be split up for days on end into patrols of three or four, they must rely for their protection on concealment and not sentries. Of course the reason for this was that sentries would mean three men every day staying defensively on guard instead of being deployed offensively to hunt and kill terrorists. The next eight years were to prove Calvert right and the army wrong. His decision was based on a sound appreciation that the enemy, being a guerrilla force, would not attack a regular camp where the chance of success would be too uncertain and the risk of casualties too great. As for the overnight camps of small patrols, if they stopped late and made sure that they were not near a track, the chances of an enemy patrol finding them in thick jungle were extremely remote. Certainly the risk was well worth taking in view of the increased patrol effort made available by the absence of sentries.

As the troops deployed from the main base to set up their patrol patterns in their own areas, both Calvert and Woodhouse became fully aware of the serious lack of training. Much of Woodhouse's time was spent in encoding and decoding signals and taking his turn on the pedal generator. That frustrated him immensely; vital though the job was, he wanted to be out honing his own navigational and fieldcraft skills. If Calvert was ever going to give him a command, he had to raise himself to a standard that was better than the norm in order to effectively train and lead others. With that prospect in mind, he began to point out tactical and battle discipline errors wherever he saw them. This was noted by both. The squadron was on active service and so benefited from a daily tot of rum. This was consumed in various guises after the evening meal; it was an almost social occasion. Woodhouse recalled one of those evening sessions when he was sitting relaxed with Calvert and Colin Park (a civilian from the Department of Aborigines):

One evening, the cipher done and the pedals still, Mike Calvert, Colin Park and myself, all feeling content with life, sat talking in the basha. I admired Colin who made a practice of moving alone in the jungle, teaching me that was the safest way for a man to go since he was almost certain to hear the movement of any terrorist party before being heard by them. It was something I was to try for myself in the not too distant future. He talked to me that evening about the control of fear, to remember that fear is shared by the enemy makes it more endurable. I was surprised to hear him talk about it – imagining him to be fearless. He was tremendously fit and an enthusiast for our cause. A year later he was killed with two others in a terrorist ambush on the Sungei Legap a few miles to the north. He often seemed to me to have a presentiment of his death in Malaya.

The conversation turned to our Australian signallers. We had six attached from the Australian army. Calvert had a high regard for Australians, seeing in them a revival of the questing spirit and zest for life that had marked the young, vigorous and expanding English nation in the time of Elizabeth I. Since he himself would have been much at home in those times, this was not surprising. Calvert looked forward to the future, when the British Empire would be led by the young white Dominions. He had a deep belief in the basic idealism of the old colonial administrators, and I began to see the Commonwealth, as perhaps he saw it, a living force striving to do right and bring justice to its entire people. Often misdirected, sometimes committing follies, but with a good aim and a kind purpose. As Britain tired so the Dominions would strengthen and shoulder some of the burden. There were people who thought of Mike Calvert as just a professional soldier happy in any war. They were absolutely wrong. He fought for an ideal, a patriotic ideal, and he believed in showing chivalry to an enemy however evil the enemy may be.

There were men in Malaya, as there have been in Kenya and Cyprus, who believed that torture against murderers is justified if the aim is to get information. A police officer once suggested this to Mike Calvert in Malaya. He was a very junior officer and his opinion carried no weight. However, the colonel went white with anger asking him how he dared to suggest that the British should sink to levels of depravity common in the Middle Ages but extinguished in civilised Europe until the appearance of Fascism and Communism in the present century. He took the young officer by the arm and propelled him out of the tent. He then related to us the story of a captured Burmese who had worked and spied for the Japanese in World War II. When asked by Calvert what the Japanese would have done to him had they caught him spying on them, he replied: 'They would kill me.' Calvert told him that the British were not like that – they had no need to kill him – they would set him free. He explained to his men that the reprieved spy and his family would repeat those words for the rest of their lives and thus many would become friendly with the British. Had he been executed his relatives would have become lifelong enemies.

Calvert convinced me that the nation which stoops to those levels is sowing the seeds of its own downfall. Like tolerance of ill-discipline in a unit, it spreads, until the thin veneer of decency in which we have learned to cloak ourselves is shattered. The trivial short-term advantages are not worth the shame, disgrace and contempt which such conduct brings. When a war is won by such methods is over, the seeds of defeat in the ensuing peace have already been planted.

There were two Chinese in the regiment at that time: Captain Y Win MC who had fought with the Chindits but did not stay very long, and Corporal Ip Kwong Lau. Ip was a Hong Kong Chinese initially attached to the Scouts as an interpreter. In 1942, Ip, a British subject in Japanese-occupied Hong Kong, had walked across China and Burma to join the British army before volunteering to become the personal escort to Colonel Francis Rome, second-in-command of the 77th Indian Infantry Brigade. Rome commanded the landing ground at Broadway in the heart of Burma and was awarded the DSO, on the recommendation of Brigadier Mike Calvert, for his leadership in the Battle of Mogaung.

Ip Kwong Lau and Woodhouse were to see a great deal of each other in later years. Since the enemy was mainly Chinese and as a race they had shown a real aptitude for guerrilla warfare, it was logical that Calvert should have urged the raising of a Chinese Squadron in the regiment. That was not the only reason that Calvert favoured a Chinese Squadron. Many Chinese made the same escape from Hong Kong as Ip Kwong Lau; they walked to Chunking and then got lifts by air over 'The Hump' at which point Calvert grabbed as many as possible to join his Chindit

Brigade. They were first-class fighters and he may have had as many as 350 at one point.

Mike Calvert was optimistic that he would get approval. Woodhouse expressed doubts (as did Ip Kwong Lau) about the political reliability of recruiting from the Chinese; perhaps they would only join in order to defect to the Communists? They were sitting on a rough bench of split bamboo, tin mugs of a hot rum concoction in their hands. The night was still and warm. Mike Calvert was serious; he looked at his empty mug before he put it down and postulated: 'No man will fight for another unless he has complete trust in him. If you trust them and if you are a leader they will follow you. I am very keen on this project and we must get it through.' He went on to say that it was necessary for the Scouts to have a successful action against the terrorists in order to strengthen their hand in getting the Chinese Squadron.

It was at that point that Calvert's priorities changed and the importance of showing results tended to conflict with the requirement to properly train the squadron. The area in which the squadron was deployed was barren. There were neither terrorists nor aborigines there. This did not, however, stop Calvert 'suspecting' that a CT camp lay within the area and he organized a bombing operation using a squadron of RAF Lincoln bombers. Aided by orange marker balloons, the bombs were dropped on the co-ordinates indicated. Many trees were shattered and the marking of the target was proved effective. The only thing missing was the CT camp!

The squadron had shown that training was sadly lacking: jungle navigation was still foreign to many of the soldiers, fieldcraft was bad, litter discipline and noise control was abysmal.

Back in the base at Dusan Tua conditions were still very basic. Accommodation was still tents. The latrines still lacked seats; there were no proper other ranks' messing facilities. Willie Wilson the adjutant was screaming out for a break and Calvert decided that Woodhouse should take the bulk of the RHQ personnel out so that Wilson could join his CO in the jungle. The group reached Dusan Tua on 19 November 1950. Woodhouse was now confident in his ability to live and navigate in the jungle and he was optimistic that when 'A' Squadron returned in early December they would be equally proficient.

He soon realized that the reputation of the regiment was sinking rapidly. Contempt was shown quite openly in some quarters. He grew increasingly worried about the lack of discipline and poor administration. He had little administrative experience himself and said that he did not initially face up to Calvert as he should have done to tell of the doubts and fears he felt about that side of the regiment's affairs. In any event, Calvert was not interested in tidy stores and meticulous book-keeping. Unfortunately he did not get the officers and warrant officers that he deserved, but men of ability who could do these necessary jobs without supervision were essential to him. The HQ was badly understaffed and Calvert's policy of getting men on to operations as quickly as possible never let the organization get going. The discipline factor seemed to Woodhouse to be the most serious problem. He was so disturbed by the situation that he was considering asking to be returned to his unit. Calvert was frequently abusive but Woodhouse was not to know that he was already sick with amoebic dysentery. In his memoirs he recalled an incident:

> One evening he and I were left alone in the mess. He accused me of having no faith in the regiment and no loyalty. He sneered at officers who served on intelligence staffs. White and angry, I fought my corner by insisting that discipline was much more important than he seemed to believe. The colonel became more and more abusive. Finally he picked up a bottle by the neck and looking at me said 'You are afraid of me, aren't you?' As I refused to answer he repeated: 'You're afraid, yes, you are, afraid.' I got up, determined to walk out without looking back. 'Sit down, John.'
>
> The sudden use of my Christian name after his tirade had its calculated shock effect. I sat down promptly. He was calm and friendly. 'You know, John, not many people will talk freely to me and so I have to wring information out of them.' He shifted his gaze to the ceiling before continuing. 'Some men talk in their cups but with some you have to make them angry – information by insult you might call it.' He chuckled and repeated the phrase. 'Of course if you don't believe in what we are trying to do then don't stay, leave the sinking ship if you want to.'

Woodhouse was shaken that the colonel seemed to have deduced so clearly what he had been considering over the past few days. He was totally convinced that the tactics of the regiment and its aim of getting control of the deep jungle were right and he said so with some force. Still visibly angry, he reiterated that without good battle discipline the squadrons would never reach the high standards that would be necessary to achieve success and his time and Calvert's time would have been wasted. Calvert made the matter of discipline seem not nearly as bad as it was and explained the difficulty he had in getting rid of bad characters. 'It is a very lonely job this one, you probably hadn't thought of that, had you? But I have never made close friends since the war and anyway a soldier shouldn't do so, it's so much worse when they get killed.'

Soon afterwards they finished talking; the air had been cleared and that night Woodhouse made up his mind. They had the right answer to the struggle for the deep jungle. Whatever the difficulties, present or future, he simply could not leave the regiment or desert the man who had made it. He would continue to do battle with Calvert over the matter of discipline but he would stay with it for as long as he could, if possible, until a victorious end. That night the end seemed a long way off.

Little did John Woodhouse know how prophetic his thoughts would prove to be.

In January 1951 'A' Squadron was judged ready for operations and was inserted by sea and by boat up the Sungei Rompin into the southeast of the country, the aim being to locate terrorist bases in the remote country. Calvert became dissatisfied with the progress (or lack of it) and sent Woodhouse in to take command. Though delighted with being given command at last, he did not like what he found!

Disused CT bases and whatever signs of enemy movement there may have been were missed because of the rivalry between troops and patrols to see who could cover the most ground in a day's march; this become known as the 'Heads down. Arse up' syndrome. Constant reprimands from Woodhouse gradually got rid of the obsession and it became accepted that stealth, not speed, was set to be the answer.

During this time with 'A' Squadron Woodhouse experimented with various tactics. He tried walking barefoot in the manner of some of the terrorists but this only lasted a few days and led to a foot infection; he tried out various forms of lightweight rations and experimented with different routines. Whatever ration he selected would be the minimum but soldiers quietly rang the changes and added small tasty touches. The favourites were *ikan bilis* (whitebait), curry powder and dried onions and some opted to carry a few small tubes of margarine or *ghee* (clarified butter).

Rations were one thing but his great concern lay elsewhere. He did the best he could to begin to instil discipline into 'A' Squadron but he was soon sent for by Calvert and returned to Dusan Tua where 'C' Squadron (Rhodesian) had just arrived. The switching of tasks and responsibilities frustrated Woodhouse; he felt he was leaving jobs unfinished. With Sergeant Eddie Waters he was attached to 'C' Squadron to advise them on their training schedule. At that time they were commanded by Major Peter Walls who would later become the C-in-C of the Rhodesian army. In the near future Woodhouse would have 'C' Squadron under command again for a three-squadron operation in North Malaya.

# Chapter 11

# Command

Early in 1951, 'B' Squadron, recruited from 21 SAS Regiment (TA) and men of the 1st and 2nd SAS regiments, arrived in Malaya. Known originally as 'M' Squadron and destined for service in Korea, they were commanded by Major Tony Greville Bell, another highly-decorated wartime SAS officer. Diverted to Malaya and taken to join up with Calvert, 'B' Squadron was taken aback at what they saw as flagrantly bad discipline and Greville Bell and Calvert clashed almost immediately. Within a short space of time Greville Bell resigned and departed to the UK. In fairness to Calvert it must be said that at that time he was suffering from amoebic dysentery and fever and he was committed to hospital soon after Greville Bell left.

The late Major Tony Greville Bell was interviewed by the author many years later and he stated that he had been immensely impressed by Calvert's war record and clear thinking on the strategies and tactics that would help to end the emergency in Malaya, of which he confessed to having had a very limited knowledge. He had been pleased to be offered command of 'B' Squadron, especially because of the number of ex-wartime SAS members who were involved. Although the original destination of 'B' Squadron had been Korea and a different form of warfare, he had not been too worried by the diversion to Malaya. He had known Calvert towards the end of the war at the time when he (Calvert) commanded the SAS Brigade and he held him in high regard at that time. Despite that, he found it impossible to tolerate what he saw as the total lack of discipline and, even worse in his opinion, the absence of pride in the SAS. When it appeared that he would not be able to separate 'B' Squadron from the 'mess', he opted to return to the UK. He expressed a rueful regret at his decision as he thought that he may well have let his men down at a time of need. This was sad because Greville Bell was a proven leader and he and Calvert, given the right parameters, could have made a very effective team.

Woodhouse was put in command of 'B' Squadron and led them on a three-month operation in Johore. Prior to departing he went to see Calvert in hospital before he was shipped back to the UK. He was putting on a brave face, and as Woodhouse got up to leave he said: 'Remember I expect a lot from you, John.'

'B' Squadron was not up to scratch in so far as Woodhouse's exacting standards were concerned. Mainly due to inexperience in jungle navigation and again, like 'A' Squadron, an obsession with speed meant that signal shots were constantly being used as poor navigation, resulting in patrols missing RVs. He also made a number of journeys without an escort as he moved between patrol bases but eventually he realized that though his speed of movement was enhanced, the tension made him very tired and after an enforced night alone in the jungle he was forced to rethink the practice. No doubt he would have remembered that occasion well!

The ear-splitting crack instantly jolted him wide awake. Was that a gunshot? He jerked himself upright. His forehead smashed into a knot on the gnarled tree trunk. In pain and confused, he stood up, staggered and lost his footing on the muddy slope. In a terrifying crescendo of noise, a heavy branch crashed to earth only a few feet from where he had been huddled alongside the huge tree roots. Shivering violently now, he hauled his weary body back into the temporary sanctuary. He remembered his father's wartime words: 'Calm down. Calm down and think.' Slow, deep breaths did the trick. His flimsy jungle clothing was soaked from the incessant rain and the insidious cold wormed its way to the very marrow of his bones. How the hell was it possible to doze off in such conditions? His jungle hat had been ripped away by the falling tree limb. On hands and knees, partially blinded by the rain and blood, he groped around for the carbine that had slipped from his wet, cold hands. Finding comfort in the feel of the sleek weapon, he checked that the muzzle was free from mud and placed it carefully within easy reach. He wiped his muddy hands on his trousers and gingerly probed the head wound with his dirty fingers. Just a minor gash; the rain mingling with the blood had made it seem worse. That had been a lucky escape; one member of the Scouts had recently been killed in his hammock by a falling tree and it was a recognized precaution that trees close to bashas should be checked as far as possible for dead branches. The time had come to take stock of the situation.

At dawn on 20 June 1951, Major John Woodhouse had made a bad decision. No! It had been a stupid decision. He was the Officer Commanding 'B' Squadron and he was quite isolated. He had no radio, he was alone, so how could he possibly be in command of anything? As first light had broken he had left Captain Jeff Douglas' position, deep in the Malayan jungle, with the intention of meeting up with 8 Troop. He had asked Douglas to send a radio message for a patrol to meet him at a well-defined river junction. Many of the maps of Malaya in those days were based on air photographs and often showed quite large patches of blank paper marked 'Cloud Cover' or 'Unexplored'. Thus river junctions were often the most accurate features. He calculated that he would arrive at the rendezvous about an hour before dark. Douglas offered him an escort, which he refused. He did not want to leave him short of men and he had reckoned that he would move faster by himself. He had travelled alone before but usually on a journey that was much shorter than the one that had brought him to this lonely spot.

There were the obvious but much exaggerated dangers to confront the lone jungle traveller. True, tigers, elephants, wild pigs, snakes and wild buffaloes (*seladang*) foraged in the rain forest, but they were rarely seen and the risk of attack from them was extremely remote. A loss of footing while crossing one of the fast-flowing rivers or a triggered booby-trap was much more likely and could have resulted in crippling injury or worse; that and the greater peril came from the fact that intelligence reports suggested that a significant number of CTs were operating in the area. That was the reason that Operation WARBLER had been mounted to the north-west of Kluang in the state of Johore.

Woodhouse had driven himself almost to the point of exhaustion. He had allowed himself a ten-minute rest stop every two hours. He had not lost concentration but hoped that his quiet progress would not alert any CTs who may be in the area.

Without the luxury of an experienced leading scout he had had to pause at frequent intervals to listen and peer intently into the surrounding vegetation. 'Learn to look through the jungle – not at it.' That had been one of Mike Calvert's wise dictums based, as it was, on his huge jungle experience with the Chindits in Burma. He had a narrow escape when he was following an animal track along a ridge. Just in time he spotted an aboriginal pig trap. These devices consisted of a sharpened stake, usually bamboo, bound to a tree branch and hauled back under great tension to be held in place by a simple trip mechanism. When the trip was activated the stake lashed across the track to impale the hapless animal. At least one member of the Scouts had fallen prey to such a device, resulting in very unpleasant injuries. The CTs had copied the aboriginal design and placed them rather higher than those used to kill pigs; their traps tended to be aimed at about human waist height. It was not just the CTs who used the pig spears; some of their aborigine supporters also set the traps to injure the British soldiers.

Alone in the alien environment a man's mind might start playing tricks. Natural jungle noises could be misinterpreted as many things including enemy movement. His sustenance for the journey was meagre. Travelling light, he carried only three tins of sardines, some hard tack biscuits and a small bag of dried fish. He had a limited allowance of sugar and tea and some small sachets of salt. One pack of biscuits and a tin of sardines had already been devoured but 8 Troop would have catered for his food requirements as they had just taken a resupply air-drop.

The torrential rain had started as usual around midday. At first it was a welcome relief after the energy-sapping heat. There was little need to worry about noisy movement. The heavy drops smashing their way through the jungle canopy set up an incessant roar like a small river in spate. No need either to worry about leaving tracks; his footprints were washed away within seconds. In the rain his vision was even more limited, as was his hearing. The same, of course, was true for the enemy. Freddy Spencer Chapman was right: 'The Jungle is Neutral'. His feet inside the ill-fitting canvas and rubber jungle boots slid around and walking on a slope became uncomfortable. Because of the need for all-round observation and the slippery nature of the ground he was negotiating he could not move fast enough to achieve any noticeable body warmth.

The rain had no effect at all on the one jungle creature that Woodhouse loathed. The leeches would still be standing and waving like grass in a gentle breeze along the animal tracks as they sensed the presence of a meal. Insinuating their way through any gap in clothing (even the lace-holes in jungle boots), they would attach themselves to the first piece of flesh they found. As their suckers penetrated the skin they released both an anaesthetic and an anticoagulant, so the bite was painless. Once attached, the leeches would drink their fill, swelling to three or four times their original size until they dropped off. The anticoagulant caused the blood to continue to run freely. Though he managed to ignore the foul little pests (the bites of which could cause nasty infections), Woodhouse shared the thoughts of many of his soldiers: he did not like the idea of the leeches feasting from his genitals. Insect-repellent applied to any gap in the clothing first thing in the morning helped to keep the creatures off, but as soon as the sweat and the rain washed it away it was useless.

Most of his route had taken him through virgin jungle, which can take many forms depending on the geography. In the deep valleys and close to major waterways the vegetation can be dense with creepers, some covered with sharp hooked thorns known as 'wait-a-while'; these could deliver nasty scratches if the trapped person simply tried to pull himself away from their clutches, and scratches can quickly turn septic if not tended. Bamboo could grow to great thickness and present dense impenetrable barriers that required cutting to pass through if it could not be circumnavigated. The sheaths which emanated from each section were covered with fine hairs that could be immensely irritating to the skin. Bamboo was, of course, also a great friend as its uses were many: it made good platforms for a bed in a long-term base camp; it could be split and used to surreptitiously channel water from streams directly into a base camp; it made excellent rafts; and it was, in itself, a survival aid as the sections invariably held good clean water and new shoots found just under the surface of the ground were nutritious. On the ridges in particular, virgin jungle could sometimes be akin to walking through an English forest. On this journey the jungle had not been especially thick and he made good progress. Reaching the RV an hour earlier than expected, he cautiously scoured the immediate vicinity for signs of enemy movement. Finding nothing, he secreted himself at the base of a tree that overlooked the meeting-point. The time for the link-up with 8 Troop came and passed. He realized that he had left in such a hurry that he had no idea as to whether the troop commander had received his instructions. The light was failing now. A night alone was inevitable. He did not relish the idea. As dusk approached, the jungle 'night music' began. From all around came the shrieks, cries and squawks of birds, monkeys and insects either making ready for sleep or preparing for the nocturnal hunt for food. Some of the calls were strident, some trilling and some harsh and weird. As quickly as the noises started, they stopped when full darkness reigned. This was their habitat and Woodhouse was the intruder.

'When in doubt, brew up' had been a maxim of the East Surrey Regiment during the Second World War and Woodhouse had started to prepare to do that when, huddled between the great flanges of the tree roots, he had dozed off only to be rudely awakened by the falling branch.

Thinking clearly once more, he began to prepare for the night's stay. He rigged a makeshift shelter. His icy cold fingers seemed to have a will of their own and knotting the parachute cord to hold down the unwieldy poncho was difficult. Every part of the resupply parachutes was used: the nylon rigging lines did not rot and were immensely strong; the individual panels made good hammocks and lightweight sleeping bags; and what was not used made excellent gifts for the aborigines. Carefully protecting his precious matches from the rain, he persuaded the reluctant solid fuel block into spluttering life under his metal mug. The roots of the tree offered cavernous inlets. Some of these mighty trees stretched well over 200ft high in their search for the sun. They developed huge roots to support their massive weight. Within those he would be well hidden and more or less safe from any further falling branches; any tracks he had made during his slippery progress would be long gone. Now it was fully dark; the animal noises faded into an eerie silence broken only by the occasional bullfrog or cricket. The rain stopped as suddenly as it had started. The clouds dissipated and now the light from the full moon dappled the undergrowth with light patches that seemed to twinkle as the leaves that shifted in the breeze interrupted the passage of light. If a man stared long enough at a shadow he would swear that it had begun to move. The phosphorescent patches on the tree bark seemed almost to be alive. There would be no enemy movement at this time so it was safe to prepare for the night. He removed his sodden clothing and picked off the blood-swollen leeches before putting on his dry gear and the canvas hockey boots he carried as night wear. Sipping the welcome mug of tea and smoking his second cigarette of the day, he conjectured on the possibilities for the next phase of his journey.

He had to assume that 8 Troop had not received his message and would have moved on from their last recorded location in ignorance of his plans. His options were to try to locate their last base and follow their tracks or to head for another known troop position. He knew that Sergeant Peter Walter, commanding the reserve troop (9 Troop), was under orders to remain static for the time being with only local patrols. The trek to Walter's area should take about six hours if the going was reasonable. He decided to forego the treat of sardines and biscuits and satisfy his hunger pangs with a handful of dried fish made palatable by immersion in the remains of his tea. Walter was expecting to be the next port of call after Woodhouse had visited 8 Troop but no arrangements had been made for a precise RV. Walter was a jungle veteran and Woodhouse knew that his base camp would be well hidden and almost certainly protected by grenade booby-traps. If he was fortunate enough to find it, he would have to exercise great caution when approaching the camp perimeter. Still, that was a problem for tomorrow and, rolling himself up in the sheet of parachute silk that he carried, he tried to get some sleep.

Sleep was only possible for short periods due to the bitter cold and the uncomfortably hard ground. The first thing he did as he awoke fully an hour before dawn was to face the discomfort of changing back into yesterday's wet clothing. Experience had taught him that it was better to accept that brief misery than to end the day with two sets of wet kit. Wet clothing is difficult to put on and he had to remove his hockey boots, but the battle with the clammy trousers and shirt certainly brought him back to full mental alertness. Before he set about making his first warming brew of tea he did a quick, silent scout around the immediate area for signs of enemy movement. He spotted his hat snagged on a branch and grimaced as he put it on, rubbing the top off the new scab that had formed on his forehead. The movement around the local area, short though it was, served to physically warm him up a little. Allowing himself the luxury of a further somewhat fishy-tasting brew while he checked his map cheered him up a little, but there was a long day ahead.

Six and a half hours later, tired and very hungry, he was in the area of Walter's troop base. He began a slow circular journey through the dense secondary jungle hoping to pick up some tracks to follow into the base camp. Secondary jungle is that which had once been cultivated and then abandoned. The access to sunlight meant that thick unruly growth occurred which could become a formidable barrier to progress. He found nothing. Had he made a mistake in his navigation? Had Walter made an error? He thought that both conjectures were unlikely. Finally, almost exhausted, he sat down despondently in the thick scrub alongside a large open and treeless space that had, months ago, been cleared by aborigines for future crop planting. Now it was thick *lallang*: a tall grass, in this case about 6ft high. Alongside the *lallang* ran a narrow track that did not bear any signs of recent movement.

What a mess! He was not in command of his troops because he had no means of contact. To walk back to his squadron headquarters would take at least three days. He had next to no food. He could only contemplate two or three lonely and desperately hungry nights and a very ignominious return to his jungle headquarters. Being out of contact for so long would probably have caused great concern in Dusan Tua. Despite the situation, he grinned at the thought: some would rub their hands with glee as the thorn in their flesh was removed, but (hopefully) there would be a much greater number saddened by his apparent demise!

A recognized routine in his current circumstances would have been to fire a shot to mark his presence; however, it was a practice that he deplored and he had forbidden his squadron to use it. In this case it would have to be an absolute last resort. After a few more minutes of wallowing in gloom he pulled himself together and decided to cast around once again. As he stood up and hoisted his pack he saw, not more than 20 metres away, the long grass swaying as something moved through it. What was it? There was a 'shooshing' noise as whatever it was moved closer. The length of the line of waving grass suggested a file of men rather than an animal. Was it a CT patrol? Nervously he melted back into the undergrowth and with his carbine at the ready he sank into a crouch. Not more than 10 yards away and off to his left flank he saw a shotgun begin to protrude from the grass; whoever was on the other end of the weapon slowly parted the grass and moved to the very edge. A head emerged and the man looked carefully up and down the animal track that separated the grass from the edge of the jungle proper. He also went into a crouch with his left hand raised to signal whoever was behind him to stop. He then raised his parallel arms to the vertical position to tell his followers that he had hit a track. He continued to scrutinize the immediate area. Woodhouse knew that this was an SAS patrol but he did not immediately recognize the bearded face. If he could see the soldier then the soldier would probably be able to see him and his reaction was likely to be a blast from the shotgun which at this range would probably be fatal. He had to think quickly before he was detected. Slowly, ever so slowly, he lowered himself into a prone position, making himself the smallest target possible under the circumstances.

These men were trained to shoot to kill on contact with the enemy. There was nothing in SOPs to cater for this situation and he made a mental note to correct that. Staying in position and hugging the ground even more closely, he made up his mind. 'SAS' he called out loudly, directing his voice away from the soldier in the hope that his amateur ventriloquism would help to disguise his position. The soldier froze and looked directly at the area from which the shout had come and, lifting the butt of the shotgun to his shoulder, he melted back into the grass. He could not see Woodhouse but the use of 'SAS' had done the trick.

A quiet voice demanded, 'Who is it?' 'Squadron Commander.' 'Stand up. Show yourself.' He cautiously stood up, leaving his carbine on the ground. He concentrated on keeping his feeling of relief out of his face and voice. 'Major Woodhouse. Where is Sergeant Walter?' 'You gave us quite a surprise, sir. You are not expected. Are you alone?' 'Yes. Well done on not shooting me,' Woodhouse replied grumpily, more to hide his own relief than as a compliment.

Secure in the troop base and having been given his stand-to position, the slight head wound was attended to by the medic. Gratefully sipping at a hot brew, he found out why he had not been met the day before. All radio signals were sent back to the regimental headquarters at Dusan Tua before being relayed to the troops. A delay in transmission had meant that the order had reached 8 Troop far too late for a welcoming patrol to be despatched.

A two-day stopover in the camp gave Major John Woodhouse ample time to reflect on his recent ill-advised actions. True, it was quicker to travel unaccompanied, but the tension over a few hours of movement caused greater tiredness and travelling alone was certainly not to be contemplated unless one was certain that a rendezvous had definitely been agreed. He also used this time to think more about his SOPs. He had always stressed that they were guidelines to action, not orders. He urged all his men to continue to think about their situation and to come up with new tactics and vary their use of standard ones. His maxim was: 'The essence of operations in a guerrilla war is twofold: be unpredictable and where possible try to bring the guerrillas to battle.' He was pleased to note that Walter was varying his stand-to and stand-down times as stipulated in his SOPs. A note from his original draft demonstrates his clarity of thought:

> The purpose of stand-to is to rehearse rapid manning of pre-arranged defensive positions. It is never to take place at set times. Regular habits and regular soldiers are God's gift to guerrillas. No prior warning of stand-to will be given.
>
> At night, position will be within five paces of bashas, which are to be sited tactically and not comfortably. On a night stand-to, all ranks will kneel or lie. No man will move once in position. Anyone seen moving will be shot without warning from the closest range possible. The firer will do all he can to fire at a rising angle. On no account will fire be returned unless the enemy can be seen. The answer to noise is silence.

The tactic of booby-trapping old CT camps was introduced and seemed to have at least one success in that bloodstains and abandoned packs were found at one camp. In August after eleven weeks the squadron, for one week, carried out a number of ambushes on the jungle fringe where it ended in a rubber plantation. Two CTs were seen and one was killed but the other escaped. Woodhouse stopped a timber lorry and had it take the corpse back to the nearest police post. The squadron was then relieved by 'A' Squadron who used the same tactics. They killed six CTs in the next few weeks, though they missed more through poor shooting.

With the arrival of Lieutenant Colonel Sloane the atmosphere changed. Sloane was a genial character, but he was both efficient and firm as he introduced better order into the affairs of the Malayan Scouts. He began to get rid of the dead wood and his actions in 'cleansing' the regiment have been likened to the Fifth Labour of Hercules in cleaning out the Augean Stables! Shortly after Sloane took over, the regiment moved to Singapore and was officially retitled as 22 SAS Regiment and a fourth squadron, made up of volunteers from the UK, was formed: 'D' Squadron. Woodhouse was put in command and this made it the third squadron that he had led in the first year of the regiment's existence. Early in 1951 information from four surrendered SEPs (surrendered enemy personnel) was later to put the squadron on trial and severely test Woodhouse's leadership abilities.

# Chapter 12

# Operation HELSBY

T he Belum valley, close to the border with Thailand, was thought to be the most isolated settlement of aborigines in Malaya and intelligence was scarce. The name in Malay means 'not yet' or 'later' but the aborigine version is supposed to be 'never, never' which in the Orient can mean the same thing. To the troops the names 'Shangri La' or 'Never Never Land' seemed to be equally appropriate. The SEPs gave their information to the police. They said that the Belum valley was completely controlled by the CTs. The Malay population of more than 300 lived in two main settlements: Kampong Belum in the west of the valley and Kampong Sepor in the east. This was borne out by reports from police informants who lived in Kampong Temengger, a similar village several days' march to the south. They said that no-one from Belum had been to visit their relatives for several months.

It appeared that the CTs held a roll-call twice a day to make sure that no-one had left. The threat of a death sentence hung over anyone who tried to escape and that sentence could be applied to relatives if the escapee was not caught. Later intelligence suggested that the HQ of the 3rd Regiment along with a company of about 100 CTs was based in the valley. Well-used tracks led north over the Thailand border where many more CTs were known to live. Despite the harsh attitude towards 'escapees', in their day-to-day dealings with the Malay people the CTs were careful to avoid antagonizing them. They needed them to produce food and they paid for it. Rice, maize, tapioca, sugar cane, vegetables and coconuts were there in abundance. Apart from that the valley was used as a communications base, for medical treatment and, because it was so far from a road, as a rest area free from government troops and police. The CTs felt that their secrets were still unknown to the government.

The task of destroying the Communist base and killing as many of its occupants as possible was given to the SAS. Planning took place under conditions of great secrecy and a very busy training regime started. Lieutenant Colonel Sloane had concerns about security even in his own base as there were many locals employed in a variety of capacities, and in a letter dated 12 August 1984 his wife wrote to the author a letter which demonstrates some of the security atmosphere at that time:

Dear Major Hoe,

I felt I must write to thank you for the very kind inscription in the front of *Re-enter the SAS*, which the McGregors sent me this week, also for the appreciation of John's contribution towards the reforming of the Regiment, which has been very much glossed over in former publications. The obituaries in *The Times* and the *Telegraph*, written by John Slim and Pat Winter I believe, went a long way towards giving him his just due, but that was a bit late, wasn't it? I would have liked him to have known that in his lifetime.

It certainly was a very interesting time. I am actually reading the book – I don't often read military accounts! You might be amused to know that I typed out the Operations Plan for Operation HELSBY, as John didn't trust the typists in HQ. There was a lot of infiltration throughout all the services. I was working at the time in HQ Malaya and had been security-vetted, so I suppose I could be trusted! It was considered rather 'infra-dig' for a CO's wife to do anything other than look after the families at that time, but I was determined to get our two sons flown out for the summer holidays and that was the only way I could afford it – no free flights in those days! Actually, there were very few SAS families out there at the time, so I could well combine the two.

The Mcgregors, Winters and Slims have remained good friends and I often see them. Of course, John Slim was originally an Argyll and was with my John in Korea.

Anyway, mustn't ramble on – many thanks again. I wish you had known John, he was an outstanding man.

Yours very sincerely,

M. Sloane

For 'B' Squadron parachute training was the priority but for the others there was a wider scope, part of which was to disguise the real operation. Woodhouse in a letter to his father noted: '… we are doing parachute training, bridge demolitions, practice raids on airfields and initiative tests. Due to the uneven standard of training caused by the poor recruits sent to us by some units we have to break up troops and do much basic infantry patrol training.' In the mess the unit officers discussed the considerable recruiting problem. Most of them thought that there ought to be some sort of selection course and that recruits with records of misbehaviour or clashes with authority should be rejected. Woodhouse agreed with much of those feelings but he always had a soft spot for the soldier who got into trouble by fighting. His belief was that the SAS needed men with strong personalities and character. Even 'bad' personalities were better than weak or colourless ones. Some had got into trouble because they were badly led. Perhaps his views were a little selfish because there are few things more satisfying in the military than to have a soldier who changes from a life of rebellion against authority to using his enterprise in leadership for the good of his regiment.

Parachute training began in real earnest. In the case of 'B' Squadron who were nearly all trained parachutists, this was to prepare them for a parachute landing in open rice fields at Belum; they did not yet know that. The airborne experts considered parachuting into trees impossible and no-one questioned that opinion at the time. Other types of more conventional training were due to the fact that the CO Lieutenant Colonel Sloane was hoping that part at least of the regiment would soon be moved to the Middle East to train for possible employment there. The records do not show with any clarity why he should have been considering that.

There were very few clearings in the jungle and most of those were littered with old tree stumps which would be very dangerous to jumpers. However, the Belum valley had some wet *padi* fields which were several hundred yards long. The drop zone selected from air photographs was bordered on one side by the fast and deep Sungei Belum and on the other by jungle. That would be 'B' Squadron's DZ.

At the end of January 1952, the training was over and the regiment moved to its new camp at Sungei Besi a few miles south of Kuala Lumpur. Here they were given their orders for Operation HELSBY. 'D' Squadron and 'C' (Rhodesian) Squadron would be flown to Kota Baharu in the north-east corner of Malaya. After a short train journey they would transfer to trucks and be driven by road and track as far as Kampong Jeli. Then a day's march on a good track would get them to Batu Melintang, a village only 11 miles as the crow flies from the Belum valley. Those miles, however, were through precipitous mountains littered with bamboo-infested jungle. One of the Malay policemen was reputed to know the way. All he would say was that the route was 'very hard' and Woodhouse had a bad feeling about the value of his guide but he was confident in his own ability to navigate.

Intelligence sources had deduced that the main CT camp was close to Kampong Sepor or probably a little to the north of the village. 'C' and 'D' Squadrons were to approach from the south-east, and to be ready to move forward to find and assault the camp after 'B' Squadron had parachuted onto the *padi* fields at Belum at the far western end of the valley.

Woodhouse was not totally happy with the plan to use squadrons *en masse*; it was quite out of keeping with previous tactical methods. It had been adopted purely because of the uncertainty of the enemy's strength (estimates hovered between 100 and 400). Another reason was the fear that the enemy might stand his ground and fight, or even attack if the regiment moved in small groups. He believed then that this was a misappreciation of the enemy.

His own idea, discussed at length with Captain Mike Pearman, a tough experienced officer, was that 'D' Squadron should find a way through the mountains and approach the Belum valley from the south. The squadron should get astride the track which lay in the middle of the valley connecting the two kampongs of Sepor and Belum. He felt that should be done a short time before the parachute landing in the west and the advance into Sepor by the Rhodesians from the east. Surely some of the enemy, from one or both ends of the valley, would use the track to escape or warn their comrades of events. His plan was not supported by either Douglas or Walls, the other squadron commanders, who feared that he would be unable to get 'D' Squadron into position without being detected. Without their support it was not on.

Woodhouse was due to leave Malaya at the end of his tour, but despite the disagreement over the tactics to be used he asked to extend his tour of duty in the country in order to take part in the operation and the request was approved. He also persuaded Pearman to stay with him. He later said that it had been a wrong decision as it was not possible to compromise on principles and expect success. Throughout the operation he was to hope for an opportunity to revert to his own plan.

On 1 February 1952, 'D' and 'C' Squadrons flew as planned in new Valetta aircraft to Kota Baharu. The first mishap was caused, as so often happened in Malaya, by prolonged heavy rains. The trucks had to stop several miles short of Kampong Jeli because the track was flooded. The days of 2 and 3 February passed in marching to Batu Melintang. The additional march caused a great deal of trouble. The jungle boots which were excellent for slow movement in the soft-floored jungle were useless on hot sandy tracks in hot sun. The rubber soles caused the feet to literally overheat and many men were blistered by the time the open-air march was finished. The troops were then resupplied by air and given seven days' rations. This, added to the already heavy burdens, brought their loads up to about 70lb per man.

The maps, made from aerial surveys, showed few details of the ground but marked rivers and the larger streams accurately. The contour lines, though often obscured by cloud cover, were good guides to altitude and were most useful in making choices of when to drop off a ridge or change direction to higher ground. Air photographs of the valley itself showed several hundred acres under intensive cultivation. The squadron commanders agreed that if they left Batu Melintang on 4 February they could enter the Belum valley on 8 February which was the date set for 'B' Squadron's parachute drop. Batu Melintang was reported to be absolutely loyal to the government, and in any case there was no contact between the village and Belum because of the wild country in between. In this, as in so much of their information, the police were proved correct.

Woodhouse was in command of both squadrons for the duration of the march, and agreed with Walls that each squadron would lead on alternate days. Further questioning of the guide only gave them conflicting details of the route he 'knew'. This did not worry Woodhouse unduly since he was confident of finding a way if necessary without the guide. The reason for accepting the added burden of seven days' rations was that they did not want to be halted for resupply; as soon as they reached Belum they all expected to have to follow up the enemy and wanted rations in hand to do that quickly.

On 4 February, in a long snaking file, the heavily laden squadrons walked round the narrow *padi* field banks to the jungle. Once inside the warmth and light disappeared, replaced by the cool dull shades of green now so familiar. The track was wide and good and climbed slowly into the mountains. Woodhouse had warned every man that he could not wait for stragglers. If a man could not keep up he must turn back and go home alone.

The men kept going as best they could but two or three were seen to be lagging. They marched from 0730 hours to 1730 with no long halts. The ascents and descent were severe, and though the track was good it still involved many scrambles over or around fallen trees. On the second day the track was, for more than four hours, the bed of a sandy boulder-strewn torrent. The sand seeped into the jungle boots and slowly scraped water-softened skin. At the end of it Lance Corporal Moseley reported to his OC that he was afraid he might not be able to keep up much longer. Moseley, a short, stocky man, had been in 'B' Squadron and had been considered a poor soldier. Woodhouse, suspecting that it was a case of he and his troop commander having taken a mutual dislike to one another, had offered him a chance in 'D' Squadron. He looked at Moseley's feet. His socks were sticky with blood and when he peeled them off, inches of white skin came with them. It was a wonder that he had got as far as he did. With two other men in similar condition, Woodhouse ordered him to stay a day where he was and then make his way back very slowly to Batu Melintang. Reluctantly Moseley nodded his acceptance.

The guide came back and told the OC that they would have to stop, even though it was only 1400 hours. He said that the next part of the track was on a high ridge with no water and would take six hours to cover. After several minutes of indecision, Woodhouse agreed to stop. He was influenced not only by what the guide had said but also by the desire to avoid more stragglers. Even so, he was worried by the prospect of losing three or four hours.

The next day he was furious when the column crossed the ridge in three hours. He was near to the front and the track went down to the turbulent river, the Sungei Belum. In distance they were a little over halfway to their destination. Walls informed him that the guide was now adamant that the track ended right there. It was a *fait accompli* and the favoured option of Pearman was to build bamboo rafts and move downstream. Woodhouse was in a quandary. They were inexperienced in rafting which was a danger in itself in the swollen river; they could easily be ambushed and he thought it likely that the enemy would be aware of attempts to approach the camp by using the river and would have set up sentries. This gave him a perfect opportunity to carry out his own plans that had been thwarted earlier! He told Walls that he would lead 'D' Squadron across the mountains and bring them out west of Kampong Sepor while 'C' Squadron could advance down the river and approach it from the east. One of them at least should find a route that brought them to Sepor by 8 February. He informed RHQ but did not disclose that he intended to move west of Kampong Sepor and directly towards it. On the same radio call he got the news that the parachute drop had been changed to 9 February.

After parting from 'C', 'D' Squadron made good progress, climbing up to 4,000ft. The third day in the jungle was very rough. The weather had broken again and mist or rain shrouded the trees, which in turn shrouded the soldiers. The men were tiring and at intervals Pearman and Woodhouse went up and down the line cajoling and exhorting the weakest to go on. Sometimes he, Pearman and the fittest of the soldiers carried two packs for a short time to allow a few worn out men to recover some of their strength. Woodhouse later said that he felt no tiredness, just a furious determination to reach the west of Kampong Sepor no matter what it cost them. There were no tracks and the column spent all day doing one of four things: climbing with hands and feet up hillsides that became mudslides after the first three or four men had passed; sliding down equally steep hillsides; stumbling or slipping up or down rocky stream beds; and cutting step by step through bamboo. Never before or afterwards did they find such hard going in Malaya.

On the night of 7 February he was uncertain of his position. Try as he might, he could not relate either the day's movement or his current surroundings to the map. He discussed it with Pearman (himself an expert in jungle navigation), but he too was undecided. Woodhouse was not seriously concerned; he thought that he could not be far wrong in his rough fix. He was feeling tired himself now and was again grateful to Ip Kwong Lau. With him as his personal escort, Ip gave him many tips on living in the jungle and he produced food, a basha and hot tea while Woodhouse wrote and coded signals to RHQ every evening. He had a vivid memory of that night:

> That night came the news that the King had died. For a few minutes I was reminded of England and was conscious of our isolation. It was hard to think of an outside world. I was so intent on our mission that all else soon faded into dimness and unreality. There was nothing in my life then but the jungle, and the overwhelming importance of getting my squadron through it to my chosen objective.

On 8 February, with their position still uncertain, the squadron climbed for most of the morning. Shortly after noon they reached the crest of a mountain ridge on the top of which they discovered a track. It was not a good track and it did not seem to have been used much, but it was the first that they had seen in two days. He knew that they must be near the steep drop of some 2,000ft or more which lay between the squadron and Kampong Sepor. The mist persisted so they were denied the chance to glimpse the Belum valley between treetops. Walking onto a flat shelf that dropped away with alarming steepness, he halted the squadron and sat down with his map to think. He was totally uncertain whether he was south-west of Sepor or south of it. Two faint tracks ran down towards the Belum valley. The one north-east seemed the best; they could not get too far west for his liking. The other track headed north. He decided to look at the north-east one but after 50 yards it became a tangle of fallen branches. That made up his mind: they would take the north track which seemed to be unblocked. He recalled:

> In retrospect I am sure that decision was influenced by exhaustion from continuous forced marching. That was our fifth successive day of jungle marching, following 20 miles of open countryside torture. Once we parted from the Rhodesians we marched for eleven hours

a day with no halt longer than ten minutes. Now I believe that I took the easier path because it WAS easier.

They scrambled down the steep mountainside and camped at a place that Woodhouse estimated was probably not more than 2,000 yards from the Sungei Belum. He thought they were probably south-south-west of Kampong Sepor.

As 9 February dawned cold and wet, it seemed unlikely that 'B' Squadron would drop because the low clouds must be obscuring the mountains and they were not to close in until after 'B' had landed. Closing down his radio to conserve batteries, Woodhouse felt a little of the strain lift. A short time later he was amazed to hear the sound of aircraft! Feeding on the adrenaline, they hurriedly put on their packs and forced a way down to the banks of the Sungei Belum where they stopped in horror. The rains had swollen the river to a massive 40-yard width well over 6ft deep. At that point the river was flanked by bamboo thickets so there was no handy tree to chop down to make a bridge. Captain Pearman made a courageous offer to swim across with a line while the rest constructed hasty bamboo rafts. Woodhouse later recalled:

It looked a very hazardous crossing but there was no alternative. With a line looped around his body Pearman jumped in and seemed to me, holding the other end of the rope, to be torn straight down river. I decided to pull him in before he drowned. When at last I landed him like a monster fish, he was very angry – he cocked his fist and I thought he was going to belt me one!

'You bloody near drowned me hauling on the line like that!'

'I'm very sorry, Mike, but I thought you were going to drown if I left you.'

'No, but you bloody nearly drowned me yourself. I was quite alright until you pulled,' Pearman spluttered. 'Just let me go the next time. I have to go a long way downstream to cross.'

'Alright, Mike, say when you're ready.'

He went in again and this time reached the far bank. It was a dangerous crossing and it must have taken supreme courage to try a second time but that was the sort of man Pearman was. In an hour we were all across ferried over on two precarious bamboo rafts.

While they were preparing to cross, Woodhouse checked his compass. He was sure that a big river would be accurately marked, even on their sketchy air-surveyed maps. A horrible doubt had crept into his mind. There was no stretch of the river west of Kampong Sepor that could possibly fit that pattern. As soon as he got across the river he hurtled north for several hundred yards hoping to find the Belum valley track. There was nothing there and he remembered with a sinking feeling how faint the sounds of the aircraft had been. They could take no part in the action that may be taking place because there was no doubt that he had led the squadron out east of Sepor. Deeply disappointed, they pushed on west until dark. That night he went round all the bashas telling his soldiers that he had blundered. The faithful incredulity with which some of the men took the drastic map corrections he gave them made him even more miserable and angry with himself. Even those who had already noted the river shrugged, saying that it could have happened to anyone. Then they looked ahead asking how quickly they could get to Sepor. Woodhouse said that they would make it by 11 o'clock.

The next day it turned out that he had fixed their position with certainty and as they walked into the open fields of Sepor they met Walls and the rest of the Rhodesians. He explained his error and asked about Wall's experience. They had come under fire from an unexpected direction, but it was ineffective and his outlying patrols had failed to make contact. It was confirmed by a later reconnaissance that if 'D' Squadron had taken the track which appeared to be blocked they would have arrived at the right time and in the right place.

'C' Squadron was occupied in sending patrols after the escaped CTs and questioning the villagers and 'D' moved towards Belum and 'B' Squadron. That evening Woodhouse planned patrols to the north and the south in the area given to the squadron by RHQ. The patrols were restricted by the exhaustion of the men who were also suffering from the anti-climax of the so far inglorious late arrival. While he was plotting the patrol pattern he heard someone walk up to him. Looking upwards from the feet, which like most of them were in boots that were split and tattered from the past week of marching, he got a shock. There with a big grin on his face was Moseley!

Moseley and two others in similar condition had decided that if they took it easy the track left by 'D' Squadron was simple to follow. Now that they had made it the medic cut the boots away from their feet. It was very hard to see how they could have made it on those suppurating virtually skinless feet. They were flown out by helicopter and within a few weeks Moseley was back with his squadron. As Woodhouse said, 'That's one sort of disobedience I don't mind!'

He took a patrol south and met up with 'B' Squadron in the west and listened to their news. On the day of the drop they had been flying from 9 o'clock until 1350 hours hoping for a break in the weather. At the last moment before the point of no return was reached in terms of aircraft fuel, the three Dakotas managed to get in low and drop fifty-four men. In the dangerous flying conditions and bad visibility it was no blame to the RAF that only four landed on the DZ. It had always been realized that a few men might miss the target, so all had been provided with 100ft of rope in case they fell into trees. A few narrowly missed the river and fell into open ground but most of them did land in trees. Only three men were injured, all of a very slight nature. All whose parachutes were caught up in the trees managed to lower themselves to the ground. From that incident the SAS learned that it might after all be possible to parachute straight into the jungle with no greater risk than onto open fields. Once the possibility was seen, the SAS vigorously pursued it with much material help from the RAF Parachute School on Singapore Island. At length a system was perfected that made jungle parachuting a normal routine for SAS soldiers.

The force took an air resupply on 11 February. They also received orders to prepare to evacuate all civilians from the area. Woodhouse thought then – and the conviction never left him – that the evacuation was a mistake. There on the centre of a CT supply route was a considerable Malay civil population. It would have made an admirable base for operations against the CTs near their homes in Thailand. It also went against the grain to abandon such a beautiful, fertile and well-cared-for valley. He knew too well what a sorry mess the cultivation would be in after even one year's desertion. It was during this resupply that Joe Durkin, in a memoir of life with the Malayan Scouts, made an interesting observation:

As the rations were being distributed Woodhouse buttonholed me and for the first time I noticed the change that had come over him in the past month or so. He was about 30 years old but now looking much older, 40 perhaps. He had lost two stones from a ten-stone frame and there was little evidence of flesh on his bones. His eyes had sunk into the sockets and his bones were prominent over hollow cheeks. His hands were taut strings covered in see-through parchment, each string defined as if on an X-ray plate. The physical change was very marked but nothing else, his iron will intact, eyes as sharp as ever, his brain in top gear. He had earned his pay, driving himself, and others, onwards – attempting everything but in the end would get nothing. It is the way of things.

About that time one worry was removed from Woodhouse's mind. One man who had been unable to keep up because his feet were so bad had not yet got back to Batu Melintang. He had taken a calculated risk over stragglers, but he knew that he would be in serious trouble if any man was lost as a result of his order to find their own way back. However, the lone straggler turned up. Like Moseley, he had courageously decided to follow as best he could. He lost the track but managed to reach a police patrol base and made his way on from there.

After the force was resupplied they were given orders that, as part of the Briggs Plan, they were to evacuate all civilians from the area. The plan was not completely the brainchild of the Director of Operations, Lieutenant General Sir Harold Briggs, and had been formulated by various committees but Briggs was the one to give it the go-ahead. It was designed to evacuate Chinese squatters (and some aborigines) from areas where they were being influenced by the Communist terrorists and rehouse them in areas under government control. The theory was that this would reduce any physical and intelligence support the Chinese were able to get from the civilians. Overall the operation was a sound success.

On 12 February 'B' Squadron captured a CT who died of his wounds soon afterwards. He proved to be a courier from Thailand who probably had not heard of the SAS presence. Woodhouse decided that the CTs would probably keep clear of the area and sent Pearman off to the south on a reconnaissance with his full troop; it was hoped that he would reach the Sungei Singor which was unexplored country some three or four days' march away. He also sent a corporal and two of his own escort to the Thai border to see what they could find. In the meantime, arrangements had to be made to move all the civilians out of the area.

Hardly had he done that when the enemy showed an unusually aggressive spirit. The SAS had begun to escort groups of Malays from the west of the valley towards Kampong Sepor ready for evacuation on foot. As they handed over a group of thirty to a Rhodesian escort only a few yards from 'D' Squadron's base, a long burst of fire spattered among the trees around them. Incredibly no-one was hurt. The enemy patrol fled before they were even seen. Twice in the next few days escorts were fired on but there were no casualties.

It was obvious that the enemy were sending patrols of two or three men down the broad valley track which the SAS had to use to move the civilians. Just before dawn, in order to catch them, Woodhouse sent the squadron out in pairs and told them to lie up off the track and about 100 yards apart. His reasoning was that when the CT ambush patrols arrived his men would probably hear them moving and one of the pairs could slowly crawl up and kill them. If the CTs were not heard, as soon as they opened fire the nearest SAS pair could cut off their retreat. The first day nothing happened but on the second day blood was drawn, yet in an unexpected way. One of the soldiers, obeying the call of nature, withdrew some 20 yards from his comrades, perhaps motivated by a sense of propriety that proved to be misplaced. He had just undone and dropped his trousers when he was shot through the buttocks. Unwittingly he had almost stumbled upon a CT patrol about to come on to the track. Luckily for him they ran off after firing and his wound was not serious.

It was plain that the 'D' Squadron plot had been uncovered and the CTs abandoned aggressive patrols. Though their shooting had been bad, those patrols indicated a local enemy commander with spirit and a good tactical sense. They had been very good at evasion and often proficient at ambushes against road targets. Very seldom, however, did they seek action against the SAS squadrons even when, at Belum, the SAS was forced to use certain tracks to move the civilians.

At this point Woodhouse was ordered to recall Pearman; his request to take 'D' Squadron out via a long reconnaissance with three weeks marching

Plate 1: Brigadier Charles Hall Woodhouse OBE MC, taken when he commanded 211 Infantry Brigade at Portsmouth in 1941.

Plate 2: Charles Woodhouse and his wife Stella, c.1949.

Plate 3: John Woodhouse and his sister Ann, 1934.

**Plate 4**: Lieutenant John Woodhouse, taken in 1943 at Palermo.

**Plate 5**: Fort McGregor (Tunisia). John Woodhouse led his first active service patrol to the fort after the near annihilation of the East Surrey troops who were defending the feature.

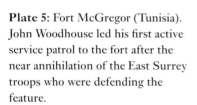

**Plate 6**: No. 78 Division Battle Patrol in Italy 1943, led by Lieutenant John Woodhouse.

**Plate 7:** Captain John Woodhouse MC is presented with his war medals by his father Brigadier Charles Woodhouse OBE MC in Vienna.

**Plate 8:** Woodhouse secures third place in the slalom event of the British Army Ski Championships of 1949.

**Plate 9:** With Helen while serving with HQ Rhine Army in Bad Oeynhausen in 1947.

**Plate 10**: Major John Woodhouse checking the route timings for the selection course that he devised in Wales, 1954.

**Plate 11**: Recruit training in the Brecon Beacons during a 1955 selection.

**Plate 12**: General Bourne visits D Squadron in Malaya, 1956.

**Plate 13:** Trooper Court of D Squadron relaxes in jungle comfort in 1956.

**Plate 14:** Sergeant Bob Turnbull MM on a march into a jungle base in 1955. Note the unwieldy equipment.

**Plate 15:** A somewhat luxurious bandit camp in Malaya. This was occupied by the Rhodesian SAS Squadron after an action with the bandits.

**Plate 16:** Sorting stores after a resupply air-drop in 1955. John Woodhouse would not have been amused! Not a weapon in sight.

**Plate 17:** Fort Brooke, one of a number of jungle bases constructed to be safe centres for aboriginal trading and basic medical treatment, c.1955.

**Plate 18:** John Woodhouse at a D Squadron base in 1955.

**Plate 19**: The entrance to 18 Troop's base on the Sungei Yum, Johore, 1955.

**Plate 20**: Elements of D Squadron waiting for transport.

**Plate 21**: Evacuation of a sick soldier in 1956. Very few Landing Zones were so generously sized.

**Plate 22:** The Belum Valley Drop Zone. Only six paratroopers landed in the rice fields; all the others landed in trees.

**Plate 23:** John Woodhouse with his parents outside Buckingham Palace after his MBE presentation in 1957.

**Plate 24:** John Woodhouse and Peggy Lacey marry at East Horsley on 29 May 1958.

**Plate 25**: Demonstrating the new tree-lowering equipment.

**Plate 26**: Father and son attend the Society of Dorset Men Dinner in 1958.

**Plate 27**: The officers of 21 SAS Regiment in 1958. Major Woodhouse, the second-in-command, is second from right in the front row.

**Plate 28**: As Officer Commanding B Company, 3rd Parachute Regiment on exercise in Bardufoss, Norway in 1959. Woodhouse is on the left shaving.

**Plate 29**: At an SAS reunion in 1959 some of the Malayan veterans get together. Left to right: Ian Cartwright, Bill Ross, John Woodhouse, Mick Reeves, Ip Kwong Lau, Paddy Winters. (No ID for the kneeling man.)

**Plate 30**: 'Hearts and Minds' during the floods in Hereford in the early 1960s. There being no fair maidens to rescue, the troops had to be content with saving sheep! (*Author's collection*)

**Plate 31**: Mike Gooley, Peter de la Billière and Johnny Watts enjoy breakfast in the Haunted House in Brunei, 1964.

**Plate 32**: Exercise 'Eagle's Nest' in the USA. Troopers Spike Hoe and Tom Pollard with John Woodhouse waiting to deploy, 1963. (*Author's collection*)

**Plate 33**: Beware the unguarded moment. Even such a mundane task as washing mess tins requires an alert sentry. Borneo, c.1963.

**Plate 34:** CO 22 SAS Regiment with Sergeants Cann and Lillico MM looking at the photograph album of Exercise 'Eagle's Nest', 1963.

**Plate 35:** As the commanding officer of 22 SAS Regiment John Woodhouse prepares to go on a light order patrol, South Yemen, 1964.

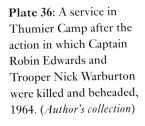

**Plate 36:** A service in Thumier Camp after the action in which Captain Robin Edwards and Trooper Nick Warburton were killed and beheaded, 1964. (*Author's collection*)

**Plate 37**: Lieutenant Colonel John Woodhouse with Member of Parliament Denis Healey when Healey visited Borneo in 1964.

**Plate 38**: The original memorial stone at the site of the helicopter crash in May 1963 in which Majors Ron Norman and Harry Thompson and Corporal Philip 'Spud' Murphy were killed.

**Plate 39**: Mr John Woodhouse at the headquarters of Gassim Monassir in Yemen watching the Egyptian air base, 1965.

**Plate 40**: John's two sons – Michael (left), William (right) – and their friend Tim Atkinson. With weapons at the ready, they stand by to repel boarders at Higher Melcombe, c.1968.

**Plate 41**: John Woodhouse as Sales Director for the Hall & Woodhouse Brewery gives a display of enthusiasm for the ales, 1972.

**Plate 42**: Ex-SAS Major Mike Jones meets Chin Peng in Thailand in 1998. Chin Peng was the leader of the Malayan Communists from 1942 to 1945 and 1949 to 1960.

**Plate 43**: In June 1984, as president of the SAS Regimental Association, John visits Auckland and meets his ex-comrade-in-arms Colonel Frank Rennie who commanded the New Zealand SAS Squadron in Malaya.

**Plate 44**: A 1998 reunion with Frank Gage, a member of the 1st East Surreys Battle Group (1943–44).

**Plate 45**: Chairman of Hall & Woodhouse Brewery, 1995.

Pulling a pint of the best bitter at the Cock and Bottle pub in Morden, Dorset, 1994.

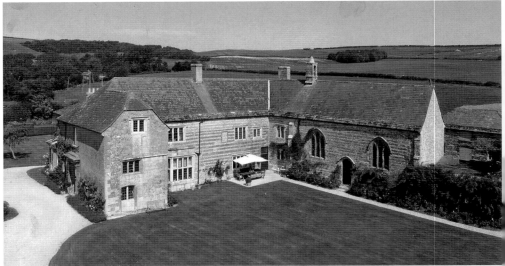

The family home, Higher Melcombe, Melcombe Bingham, Dorset in 2017.

Times. 27/4/99

# Nato strategy

*From Lieutenant-Colonel
John Woodhouse (retd)*

Sir, Nato targeted and hit the Serb TV
station in Belgrade knowing it was on
air and staffed by civilians. The
deaths that resulted are surely not col
lateral damage but murder.

Yours faithfully,
JOHN WOODHOUSE,
Higher Melcombe,
Melcombe Bingham,
Dorchester, Dorset DT2 7PB.
April 26.

An angry letter to *The Times* in 1999.

to the south along the Perak/Kelantan border was not approved. Probably the squadron was not really fit as they were still paying for over-exertion in the first week of Operation HELSBY; this showed in the high rate of sickness through fever and septic sores. After the sad destruction of the food crops they prepared to escort the civilians out. A local brigadier flew in by helicopter to view the situation. The only remark that Woodhouse remembered him making was to remind the squadron commanders that they were responsible for ensuring that no civilians were killed by enemy action on the way out. How, in a country where all movement had to be in single file, could this guarantee be given?! Woodhouse handed over to his second-in-command and opted to walk out with a three-man escort; that took just three days.

HQ FARELF (HQ Far East Land Forces) were delighted with Operation HELSBY and deemed it a great success. In their opinion a number of achievements had been made. An administratively difficult operation had been undertaken smoothly, despite severe weather. The parachuting concept had been proven. A major CT base had been disrupted and maybe closed down and that had to have an adverse effect on the enemy's morale. In addition, self-contained troops had crossed some of the worst terrain in the country on schedule. Whatever else, HELSBY served to heighten the appreciation of the SAS at an important level of the hierarchy. Woodhouse was not so happy. Although he supported the logic behind the Briggs Plan, he felt that any plan should be capable of modification given the right conditions. He was convinced that a squadron of the SAS should have remained in the area to straddle the important line of communication and supply; to continue with a positive hearts-and-minds campaign with the civilians rather than move them all out. On the plus side, however, was the fact that almost certainly the SAS would have support for continuing to master the business of parachuting into the jungle. The physical fitness and stamina of the squadrons had been displayed to a most remarkable degree and lessons had been learned about the pros and cons of the SAS operating in strength. Although it may not have been obvious to Woodhouse (who still berated himself mentally over the navigational error), he had proved that his own mental and physical strength was second to none. His status as a respected leader was enhanced even further.

His predictions about the CTs reoccupying the Belum valley were once more proved correct. In July and August 1953 a thorough reconnaissance of the area was conducted by three troops of 'D' Squadron under command of Major Dare Newell. They found that the main track was being constantly used by up to twenty men at a time; a further aborigine settlement of about sixty people had been made to the north of the original ones; areas of 100 sq yards were under cultivation with tapioca, sweet potatoes, maize and onions already ripe for consumption. It also became apparent that the cultivation once destroyed on Operation HELSBY was once more providing food for the CTs. Later operations would clear the area once and for all.

Another tactic that was started off by 'D' Squadron in part owed its inception to John Woodhouse's first reaction to Kampong Aur on his first trip into the jungle. A series of forts was now being planned, the purpose of which was to provide easily defendable bases deep in the jungle from which the police could dominate the surrounding countryside and prevent the aborigines from being exploited by the Communists. This proved to be a very effective strategy.

The forts were eventually a great success, but during the planning phases for the bases another CT tactic involving the aborigines came to light. During Operation GALWEY (October 1953 to June 1954), Lieutenant Fotheringham of 'B' Squadron took his troop into the area north-west of Pahang from the squadron base on the Sungei Telom. He was fully aware that a large party of aborigines was due to arrive in the base area and it was not long before they heard the aborigines 'chattering like a tree full of monkeys' heading towards them. The patrol moved off the track to give the party free passage and made no serious attempt at concealment. They were spotted almost straight away and immediately came under accurate small-arms fire from a group of CTs who had concealed themselves among the tribesmen. Fotheringham was killed in the first stages of the fire-fight during which his patrol was inhibited by the presence of the aborigines, none of whom was injured. There were no recriminations or reprisals when they began to filter back into the base area. That was in stark contrast to the treatment the CTs would have meted out and it became a factor in the cementation of good relations.

The CTs' actions on this occasion were not unique but it was the only one that involved the death of an SAS soldier.

Woodhouse was put in command of HQ Squadron for a short time to reorganize where necessary and then he was informed that he would be flying back to the UK in March. Before his departure date he was sent back into the jungle to train a troop of reinforcements which included tracking training with Ibans who had been sent over from Sarawak. The troop included two newcomers on their selection who were to become widely known and respected throughout the SAS: Captain John Slim (later to command 22 SAS Regiment) who Woodhouse had known in Hong Kong when he was the adjutant of the Argyll and Sutherland Highlanders having already seen active service in Korea, and Bob Turnbull (an ex-Royal Artillery bombardier) who became famous in the regiment in the '50s and '60s for his outstanding successes as a troop sergeant and warrant officer (he was awarded the Military Medal in Malaya). The latter was also a remarkably good boxer who specialized in early knockout punches because – in his words – he was not fit enough to go more than a couple of rounds! A good proportion of men, including Turnbull, became very expert at the tracking skills that were second nature to the Ibans and a number of later kills were directly attributable to those abilities.

During this training phase Special Branch handed over a surrendered terrorist who, under police questioning, claimed that he no longer wanted to be a terrorist and he would help by guiding troops to one of the camps in the deep jungle in the Perak area where Chin Peng and other senior leaders lived. Woodhouse selected about twenty of his soldiers and, with the prisoner and an interpreter, set off to deal with the camp. Some days later the prisoner claimed that they were within range of the target. Reckoning on having two to three days, the party adopted the appropriate SOPs and slowed down the pace of their movement. Their suspicions were aroused when the Chinaman led them across the same river three or four times. Woodhouse had a serious confrontation with him but he continued to say that he knew the whereabouts of the camp, though he admitted that he had gone astray. After two hours of walking it became increasingly obvious that either he was totally lost or, more probably, the whole story was an invention. Woodhouse was later to record:

To my shame we applied pressure by making him sit in the sun without water for a few hours and threatening his death if he did not lead us to the enemy. This was the only time that my treatment of a prisoner fell below the expected standards and the shame of it stayed with me (and still does). I was later to emphasise that the correct treatment of prisoners was imperative.

The prisoner wilted and admitted that he had made up the story and used it to get out of prison because he thought that the Chinese would raid the jail and kill him for becoming a turncoat.

John Slim rejected his OC's sense of guilt! Sitting in the sun may have been uncomfortable but it was hardly torture. In fact it was no more uncomfortable than them spending about ten days wandering around the jungle on a busted flush.

The prisoner was given a small escort and sent back to the police post. During the next couple of weeks both Slim and Turnbull were sent off individually to carry out various tasks. Slim, who had spent part of his youth walking in the jungles of India and Burma had no problems with these lonely travails. Turnbull, who had no prior experience in the jungle but was a natural navigator, acquitted himself well. The time came for the troops to be recalled to base.

Woodhouse wanted to be back in base as quickly as possible and decided that he would walk the 15,000 yards or so out to the road head with a small party that would move much faster than the main body. He instructed Slim and Turnbull that they would be his escort and they should be ready to move the next morning at 0530 hours. Slim decided to give Turnbull some friendly advice. He told him to get his gear packed right away and to forget hammocks or other comforts for this night. He should put his pack on his back and go to sleep relaxing against a tree trunk with his rifle in his hand. Slim told him that it was his guess that Woodhouse would probably be ready to move at 0430 hours and he would be really stroppy if he and Turnbull were not ready to go. Sure enough, Woodhouse came very quietly to their position at about 0445 hours and was surprised when both stood up, packs on their backs, rifles in hand and all set to move. He was possibly a little annoyed at not catching them out! Not a word was spoken and away he went as fast as the jungle would allow him. He took only a couple of very short breaks on the whole journey; less than five minutes in which Slim and Turnbull were tested on their navigation. On the march they were tight behind him all the time trying very hard not to look tired. The road head was reached and the Jeep was waiting. Again, not a word spoken until they reached the camp at Kuala Lumpur and dismounted. At that point Woodhouse commented: 'I shall tell the Colonel that you have done quite well and he should keep you both. John, I will want you to command one of my troops.'

John Woodhouse left the country with very positive feelings about 22 SAS Regiment:

> The time came for me to leave Malaya. I was to fly home with Mike Pearman. As the train crossed the well-known causeway from Malaya to Singapore I wondered how long it would be before I saw it again. After spending all but four of the past eighteen months in the jungle, I was certain that the SAS could wrest control of the deep jungle from the Communists, but not sure that it would! I decided at that moment that I must get back to see that happen. Before it did there were three essential conditions to be met:
>
>   The men for the Regiment must be carefully selected
>   The internal administration and discipline must be good
>   Calvert's tactics, together with the risks inherent in them, must be accepted.
>
>   I sought support and publicity for the third condition after I left the Regiment by writing an article for *The Army Quarterly* in April 1953. The theme of it was that the primary aim and main problem of all anti-guerrilla operations is to bring them to battle. The chance of doing this is increased by using small parties in preference to a few big and noisy columns.

The concept of using small patrols living for long periods in deep jungle and winning over the hearts and minds of the aborigines was right. Of that there was no doubt. The execution, however, was weak. Some of the officers and soldiers were not sufficiently dedicated and a special force, above all else, would require determination and dedication. The new CO John Sloane had worked wonders with base morale but though he was admirable over discipline and good administration, he was quite cool to the concept of small patrols. Woodhouse, who had shown leadership of the very highest quality, was now sure that he wanted to return to Malaya. It so happened that events of which he knew naught at the time would make him keener than ever to return.

# Chapter 13

# The 'Z' Reservists and Beyond

In early September 1952, back in England, John Woodhouse was feeling distinctly nervous as he headed north to the army training grounds in Otley, Yorkshire. He was to take command of a group of 'Z' Reservists and supervise their annual training. 'Z' Reservists were all ex-regular officers and men who had opted to remain on the Reserve List to be called back to the Colours in the event of a sudden requirement for well-trained troops as first-line reinforcements. They had the same obligation as the Territorial Army to undergo annual training. The group in question, known at the time as 'Z' Squadron, consisted of about 100 soldiers with wartime experience, many of them in 1 and 2 SAS regiments. They had been blistered onto 21 SAS Regiment (TA) for accounting purposes. Some of these would be men who had seen hard action in North Africa, Italy, France and Germany and to take even temporary command of them was a daunting prospect, but Woodhouse need not have worried. With him at that point were Mike Pearman from Malaya and Eric Newby, his old friend from his prisoner-of-war days. Newby had been in the SBS during the war and he almost immediately left Otley to paddle his canoe in Scottish waters.

On the first night, in a cold Nissen-hutted camp, there was a very noisy but jolly reunion as hearty slaps on the back and in some cases tears were the norm as old comrades-in-arms reacquainted themselves and caught up on events since the war had ended. In the next ten days on exercise on the North Yorkshire moors and the Cumbrian Mountains they showed John Woodhouse that they had lost none of the skills they had learned behind the German lines eight years earlier. Most of them had maintained a high level of fitness that had obviously been self-imposed. He listened and learned from those outstanding soldiers as they exercised most effectively against the regular police and army units. It aroused his interest in the possible future use of

SAS troops in both limited and intensive warfare. His belief in their value (quite outside the jungle theatre) was really fired up from that time as his realization that there was a much wider scope of use for the deployment of 22 SAS began to solidify. At that point he again began to consider the possibility of disbandment when peace eventually came to Malaya.

The ex–SAS members of 'Z' Squadron, who were not fazed by superior rank, quizzed him about his experiences during the war and in Malaya with the same intensity as he questioned them. Their questions and observations were acutely pertinent and Woodhouse warmed to those extraordinary soldiers. In turn, in him they recognized a kindred spirit. He learned the detail of the wartime regiment's selection system and harsh training techniques devised by Jock Lewes, and that was invaluable to him as he had also been tasked with setting up a formal selection course for 22 SAS Regiment. Each and every one of the wartime SAS veterans gave the opinion that a hard selection phase was critical. Apart from anything else, Woodhouse could see it became very much a binding factor between the soldiers all being aware of the severity of the selection process. That short period of involvement with the reservists showed him how close the bonds of shared hardship and mutual respect can be forged among soldiers. The men talked freely of difficult operations, of the violent deaths of comrades, of close calls, of the horrors of war such as the revelations of Belsen, and the difficulties of settling down to 'Civvy Street'. A surprising number had joined the police force and some were considering re–enlisting into the army again.

It is interesting to note that in the early 1950s at least six members of David Stirling's original 'L' Detachment or 1 SAS Regiment became active in Malaya with 22 SAS Regiment: Major Tony Greville-Bell (1 SAS) commanded the original 'B' Squadron, as did Major 'Gentleman Jim' Almonds ('L' Detachment) and Major Alistair McGregor (1 SAS); Major Pat Riley ('L' Detachment) re–enlisted into the army, though not a member of 22 SAS Regiment, was in close liaison regarding intelligence and other support matters; Major Johnny Cooper ('L' Detachment) commanded a squadron and was a key part of developing parachuting into trees; Warrant Officer (later Lieutenant Colonel) Joe Schofield and Warrant Officer Bob Bennett ('L' Detachment) joined a squadron in Malaya and later became the regimental sergeant major of 21 SAS Regiment. In later years this was a source of pleasure to John Woodhouse.

After the two weeks' training was over Woodhouse turned his mind to the next task he had been given. He was to organize a selection course for the volunteers who were kicking their heels awaiting passage to Malaya. At that time the volunteers for the Malayan Scouts (SAS) who were awaiting their selection course and transport to the Far East were put into a holding camp at the Airborne Forces Depot (AFD) in Aldershot. Woodhouse did not like what he found in Aldershot! The men were treated contemptuously by the command element of AFD and spent the majority of their time on fatigues. Disgustingly, some volunteers were stripped of their rank because they did not feature on the AFD establishment. Lacking any form of leadership with no SAS officer to look after their interests, billeted in sub-standard accommodation and being paid only spasmodically led to a miserable existence and morale was at rock bottom.

The situation, with a great deal of imagination, could be put down to the AFD having no idea of what was going on in Malaya. However, in reality it was the fact that the SAS members were not yet parachute-trained that made them 'crap hats' and automatic outcasts. In October 1952 Major John Woodhouse and WO2 (Company Sergeant Major) Bob Bennett, a founder member of David Stirling's 'L' Detachment and 1 SAS Regiment who had himself suffered a short period of inactivity at the AFD, reported to the old Victorian barracks. Mingling with the men, Woodhouse and Bennett set about trying to put some pride and spirit back into the twenty who were awaiting their posting to Malaya. He was helped enormously when the SAS Colonel Commandant, General Sir Miles Dempsey, paid a visit. Dempsey had been the honorary colonel of 21 SAS Regiment from 1948 until 1951 when he became colonel commandant of the SAS and remained so until 1960. He talked freely to the men and told them how much he had admired the actions of the SAS in the Western Desert, Italy, France and Germany. Dempsey, in the presence of Woodhouse, also made it very clear to the Parachute Regiment commandant of the depot, Colonel Pine Coffin, that there was no question of the SAS ever being taken over by the Airborne Forces. Woodhouse, motivated by an urgent desire to capitalize on Dempsey's morale-boosting statements, decided that he would press ahead with all speed and begin the first selection course with the current volunteers at AFD.

From his time with Calvert, his chats to Dare Newell and long discussions on the 'night train' in addition to his exposure to the men of the 'Z' Reservists, he knew what he wanted from every SAS volunteer. The man must be intelligent; he must be ready and able to act on his own initiative; he must be able to work without supervision; he must be self-disciplined; he must be capable of great physical endurance; he must be good-tempered and patient but he must also be capable of working as a team member.

This was all very well in principle but Woodhouse had no staff, no transport and no stores. He had decided that North Wales was to be the testing ground, but the only way he could get the men there was by using rail warrants reluctantly provided by AFD. On arrival, using his own money, he purchased Ordnance Survey maps of Snowdonia. Individual ration packs were not available so he scrounged bulk rations for ten days from the Welsh Regiment based in Brecon. Not everyone had a map and a compass. That first pilot course involved some initial instruction on map-reading, practice at target reconnaissance and the physical effort of criss-crossing Mount Snowdon. The latter became a real ordeal for Woodhouse due to a recurring bout of malaria. On one occasion there was a visit from the local police who were investigating a break-in into a local mountain hut. They suspected (and rightly) that the soldiers had a hand in it. Woodhouse was desperate to avoid the news reaching the Airborne Forces Depot and successfully interrogated the men, extracting a confession from the guilty pair and then he won over the policemen, persuading them to agree to settle for a full and immediate compensation to the hut owner. Woodhouse personally footed the bill for the damage and reclaimed the money from the guilty parties later. This, of course, avoided the need for lengthy paperwork and an official investigation.

In interview John Woodhouse made light of this, the first SAS selection course, claiming that it was superficial and badly managed due to the absence of motivated staff and facilities. He was right and he was wrong. His course programme content was enlarged, refined and added to and became tailor-made for the objective. It served as a basic template for courses to be run in the Brecon Beacons with very few changes over the following years. He passed more than half of the volunteers, which he later said was probably rather generous of him. That albeit short-lived experience allowed him to chat with some authority to Dare Newell about his ideas on what a formalized selection course for the SAS should consist of and what administrative backing would be needed. He foresaw that the course should be based independently of the location of 22 SAS Regiment wherever that was going to be sited. His prompt actions in getting the volunteers out of the AFD did not go unremarked by those soldiers; it demonstrated to them that the SAS was not going to be walked over by the Parachute Regiment.

His duties with the SAS temporarily completed, Woodhouse managed to get a place on a joint Anglo-Brazilian expedition to explore the Mato Grosso area of the Amazon basin, but this was cancelled at the last moment which left him free to be posted, in December 1952, as adjutant to 4th Battalion, the Dorset Regiment (TA) in Dorchester. This appointment had been filled by his father thirty years earlier. He found the battalion to be a highly efficient unit. The more senior officers and NCOs had war service and the unit was much more battle-worthy than its regular brother unit, 1st Battalion, the Dorset Regiment which at that time was largely composed of National Servicemen. He developed a great and enduring respect for the Territorial Army that never left him.

For two years he enjoyed the relaxing social life of the Dorset 'County Set': dinner parties, Hunt balls, weekend tennis matches and rambling along old Roman roads with his friend from the PoW days, Eric Newby. During this time he became very close to Mary Lock, the daughter of a well-known Dorchester solicitor. He had known Mary and her brother, Henry, since childhood. This was the point at which he began to seriously consider the desirability of marriage. The Hall and Woodhouse Brewery and Higher Melcombe may one day depend on him to produce heirs. Though he and Mary were very fond of each other, it was not love and marriage was therefore out of the question.

Never, throughout his two years' separation from the SAS, did Woodhouse's interest in that form of soldiering wane. Latterly he was in constant contact with Major Dare Newell who had taken over the role of liaison officer between the SAS and the War Office. Newell had commanded a squadron in 22 SAS during the period 1952–54. His work with Force 136 had revolved around helping the Chinese Communists to fight the Japanese occupiers of Malaya; some of those guerrillas now formed the core of the fight against British occupation. Woodhouse was also in regular correspondence with some of the current SAS officers and was up to date with most aspects of the regiment's operations.

Apart from his other duties, Newell made himself responsible for recruiting and supervising the selection course which was now based at Dering Lines in Brecon. Woodhouse planned his return to Malaya and made contact with Newell. He was insistent that he wanted to take the selection course himself, even though he would have been welcomed back into the fold without that formality.

SAS selection now had a small staff under Lieutenant Douglas Bruce Merrie with instructors Sergeants Bill Ross (who had already distinguished himself with the regiment in Malaya) and Tim Holt. Holt, ex-Manchester Regiment, told the author in interview how appalled he had been at the poor disciplinary standards and turn-out of the Malayan Scouts. He had been with Ferret Force before volunteering for the Scouts and he was already a seasoned soldier with good jungle experience. A storeman, a clerk, cooks, mechanics and a few drivers completed the staff. Well, it almost completed the staff: Corporal Ip Kwong Lau returned to the UK as a fully-fledged member of 22 SAS and he ran a small canteen for the men on selection. Some years later he was to open a successful Chinese restaurant and takeaway in Hereford.

Woodhouse joined a course of twenty-eight volunteers.

The first event on that early course began at 0600 hours with a two-day endurance march to be completed individually with no assistance or encouragement of any kind from the staff. The truck left the camp at exactly 0600 hours; anyone late was left behind and failed the course. They were dropped off in the snow-covered ground at the little station of Tal-y-bont. 'Listen,' said Ross, 'follow me and keep up.' In later years the endurance march came at the end of the initial selection process and certainly did not have a member of the permanent staff on which to focus.

Ross was a big man of few words. Woodhouse kept up with him until, after three hours, he stopped at a deserted railway hut. There he was sick on the rails and felt exhausted. Most of the volunteers trailed in behind him but a few had already given up. He recovered quickly and for ten more hours kept up with Ross. The only words he spoke were 'Try one of these', passing him a boiled sweet as they began what turned out to be the final ascent and descent of the day. They spent the night in a bare, cold Nissen hut.

At intervals on the second day the volunteers would arrive at a road in a valley where a lorry would be parked. Tea and a ride back to barracks were on offer to any whose resolution had wavered. It was also a ride out of the regiment! They were not told how far they had to go, nor was any help or encouragement offered. Endurance, self-motivated, was only one aspect of selection. There were initiative tests, for example to report on the layout of an ammunition store. Could the students sketch a plan of a railway yard; could they navigate themselves across country by day and night? The volunteers were also closely observed to see how they got on with one another, a character assessment of which they were not aware.

Six out of the twenty-eight were accepted on that course. That percentage of one in five or six was remarkably constant. Woodhouse got to know Dare Newell, who visited the course, even better and joined him on the next course to help in the selection of four officers. Their views nearly always coincided and they remained close friends for thirty-five years until his death. On that course one officer, Mike Hawkins of the Dorset Regiment, managed to pass.

Over the following years the SAS selection course continued to seek the same characteristics in the volunteers and maintained the very demanding physical and mental tests. Eventually a period of three months' 'continuation training' was added to the course; this compensated for the fact that successful volunteers no longer headed immediately for the jungles of Malaya.

*Chapter 14*

# Return to the Jungle

In March 1955 Major John Woodhouse returned to Malaya to witness some changes. No. 22 SAS Regiment was now under command of Lieutenant Colonel George Lea (later lieutenant general). Lea was a big man in every sense of the word; he was not a volunteer for the role of CO but he accepted the job with alacrity and was already stamping his character on the regiment. He was well aware of Woodhouse's reputation as a jungle warrior, excellent trainer, shrewd tactician and unsurpassed leader. He was mentally debating whether to put him straight into command of one of the British squadrons of which there were now three, or to keep him at RHQ to oversee an increase in strength. In the event the increase was not to happen until later in 1956 when a squadron made up exclusively of members of the Parachute Regiment was established and a New Zealand SAS Squadron was formed and committed to Malaya.

Not only was it a different regiment to which Woodhouse had returned, he was also a different man. His study of Mike Calvert and his methods, the exposure to the 'Z' Reservists, his growing relationship with Dare Newell, his understanding of the low esteem in which the SAS was then held by certain departments of the War Office and his periods of quiet reflection in the mountains of Wales and the rolling countryside of Dorset had served to crystallize his thoughts on the future of the SAS. His confidence had grown considerably, and in conversation or debate he made his well-thought-out points forcibly and with eloquence. The Malayan campaign was not going to last forever and though he had no doubt that the efforts of his regiment would become more and more significant as the expertise grew, what would the future hold? The War Office had already ordered the disbandment of the wartime SAS Brigade on the grounds that there would be no requirement in future conflicts for Special Forces; they could just as easily repeat the disbandment order whenever the Malayan campaign came to a conclusion. After all, the current SAS Regiment was manned by jungle fighters with little apparent desire for conventional soldiering. Those thoughts were constantly at the forefront of his mind over the coming years. It was time to think even more deeply about those conversations on the night train and begin to 'sell' them as he had advised the regimental officers at the time.

George Lea lived in the officers' mess in Ampney Road and he and Woodhouse spent much time there in conversation over the first few days. Since Calvert's departure the SAS had benefited from two very effective commanding officers. Both Lieutenant Colonel John Sloane and Lieutenant Colonel Oliver Brooke had left their mark. The administrative system was, though still far from perfect, much improved and base discipline was significantly better. The regiment now had its own signallers and overall communications were much improved.

The business of parachuting into trees had been perfected and a number of operational jumps had been made without serious injury. The clever design of the equipment for jumping into trees evolved between the RAF and members of the regiment who had experience of the business. Jumping into trees was hazardous in any event and prior to hitting the tree canopy the parachutist would release the rucksack attached to his chest harness to hang at the end of the tethering rope just beneath his feet. In effect he would be standing on the rucksack and gain some protection from the upper branches of the trees as he fell through the leafy canopy. He would protect his manhood as best he could and cross his arms over his eyes in order to shield them. He thereafter hoped that his main canopy would snag securely and leave him dangling in an upright position. He also hoped that he would not hit a hornets' nest! The parachutist wore a canvas 'bikini' which had a double-stitched slot going all round the waist section. Attached to the front was a metal hoop shaped rather like a bottle-opener; through the hoop and the slot around the waist there ran a webbing strap. One end of the strap was designed to be tied to a handy branch when the parachute snagged as the man dropped through the trees. The 'long' end was stowed in a canvas bag strapped to the left leg; once securely snagged the parachutist tied off the 'short' end and released the canvas bag holding the long strap. The time it took to hit the ground gave an idea of how far away terra firma was; he then removed his rifle from the sack and secured it round his neck, then unhooked his rucksack to dangle below him. Once securely tied to the branch he could abseil, under good control, to the ground. If one had the misfortune not to be snagged in an upright position, then the required contortions to set up the lowering gear could be painful and time-consuming.

Captain Hugh Mercer, along with a very co-operative RAF PJI, Flight Sergeant 'Nobby' Clark, was mainly responsible for developing the hazardous techniques of parachuting into trees. Mercer was an ex-Indian army officer who had been wounded in action while with his Baluch Regiment. In retreat he was left behind with other wounded soldiers and picked up by the Japanese army. He survived the harsh treatment meted out by his captors in Rangoon jail where he remained until the end of the war. A first-class soldier, he blended well into the SAS and became the second-in-command and it was in that capacity that he led the way in developing the parachuting techniques and equipment.

The parachutes in the 1950s were not steerable and to lessen the effects of wind the drop altitude would be as low as possible, sometimes down to 450ft. When reserve parachutes came into being they were often ignored. Low-altitude drops meant that there would be little, if any, time for the 'chute to deploy. With the better equipment and techniques, tree-jumping became a matter of course and casualty figures were low.

Woodhouse was forthright in putting his views to his new CO. He stated that though there was no doubt a marked improvement in the regiment, he still believed that battle discipline left much to be desired and that training and retraining were simply not hard enough. He was delighted that Lea agreed with him and even more so when he was given command of 'D' Squadron. First though he had to qualify as a parachutist. He amusingly recalled:

George Lea arranged an individual ten-day course for me. All my life my manual dexterity and physical co-ordination has been poor. I had to do eight jumps from a Valetta aircraft over Singapore Island. I found no joy whatsoever in parachuting, only satisfaction in completing the course after suffering mild concussion on my seventh jump from an inept backward roll on landing. A fact I did not report in case it caused a delay in my qualification. I also had to learn how to lower myself after parachuting into trees which was a technique developed by the regiment. This was taught by using the equipment fixed to the hangar roof. My lack of dexterity caused such an inextricable tangle that I became the first pupil (and probably the last) to be rescued by ladder! The circulation in one of my arms had been so severely restricted that for several days I could get no grip in that hand. I could not pull on the rigging lines with it when parachuting and had also to conceal that disability. My RAF Parachute Jump Instructor and I were equally relieved when my course was completed.

Woodhouse's first action on taking command of 'D' Squadron was to move it away from the temptations of the bars and into huts on Maur beach. Close by was a large jungle-covered hill that was ideal for the retraining on which he insisted. Shooting, navigation and fieldcraft skills were honed and most evenings included the now standard 'Chinese Parliament'. This session stemmed from information obtained from a responsive prisoner. He told how the CTs every night held discussions about the day's events and future plans. Everyone had his or her say and was free to make any suggestions or criticisms. John Woodhouse thought that this was a fine way to collect ideas and observations from the soldiers and in turn they were gratified to have their opinions sought and they felt that they were making a greater contribution to their troop. Each man had his say about whichever of the wide-ranging topics was being discussed. John Woodhouse used his preparation for those sessions to indulge in some personal introspection: he would mentally go through his actions of the day and decide whether anything could be improved. In this way some SOPs were refined. The advice of Dick Noone, the head of the government's Aborigine Department, was sought. Noone thought that they were on the right track towards gaining the confidence of the aborigines by their patience and understanding; they tendered medical assistance and gave rewards for accurate information. Always the tribesmen were treated with respect. Noone was a great source of information regarding customs and habits of the aborigines. One of the CT enemy leaders, Ah Tuck, was both respected and feared by the aborigines; they were the only source of support for the CTs. In the end friendly patience and understanding would succeed over Ah Tuck's harsh methods. Ah Tuck was killed in a face-to-face confrontation with Sergeant Bob Turnbull some two years later.

Not everything was serious. While in Muria, the squadron second-in-command, the inimitable Captain Stuart Perry, organized a memorable party in the officers' mess. This was financed by running a roulette game where the mess was the banker. There were anxious moments when the mess came close to bankruptcy but the guests, nurses from the military hospital in Kuala Lumpur and local European civilians who had shown hospitality to the squadron, effectively financed the party. On different occasions there were all-ranks beer-drinking sessions round a great fire on the beach. Held after dark, they usually had a background of tremendous tropical storms out to the west over distant Sumatra.

On 2 June 1955 'D' Squadron flew to Ipoh and were met on the airfield by Brigadier Moore. Picking up their rucksacks, they emplaned in fours into the waiting helicopters. Brigadier Moore remarked to Woodhouse: 'It is quite amazing watching the SAS do anything, nobody seems to give any orders, nobody falls in, but everything happens and the job gets done.' This, of course, arose from 'D' Squadron's system of discipline instilled by Woodhouse. The stress that was put on every rank using their initiative resulted in troopers taking their own actions to correct faults or omissions. Officers and NCOs were not to check and fuss over troopers. If things were forgotten men would be punished, but they had to think for themselves.

Helicopters ferried 'D' Squadron to a police post from where they moved on foot via the Sungei Chegar and from that location the four troops, each of between twelve and fifteen men, carried on to their respective operational areas based on the Sungeis Legap, Mu, Korbu and Yum. Squadron Headquarters was sited initially on the upper slopes of the 4,000ft-high Gunong (mountain) Chingkas. This, Operation SHARK, was to be 'D' Squadron's responsibility until the end of August 1955; it was also the forerunner of many full squadron operations.

One thing that should be noted at this point is that helicopters were still very much in their infancy and Malaya was the first major 'war' deployment of those wonderfully versatile machines. There could surely be no harder testing ground than flying to make casualty evacuation flights from tight, restricted jungle LZs, very often under severe weather conditions. Crashes were not uncommon and the SAS lost a number of men over the years. It took a particular type of man to fly the helicopters of 194 Squadron in Malaya, just as it took a particular type of soldier to join the SAS. What is certain is that both types of soldier had the greatest respect for the other.

From the onset of Operation SHARK Woodhouse was determined to improve battle discipline and work through the newly-written SOPs. Over his time so far in Malaya the SOPs had grown from three pages to six. He was at great pains to point out that they were guides, NOT orders, and that it was the duty of all ranks to think about and apply new tactics because it was essential in a guerrilla war to be unpredictable. In a section of the document aimed at commanders, he pointed out that they were in command of some of the best soldiers in the army and this required exceptional standards of work and efficiency from those in the privileged position of command. Almost echoing Mike Calvert (and why not?), he stated:

> Unless you are genuinely interested in the well-being of your men, you had best find another job which takes you as far away from them as possible. If you look after your soldiers, you can and must expect them to work to the extreme limits of human endurance on operations. If you do the former, they in turn will not fail you. Insist on meticulous observance of battle discipline, especially when you and your men are tired. This is a matter of will power – yours, not your soldiers.

His discipline was quite rigid. At the police post he had allowed the squadron quartermaster sergeant (SQMS) to persuade him to take him on the operation. He had stressed in his briefing that anyone unable to keep up would have to make their own way back to the post. Predictably the SQMS was not 'jungle fit' and was quite exhausted by the second day. Woodhouse refused to give him an escort and brusquely ordered him to return to the police post alone. It took the SQMS three days to make it back to the post and Woodhouse suffered many twinges of conscience as he waited for the news of a safe arrival. This operation was the one that earned him the reputation of being a martinet in terms of discipline. He once punished a soldier who had an accidental discharge of his rifle by taking away his weapon, giving him a grenade and moving him 100 yards or so outside the base perimeter to carry out a lonely vigil for the whole of the night. This meant that the soldier would get little or no sleep that night. SAS lore says that the unfortunate man was told to carry the grenade for a week with the pin extracted. However, in an interview Woodhouse disputed that but did say that he had once, under similar circumstances, removed the pin from the grenade he had given to the offending soldier but that had only been for a couple of hours. He confessed to having had an accidental discharge himself which resulted in him carrying out the same sentry duty and also paying a hefty fine into the 'D' Squadron account to fund more beer at the next party. Another tale is that on one occasion when Woodhouse was returning to a patrol base he was fired at by one of his sentries and the soldier was put on a charge, for missing! This was confirmed by Woodhouse, who grinned and said the matter of the charge was for effect, no punishment was given.

Ian Cartwright, then a troop commander, gave a further example of his OC's determination, which through iron discipline became almost legendary. As the OC of the squadron he spent little time at his headquarters. He tended to travel with a signaller and one or two other men between troop bases; often he would deliberately visit sites where a troop may have spent the night before his RV. On one occasion he discovered a cigarette butt in a used camp site. On joining up with the troop in their new base he ordered the troop commander to immediately return to the site and bring back the cigarette butt (which he had marked).

That apparently was not the only time that Woodhouse ordered a patrol to retrace its route to right a wrong. The second occasion was more gruesome. When a CT was killed, the body would be propped up against a tree and photographed for police records use. During one patrol a contact resulted in the death of two CTs. The patrol buried the bodies but forgot to photograph them! Woodhouse sent the men back to dig up the bodies and take the necessary pictures. Not a pleasant experience!

He had long been dissatisfied with the need to air-drop food resupplies every four days while they were using the standard army ration packs. Air-drops or helicopter resupplies obviously gave away the SAS locations to the enemy. He devised a ration pack to last for fourteen days: breakfast was an oatmeal block and tea; biscuits and a 2oz tin of cheese or a tin of sardines for a midday snack; an evening meal to consist of half a tin of corned beef, rice and hardtack biscuits. This was not a popular menu, but though not suspected at that time it was the forerunner to the SAS eventually being supported with lightweight dehydrated rations. Offset against this was the resupply, every fourteen days, of food that included fresh meat, bread and rum: 'big eats' days. The new ration lightened rucksack loads, reduced the amount of litter to be hidden and greatly improved security; that was grudgingly accepted by all. Despite the medical advice given to the regiment about the dangers of such a diet, there were no cases of malnutrition, liver or kidney damage recorded during the Malayan campaign. There were, of course, cases of hepatitis, leptospirosis and dengue fever but these were attributable to other causes. Paddy Finn, a member of 'D' Squadron at the time and later 'A' Squadron, recalled in a letter to the author '... when John Woodhouse was our squadron commander in Malaya he would swap all his tins of meat for our sardines and hardtack biscuits. That was what he lived on ....' The carriage of large, heavy loads was very much assisted by the issue of Bergen rucksacks. Large waterproof bags kept clothing dry and the side, rear and top pockets meant that there was no need to unpack the main compartment to find items for the brew breaks.

During this operation Woodhouse also experimented with what was to become known as the 'hard routine'. He conjectured that there may be occasions when the troop or patrol sensed that they were in close proximity to the enemy and needed to take every precaution to hide their presence. In such circumstances there would be no cooking, no smoking, no use of toothpaste or soap, no cutting to make bashas, no speaking except in whispers, stand to before last light and again before first light, and after first light move off for about an hour before making the morning brew. All litter was to be carried away. This discipline was to be refined even more in Borneo in later years. In his own words, Woodhouse recalled:

I was seldom in SHQ for very long. I moved from troop to troop with an escort of two or three soldiers. I got to know the area well. I kept a critical eye open for anything wrong. We mostly lived the hard routine as we travelled. If I found fault then I had it out with the Troop Commander on the spot first and then with his men. Exhorting, cajoling, explaining with persistence was initially exhausting for me, it seemed to be a one man crusade, but – it was also rewarding. I have to say though that in the early days of that command it almost broke my heart as my words seemed to bounce off the ears of my soldiers but suddenly it seemed to click and come together. Our Chinese Parliaments became something to look forward to and I truly enjoyed those wide-ranging sessions. There is often a wide gap between knowing what is right and actually doing it. By the end of that three-month operation I had greatly narrowed that gap and increased my and my soldiers' pride in 'D' Squadron.

On 22 March Woodhouse was recalled to HQ Squadron in order to train newly-joined officers and to take a look at how the efficiency of the squadron could be improved. He found it a mixed bunch. He quickly reduced the strength from 123 men to 116 by taking them out on a series of overnight ambush patrols. One batch of new arrivals was treated to a ten-day patrol along the River Mu; the group included four new officers.

In a letter to the author Vic Steyerman, often one of the escorts, recalls time spent with John Woodhouse:

> Not only, of course, was I one of the very few National Servicemen to have had the privilege of being allowed into the Regiment but I was also chosen whilst on the very first revamped selection course in Wales initiated by John Woodhouse and indeed it was he who allowed me to travel back to Malaya with him. Thereafter and for another year or so I was in his team on various jungle operations.....
> I have always considered that five men have had a great influence in my life and, although only in his company for a comparatively short period, Major Woodhouse, as he was then, was certainly one of them. He, of course, would not have known about this impact on my life but I am quite sure that I am not the only man to have benefited from his talents. In my mind he was a real man, a great jungle fighter, a natural but quiet leader and a soldier whom we should all be proud to have known.

In his diaries there is a note detailing some statistics:

In the five months from April 1956 the SAS killed 25 terrorists. The NZ Squadron (with 90 men compared to 60 in each of the British squadrons) was the most successful. These successes gradually swung the aborigines to support us in preference to the CTs. When a NZ soldier was killed in action I went with others to his funeral. The cemetery was on a hill overlooking the cultivated valley in which Kuala Lumpur lies. Black rain clouds hung over the jungle-covered hills, but late afternoon sun lit up the valley. The crosses of 20 SAS soldiers lay in this place – part of the price of freedom. I thought of the misery war brings, not so much to us soldiers, but to our homes. The bugle calls of Last Post and Reveille were accompanied by distant thunder. It was very moving.

The main organizer of aboriginal support for the CTs was Ah Tuck who became the focal point for a number of full squadron operations. He was a vicious man who was feared by those aborigines and he covered a wide geographic area. With that in mind, Ip Kwong Lau made many forays into aborigine settlements disguised as a CT and pretending to be lost after an action against the security forces. When, a day or two later, one of the patrols called in to a village, the aborigines did not tell of Ip's visits. No doubt it was fear of Ah Tuck rather than any sense of loyalty, but despite the lack of positive information the net was slowly closing in and later, in 1957, Sergeant Bob Turnbull, during Operation CHIEFTAIN, had a head-on meeting with Ah Tuck and shot and killed him with his shotgun at a range of 25 yards. Woodhouse was not to learn of that action until some weeks later. That ended Communist control of the area. Before the killing Woodhouse had a visitor: Brigadier 'Digger' Tighe Wood who was on the administrative staff of HQ Malaya. He had commanded a parachute battalion before his appointment. Before he visited Woodhouse he did not believe that the SAS did anything that could not be done by the Parachute Regiment. In a letter afterwards he wrote: 'I did not before realise the calibre of your chaps nor the task that they perform in the jungle. I was deeply impressed by them as individuals and in their spirit and belief in 'D' Squadron. ... You have recruited a very staunch supporter of the SAS in me.'

Another letter to the author was from Mike Dillon, a veteran of those early 'D' Squadron days, who wrote:

The formation of 'D' Squadron was a wonderful escape for John Woodhouse (and myself). I had great trouble getting away from HQ Squadron and SSM Bob Bennett. But I made it, though it meant coming down to corporal. But soon I was made the acting Troop Sergeant of 16 Troop. In the beginning 'D' Squadron formed up for training, fitness and battle discipline. We operated in small patrols in a quiet area before being moved to deep jungle in the North Johore/Negri Sembilan area where we built Fort Clapham. At that time John stayed in Dusan Tua gathering the new arrivals and forming 17, 18 and 19 Troops. I cannot remember any other officers, or even a SSM, at that time....

Soon this phase was followed by the arrival of John and the other troops. He was experimenting with surveillance tactics at that time. It was a new concept. We were not allowed to speak – whisper if absolutely necessary. No washing. No teeth cleaning. No daylight feeding. No cutting branches or twigs. The rations we had at that time were not suitable for cold eating so cooking and brew up were at night after a long stand to. All that was later used as a technique in Borneo, albeit more developed and with better communications and back up....

All that is just to show where I fitted in with John Woodhouse. He gave me the best Confidential Report I ever had. He even brought in a birthday cake for my 21st birthday hidden in his Bergen. He whispered 'Happy Birthday'. He was the best OC I ever served with. A real man and a real leader.

The next visitor was Major Harry Thompson, a red-haired giant of a man who was to replace John Woodhouse as OC 'D' Squadron. That he did with great success. Woodhouse was instructed to return to the UK to take up the post of second-in-command of 21 SAS Regiment based in London.

*Chapter 15*

# The TAVR

During the long journey back to the UK and the short period of home leave that followed, Woodhouse applied his mind to some of the problems that he foresaw could possibly affect the future of 22 SAS Regiment. The effect of one or two tours of duty with the regiment was beginning to create some ripples. In the case of some officers their careers were suffering as accusations of disloyalty to their parent regiments were made; on occasions they were debarred from jobs that would normally have been part of their upward progression in rank. For other ranks there were similar problems. Technically, after passing selection they were given a three-year tour of duty before being recalled to their parent regiments. Probably about 90 per cent of those regiments ignored this ruling, content in the knowledge that their soldiers were getting good experience with the SAS. On joining the regiment soldiers were obliged to drop their rank and begin again from trooper. Some parent regiments allowed them to keep their past rank and even progress upwards on a 'shadow' roster. The biggest problem was with the 'non-teeth' arms. Many ex-corps men held technical trades and periodically they had to be recalled to upgrade their trade qualifications upon which promotion depended and often pressure was put on them to return 'home'. This system posed a danger to the SAS in that experienced soldiers could be taken away at any time. The effect was twofold: a loss of valued expertise to the regiment and a feeling of insecurity in the minds of the soldiers. A permanent cadre for the SAS would be an ideal solution. A third factor was the value of active service experience in the jungle. There was no doubt that it honed the skills of individual soldiers in many ways; should this, thought Woodhouse, become a part of the selection course, even if the campaign in Malaya came to a sudden end? All these problems were to be thrashed out in tandem with the loyalty, far-sightedness and energy of the ubiquitous Dare Newell.

John Woodhouse had mixed feelings on his posting as second-in-command of 21 SAS (Artists) (V) Regiment. A large part of him wished that he could have had the good fortune to remain for a further tour with 22 SAS Regiment in Malaya; he sensed that the emergency could end within the next two to three years. He was confident that the British army would have defeated the Communists without the efforts of the SAS, but he thought that the regiment had positively shortened the campaign. Indeed, many years later an experienced ex-officer of 22 SAS (Major Mike Jones) met the Communist leader, Chin Peng, and had lunch with him in a border town in Thailand. Chin Peng had spent the majority of his time in command either in the deep jungle of Perak or in Thailand. During that meeting he categorically stated that it was the disruption of his courier routes and the gradual loss of co-operation of the aborigines due to the effectiveness of the SAS that foreshortened the war. Chin Peng steadfastly maintained that his aspirations at the time were the best for both China and Malaya.

Woodhouse had no prejudice against the Territorial Army; indeed, he had enormous respect for those 'part-time' soldiers who worked so hard and enthusiastically. His experience as adjutant in the Dorset Regiment and with the 'Z' Reservists had provided him with a solid basis for that respect. The system then was that a Territorial Army commanding officer would have a regular army officer as his second-in-command and vice versa. Woodhouse knew that the CO of 21 SAS was a wartime hero of the Special Boat Service: Lieutenant Colonel David Sutherland. Sutherland, still an active member of MI5, had taken over the regiment in January 1956 from another equally distinguished wartime hero, Colonel Ian Lapraik.

During the short time between leaving 22 SAS in the jungles of Malaya and arriving at the 21 SAS Regiment's HQ in Duke's Road, London, he had applied his mind to the theatre of war in which 21 SAS was scheduled to be involved. He carried with him two strong convictions: the use of small parties of intelligent, self-disciplined and motivated soldiers that was proving so successful in Malaya would prove equally successful in adapting to other conditions in other theatres of war; and the energy and dedication that he had witnessed in the TA could be harnessed to further those convictions. Just before Woodhouse took up his position as second-in-command 21 SAS, Major Dare Newell had taken an appointment as GSO2 in the Directorate of Land/Air Warfare (DLAW) at the War Office. This was an excellent placement of Dare, giving him fast access to a number of incumbents who were important to the future of the SAS. This close proximity for the next two years ensured that Woodhouse was happily drawn into many of the discussions about the future of the SAS and often supplied written dissertations in support of the lobbying.

Sutherland's initial briefing to his new second-in-command was succinct. The annual two-week TA camp had recently taken place on Salisbury Plain and it had, in Sutherland's eyes, been a shambles. Woodhouse would have his work cut out in devising training methods to bring the soldiering skills up to date. He was by then the most experienced officer from 22 SAS with an excellent reputation for toughness, innovation and leadership. It was during his early days with 21 SAS that he was made MBE for his services to the regiment in Malaya. The recognition pleased him very much and confirmed to him that his energy and patience with 'D' Squadron had been expended along the right lines and gave him even more confidence with which to pursue his dreams of seeing a permanent SAS Regiment in the British army's Order of Battle.

Woodhouse's tour with the TA lasted for two years, during which he became widely respected by the regiment. He forged a better relationship between the regulars of 22 SAS and the TA soldiers by informally having regulars attached to 21 SAS during exercises. He wrote the first set of SOPs for the regiment and paid close attention to officer training. He organized and supervised a series of TEWTs (Tactical Exercises without Troops) that were designed to stimulate original thought in devising new tactics, improving SOPs and to explore possible commitments both during the Cold War period and a possible nuclear war. In this way he began to get to know the strengths and weaknesses of his officers as they in turn began to respect and appreciate him. He was greatly assisted in his endeavours by the presence of the late Captain John Spreull (already a veteran troop commander of 22 SAS who later became OC of 'A' Squadron). At that time he was filling the post of adjutant. Additionally there were six or seven warrant officers and sergeants acting as permanent staff instructors. Equally pleasing was the knowledge that Bob Bennett was the RSM. What a team that was! The duties of a second-in-command of a Territorial Army regiment include taking over from the CO should that become necessary for any reason, but his main focus is on organizing and supervising the training of the regiment to enable it to meet the wartime role. He brought a new dimension to the training exercises he organized. In particular he liaised with the military in Denmark to ensure that his troops were truly tested on the annual exercises. Those exercises were always demanding. The Danes employed children and reservist soldiers to scour the countryside looking for alien tracks. Pictures of the soles of British army boots and uniforms were pinned up in the villages and children were rewarded with sweets if they were able to spot the signs of infiltration. Quite often troops from 22 SAS would also take part in those exercises.

In preparation for the Danish scenarios, Woodhouse designed many Escape & Evasion exercises for 21 SAS in the UK. In those days it was not unusual for the position of an RV to be deliberately leaked to the enemy by the controllers in order that some participants at least would get practice at resistance to interrogation. He went on a number of those exercises himself and two memories came from different members of the regiment. They are concerned with an exercise that took place on the Romney Marshes in the winter of 1963. Snow was thick on the ground. One member of the regiment who had been captured at the same time told how Woodhouse, a fellow prisoner, had bumped into him and whispered 'Don't let the buggers know who I am – I'm pretending to be a private.' With that he hawked, spat and wiped his nose on his sleeve and was heard to mutter 'Don't like this fookin' cold.' The enemy guards never suspected that they had the 21 SAS second-in-command in their grasp. The other member recalled that he was hiding in some scrub by a river waiting to see if the coast was clear when he heard something close by. It was Woodhouse about to cross the river. What impressed him the most was that in the dead of night his CO was walking backwards into the river so that he would not be tracked!

Major Roy Fielder, a 21 SAS veteran, recalled an incident:

Early in 1957 I was a 23-year-old corporal when the 21 SAS second-in-command – John Woodhouse – asked if he could join my patrol. Astonished at being *asked* rather than *told* by this distinguished soldier, maybe I was affected by this unexpected addition to my patrol. I neglected to use my compass and in dense woodland managed to take my patrol in a complete circle. In a pub after the exercise I encountered John again. I made my apologies for my Horlicks in navigation, expecting a bollocking. John simply said 'Yes, but you won't do that again will you?' He then added 'But I did admire your fieldcraft'! Years later, and then deeply involved in management development, I realised that often people already understood where they went wrong and simply needed encouragement not to repeat the error. To add, as John did, a compliment can be a powerful incentive. But then he was a very remarkable leader.

Included in his busy life were many meetings with Dare Newell, said by many to be the ultimate SAS visionary, discussing the ways and means of furthering the chances of the survival of 22 SAS. Also deeply involved in those discussions were David Stirling, David Sutherland, Hugh Gillies, Brian Franks, manager of the Hyde Park Hotel, chairman of the SAS Association and a former highly-decorated CO of 2 SAS and, of course, the equally highly-decorated Colonel Ian Lapraik.

Woodhouse was, on several occasions, invited to lecture to FCO candidates under training. Those lectures were on the background and capabilities of the SAS, their post-war activities and his own theories on counter-insurgency and counter-terrorist operations and the importance of accurate and timely intelligence. He was to repeat those instructional sessions in the 1960s. It was clear that he was well-regarded as he was asked to stay in touch after his retirement. One aspect of Woodhouse's career was fast becoming a problem. He had failed the Staff College entrance exam (1954) and he was not keen to try it again, but without a staff qualification under his belt his promotion prospects were very limited. A year at the Staff College was considered essential for promotion above lieutenant colonel and important in even reaching that rank. He actually, for the first time in years, considered leaving the army and beginning a second career in the family brewing industry. Fortunately for the SAS his former CO, George Lea, took a persuasive stance and talked him out of retiring.

In his Confidential Report on Woodhouse, Sutherland wrote:

During his tour as 2i/c this officer has made a very significant contribution to the evolution and progress of the Regiment. This contribution stems from personal ability and practical experience. He is by nature modest, thoughtful and reserved. This deceptive exterior conceals a determined and resourceful character and an acute brain. He has many interests outside the Army and is well read. He is himself clear and economical on paper, and although not staff trained, has the temperament, ability and professional knowledge to make a good staff officer.... He leads in a quiet, economical and purposeful manner which is most effective. He is popular, completely reliable and thrives on responsibility.... Taken all round he is the best post-war officer of his rank that I know and the best 2i/c this Regiment has ever had.

That report, added to George Lea's exhortations, persuaded him to stay in the army for at least a little longer. During his tenure in London the amalgamation of the Dorset and Devonshire regiments was announced. They were to become the Devon and Dorset Regiment. This, at a stroke, took away the intense loyalty to the Dorsets that Woodhouse had felt so strongly throughout his career. He began to cast around for alternatives and spoke to his contemporary, Tony Farrar Hockley, enquiring as to whether he thought the Parachute Regiment would accept him. Encouraged by Farrar Hockley's very positive response, he applied for a transfer from the Dorset Regiment to the Parachute Regiment. This was put on hold until his tour as the 21 SAS Regiment second-in-command was completed.

Something far removed from his military duties had been occupying much of his thoughts for some time. One day a share of the Hall & Woodhouse Brewery could pass down to him and surely it was his duty and indeed, deep desire, to not only fully support the family business but to have his own heirs. Always shy and inhibited with women, he had had little prolonged social contact outside his friendships with Helen and Mary Lock. He was in an occupation that offered little by way of a social life leading to meeting many women and in early 1958, he quietly turned to a London-based marriage bureau. His third meeting with possible suitors was with Peggy Lacey. Peggy was a daughter of George Lacey, a

London solicitor, and she was the same age as Woodhouse (35); she had been a member of the WRNS during the war and then she became a nurse at St Thomas's Hospital in London. She was looking for security and he was looking to establish himself as a family man. She was very attractive with a warm, engaging personality and a vibrant sense of humour. Her wartime service had given her at least an understanding of service life and the probable demands it would make on a relationship. They got on very well together in an easygoing way and they were married on 29 May 1958 with Bruce Mercer (a Malaya veteran) filling the post of best man. They went on honeymoon by train to Salzburg and Vienna while still getting to know each other. John's memoirs record:

> I was to be blessed and loved much more than I deserved by Peggy. She was not an organizer and I was often short-tempered, leading to occasional stormy interludes. She was immensely loyal and never complained, no matter what life threw at her. She had a gift greater than any other, the gift of inspiring affection and laughter in all who knew her.

The marriage brought a totally new dimension to John Woodhouse's life. His visits to the family had always been warm and welcoming, but a wife broadened the horizons considerably and Peggy took a great interest in Higher Melcombe and its history. The life of a bachelor, especially one in command, could be lonely, despite the love of the work. Later he was to be particularly appreciative of how Peggy easily and smoothly immersed herself into village life at Melcombe and into the SAS fraternity. Her support for him was uncomplicated and total.

At the end of his tour with 21 SAS Regiment Woodhouse was well-known and respected throughout the SAS family. His earlier wishes were met and he was posted to 3rd Battalion, the Parachute Regiment.

While he had been working hard with 21 SAS Woodhouse was also well aware, through Dare Newell, of the events that were to greatly assist in establishing a firm future for the SAS. Lobbying was taking place to ensure that the SAS was requested to take part in quelling an uprising in Oman. Around 600 rebels had positioned themselves on the 8,000ft-high Jebel Akhdar Mountain where they considered their stronghold to be impregnable. In late October 1958, having been briefed on the facts by Major Frank Kitson (the eventual commander-in-chief of UK Land Forces who later became a friend of the SAS), Lieutenant Colonel Tony Deane-Drummond, then CO of 22 SAS Regiment, was pushing strongly to have his men deployed to Oman. Knowing that hostilities in Malaya could soon cease, he figured that it was imperative to prove his regiment's value in other theatres. At the same time he knew what he was asking of his soldiers. 'D' Squadron was currently operating close to the Thai/Malay border where they had been for six weeks or so. It would be a difficult move from steaming jungle to the fierce dry daytime heat, freezing nights and savagely steep mountains of Oman.

In an interview Deane Drummond said that it was the extreme change of climate that initially worried him the most. He had every confidence in his soldiers, but he still contacted John Woodhouse who assured that in his opinion the fitness and pride of the squadrons would win the day. Deane Drummond, aware that the SAS needed to demonstrate an ability to move quickly from one theatre to another and go straight into action, decided that the gamble was worthwhile.

When the order was given 'D' Squadron, by raft and forced marches, made it to Kuala Lumpur in forty-eight hours! By 18 November the squadron, re-trained and re-equipped, was on the ground in Oman. By anyone's standards that was a truly remarkable achievement!

Amazingly the move from the Far East to Oman was conducted in total secrecy so far as the general public was concerned and the brilliantly successful operation lasted just over three months. The effect of this was, in no small way, helpful to the efforts of Newell, Gillies and Woodhouse *et al* in the lobbying for the future of the SAS. It has been mooted that the Jebel Akhdar operation was the turning-point in rescuing the SAS from extinction, but it is eminently arguable that the real turning-point came a few years later.

*Chapter 16*

# The Red Beret

When Woodhouse reported for duty at Aldershot, the 3rd Parachute Regiment was under the command of Lieutenant Colonel Michael Forrester whose second-in-command was Major Roly Gibbs who would later rise in rank to field marshal and, along the way, become a good friend to the SAS. Woodhouse was disappointed when he arrived to find that there was no vacancy to command a company and temporarily he was given a thankless task. There was an ongoing experiment to find ways of speeding up deployment times and generally smoothing out the cumbersome process. Many hours were spent packing, unloading and repacking supermarket-type trolleys, flat-bed trolleys and even wheelbarrows with equipment and ammunition and manhandling them around the barracks. An ever more frustrated Woodhouse was in charge of the fiasco. This ill-fated experiment went on for about three months before being abandoned and, to his surprise and great pleasure, he was given command of 'B' Company with instructions to make ten parachute jumps with different types of weapon containers.

Though still not over-enamoured with the physical act of parachuting, Woodhouse did enjoy commanding the Paras. In his words: 'The men were full of zest needing an iron hand to control with the thinnest of velvet gloves.' He settled in well and enjoyed a good 'bedding-in' exercise in the form of a company drop into Bardufoss, North Norway.

In December 1959 Woodhouse was most surprised to learn that the SAS had requested that he return to the fold to take the job of second-in-command of 22 SAS Regiment, which had recently returned from Malaya via the superb successful operation on the Jebel Akhdar in Oman. They were currently based in Hanley Swan barracks near Malvern in Worcestershire. Woodhouse was in a quandary.

He knew that the SAS was not yet clear of the threat of disbandment. If he stayed with the Parachute Regiment there was a good chance that he would get command of a battalion within about three years. That was an attractive option. He knew that the SAS would never fight as a complete regiment on the ground under personal command of the CO, unlike a Parachute Regiment battalion that most certainly would, and that was a prospect that had great appeal: in action and leading from the front. The beloved Dorset Regiment was lost to him for ever more and he had begun to feel real affinity with 3rd Battalion.

On 8 November Peggy and he had been blessed with a son and heir, Michael, several weeks premature and it was probable that he would not be released from the Queen Alexandra Hospital in Aldershot until Christmas and here, with 3rd Para, he was close at hand in case of complications. After careful consideration and a long discussion with Peggy, he thanked Para HQ for being so even-handed in giving him the option of going or staying and told them that he would stay with 3 Para. The decision was gut-wrenching. Woodhouse had never lost his desire to try to influence the future of 22 SAS Regiment, but if he left the Parachute Regiment now there would probably never be a way back and the alternatives were hard to stomach.

The SAS mafia must have gone into immediate overdrive because that very night Woodhouse received a telephone call from Dare Newell. Newell, now in charge of what had become RHQ SAS, was still holding the vital SAS co-ordinating role in London and he earnestly pleaded with Woodhouse to reconsider his decision. He was the only SAS officer with the field experience to set about laying the foundations of an updated training schedule for 22 SAS Regiment. His leadership was of the finest order and he was very politically aware of the problems the regiment was to face in the near future. Although the successes in Malaya and Oman seemed to have given the SAS a breathing space, there was a long way to go before permanence would become even a possibility. In the meantime 22 SAS needed a second-in-command of the highest ability and reputation to support Lieutenant Colonel Dare Wilson who was totally new to Special Forces soldiering but was shortly to become the next CO. In a phrase that would stick, Newell told Woodhouse that he needed a 'Keystone for the SAS' as a strong negotiating-point in his lobbying in the War Office corridors of power. For whatever his proposals to the War Office might be, they would be reinforced by having the ability to call on a highly-experienced, current and well-respected officer serving in a senior capacity with the regiment: an officer who had, from the very beginnings, been instrumental in the regiment reaching the high level of efficiency that it enjoyed at the end of the Malayan campaign and throughout the short, sharp operation on the Jebel Akhdar.

Woodhouse did indeed change his mind and was very embarrassed to inform Para HQ of the fact. Roly Gibbs said that he was not in the least surprised and wished him luck. Woodhouse was not, however, to be released from 3 Para until the end of the year and in some ways that was a good thing. The current second-in-command of 22 SAS, Major Bob Walker Brown, was very highly regarded. He wrote to Woodhouse in October 1959 after the regiment had returned from a short exercise in BAOR. One worrying paragraph stated: 'I consider that apart from the high calibre of the men the Regiment is in bad order. There is so much flagrant ill-discipline and inefficiency, and bloody awful behaviour by officers that I was thoroughly ashamed of the Regiment in Germany.'

The highly-respected Bob Walker Brown DSO was an ex-Highland Light Infantry officer with a good war record with his own regiment and 2 SAS Regiment and he was not a man to pull punches, nor was he prone to exaggeration. Though Woodhouse was depressed by the tone of the letter, he also found himself getting quite excited! Here indeed there appeared to be a major challenge to his abilities. He thought that the crux of the problem was probably a lack of incentive for the soldiers; they had been on active service from the moment the regiment had been formed back in 1950. This was unique in the modern annals of military history. Nine years of continuous active service and there seemed to be no potential for further action on the horizon. The world seemed to be a fairly peaceful place, or at least peaceful as far as the possible deployment of British troops was concerned. At that time there was no operational role for the SAS in Europe. Many of the experienced soldiers would be thinking of their own careers. What would be their status if they were to be sent back to their parent units on the disbandment of the SAS? However, probably the major and immediate concern was the comment on '... bloody awful behaviour by officers....' If the officers were not up to scratch, what chance was there for the men? During his remaining few weeks with 3rd Para he exercised his mind with what his priorities would be in 22 SAS Regiment. The SAS had to have first-class officers, not only for the obvious reasons of short-term leadership of their troops but they would have to spread the word about the regiment after their three-year tour. Also, of course, was the fact that they represented the pool from which future squadron and regimental commanders would be drawn.

*Chapter 17*

# Back to the Beige Beret

He rejoined the regiment on 1 March 1959 and assumed the appointment of second-in-command to Lieutenant Colonel Tony Deane Drummond. He was immediately tasked to inspect each department of the regiment and prepare a comprehensive report for Lieutenant Colonel Dare Wilson, who would assume command on 16 April. His report was scathing: HQ Squadron was critically understaffed but the main cause of the huge administrative inefficiency was, in Woodhouse's opinion, the negligence of officers throughout the regiment combined with a total ignorance of administration. The Pay Office, Orderly Room and Catering Department escaped with scant criticism as they functioned reasonably well with their own specialists. In particular the Operations Centre was condemned. There was no full-time OC, a fluctuating staff with little interest in their ill-defined jobs and no intelligence collation; 22 SAS Regiment had no operational role for a war in Europe. The lack of time precluded a close inspection of the two sabre squadrons and the selection course that was based in Dering Lines, Brecon; only the administrative aspects of those three organizations were looked at. They were found to be wanting but not in a serious way. What weaknesses there were in those departments stemmed from inadequate QM support from HQ Squadron.

The Woodhouse report was approved by Dare Wilson. He was in total agreement that a successful regiment had to have a very efficient administrative base. This also would be one of Newell's debating points with the War Office: it had to be shown that, if necessary, 22 SAS Regiment could operate independently. At that point it was decided that wherever possible recruits to the regiment, after passing the selection course, would be awarded the SAS insignia but would not be considered fully trained until they had passed a jungle training course. There was little to be done in the immediate time frame as the regiment had been rehoused in a hutted camp in Hereford in April 1960.

The basic organization of the squadrons was confirmed in that each of the four troops would have a specialist skill: mountain, boat, free-fall parachuting and Land Rover. Each troop should have an officer and fifteen men in order to field four patrols. Within each patrol there would be a signaller, an explosives man, a medic and a linguist. In those early days, for obvious reasons the linguist tended to be a Malay speaker. SHQ would comprise the OC, SSM, SQMS, squadron clerk, a driver and a storeman. There were insufficient officers available to allow for a squadron second-in-command.

Wilson's immediate priorities were to properly man the HQ departments and get them working efficiently. The sabre squadrons could not possibly function effectively without proper HQ Squadron support. The key departments of QM, Medical Centre, Operations Centre and MT all required an OC and at least one SNCO in supervisory roles: some of those jobs were given to existing members of the regiment and others required 'outsiders' to be drafted in. To Woodhouse, as second-in-command, fell the task of devising training aims and organizing realistic exercises to meet the emerging NATO wartime roles. In his own words: 'I greatly enjoyed organizing training and I worked closely and harmoniously with the CO, Dare Wilson.'

As had now become the norm, Woodhouse's opinions and ideas were at the forefront of Dare Newell's efforts in the War Office; though Newell was fighting for an official establishment, essential to his machinations was the availability of the 'Keystone'. Apart from the constant need to get a positive statement about the future of the SAS, other requirements were being mooted. Woodhouse was aware that some of the experienced SAS soldiers who were leaving to rejoin their parent regiments were motivated by the need to earn more. In many cases, by picking up their shadow ranks their take-home pay would be noticeably better and they could plan a balanced career. Woodhouse suggested that two things would improve this situation: specialist pay for fully-qualified SAS members and the establishment of a permanent cadre. Both of those requests now formed a major part of Newell's lobbying. New SOPs were being produced with each troop assisting with ideas based on their specialist activities.

Officer training took on new proportions as Woodhouse concentrated on instilling pride and efficiency into them through exercises, study groups and personal example. To be fair to the officers in the administrative departments, they were not always supported well. Quartermasters need good RQMSs and SQMSs who could adapt quickly to peacetime accounting, which was much more rigorous than that used in Malaya! The same was true of the MT and Catering departments. Woodhouse did recognize that fact and took steps to resolve it. QM and MT were sent on the appropriate courses.

With Newell he had met the SAS founder, David Stirling, on a number of occasions and he was pleased to think that he had become instrumental in moves to restore the original SAS ethos to the regiment. Stirling in turn had developed a very high regard for Woodhouse and he lent his own input and vast range of senior political contacts to the efforts of the SAS lobby group.

The regiment was tasked by the War Office with organizing the first Army Combat Survival course which included a Joint Service Interrogation Unit (JSIU) commanded by Squadron Leader Parker. The brunt of the organizational work fell on the shoulders of Woodhouse and he welcomed it. This was another chance to learn more that could benefit the SAS. Later on a combat survival exercise became part of the selection course. This task coincided with the presence of the first two attached personnel from the US Army Special Forces: Captain Elliot 'Bud' Sydnor,[1] and Master Sergeant (MSG) Richard 'Dick' Meadows who was a survival expert and played a major role in planning and executing the course which was a marked success and became an SAS responsibility for some years.

After a year as second-in-command the time came for Woodhouse's annual report written by his CO:

---

1. Many years later I interviewed Bud Sydnor while researching *The Quiet Professional* and I asked him about his thoughts on joining 22 SAS. He replied that though the soldiers were very fit and well-disciplined they were, after all, just first-rate jungle soldiers. I was obliged to inform him that although 'Jebel Akhdar' translated as 'Green Mountain', it was not carpeted by a rain forest!

Major Woodhouse has had an eventful year in which training has been carried out in many countries and much of the planning and staff work has fallen on his shoulders.... In all his work he has proved a most loyal, enthusiastic and hardworking officer.... His experience in the SAS is now very extensive and covers many theatres. As a newcomer to the SAS I have found his experience, judgement and support invaluable.... Few officers I have known command such respect and affection with all ranks and I can think of no one more suitable to command a regular SAS Regiment.... His drive, determination and administrative ability .... make him exceptionally well qualified for command.

Behind the scenes, and initially without the knowledge of Woodhouse himself, his supporters were hard at work. Newell had approached General George Lea (Woodhouse's one-time CO in Malaya who had once talked him out of leaving the army) to explore the chances of him being given a Grade 2 staff appointment. This would normally only be open to an officer who had passed the Staff College course. Without having held such an appointment it would be unlikely that Woodhouse would achieve promotion and this did not suit the longer-term plans of the SAS supporters. Lea was indeed in a position to make such an appointment and agreed enthusiastically that it was the right thing to do, but it would mean that Woodhouse would have to cut short his tour as second-in-command of 22 SAS Regiment! Newell made the proposal to Woodhouse and urged him to accept it; he had, after all, as second-in-command, already made a very significant contribution to the long-term future of 22 SAS. Woodhouse accepted the validity of Newell's advice, but he still had feelings of guilt as he secured the support of his CO and agreed to be posted to Aden as GSO2 of the six-battalion force that comprised the Aden Protectorate Levies (APL). That the decision was not taken lightly shows in this letter to Dare Wilson:

My dear Colonel,

I have considered the question of my change over to a Grade II staff appointment and asked my father for advice in addition. I enclose his letter.

I have come to the conclusion that I could accept, but only if I know in advance that you would get a Second in Command who would, in every way, be entirely acceptable and satisfactory to you and the Regiment. This is not just a matter of loyalty, I would be really unhappy to leave and find it impossible to do so if I thought that this problem of replacement would not be met to everyone's complete satisfaction.

I would prefer, if possible, to complete my tour here and then get a Grade II staff appointment if I am not selected for command. Failing this I would like action to be considered as proposed in the above paragraph.

If it is not possible to find, at very short notice, a suitable replacement for me, I should be very happy for this whole matter to be quietly dropped, in which case no one will be any the wiser and I shall never feel in the slightest degree disappointment at the future course of events, whatever they may be.

I should like to add that I am most appreciative both of the confidence you and Brigadier Lea have shown in me, and of your attitude to the proposal.

This is not an easy Regiment to get into but it is even harder to leave it than to join it! If I go, and if I never get back, I shall certainly regret having gone as it will be with very mixed feelings that I await the outcome of this matter.

Please excuse me writing but I find it easier to set out my reasons on paper and we can discuss them afterwards.

Yours ever, John

The matter was resolved to the satisfaction of both Wilson and Woodhouse. Shortly before the move to Aden, Woodhouse was on exercise in Denmark when he was delighted to hear that Peggy had given birth to their second son, William John, on 2 May 1961.

*Chapter 18*

# Staff Duties

The APL was an Arab force with mainly British officers at the HQ and British COs of the battalions which were under the overall command of Brigadier Derek Wormald, who was not best pleased to have an unqualified officer to fill the GSO2 vacancy.

In 1961 Aden was held as a colony and staging post for troops bound for the Far East. At that time there was only sporadic violence in the country between rival tribal groups which was easily contained by the Levies. Once a week Woodhouse attended a conference chaired by the provincial governor of the West Aden Protectorate, Sir Kennedy Trevaskis (some years later his son, Jeremy, would join 22 SAS Regiment), with Wormald, the chief of police and district officers; occasionally there may be a senior officer of the RAF present. Quite often the RAF would be tasked to bomb the forts of rebel tribes after first warning them to evacuate the villages. This was not a 'Hearts and Minds' operation; it was very much 'Carrot and Stick' in that gifts of rifles would be made to co-operative tribes.

Woodhouse's duties were to act as the senior staff officer of the APL, organize training and the moves of battalions and act as the personal representative of the brigadier. He did not find Wormald easy to work with, nor did Wormald initially have much confidence in Woodhouse! However, the relationship did gradually improve, as comments from his annual report show:

> As an unqualified officer for a staff appointment he has had some difficulty in coping with his present job, particularly as the military and political situation is unusual... he has done quite well and is improving as a staff officer... he abounds with energy and bounces into my office in an almost frightening manner... he is most conscientious and uses his initiative to good effect... he is a capable organiser and ensures that his instructions are carried out

thoroughly... he mixes well with those with whom he comes in contact, and is well suited to joint staff work.

There was no recommendation, however, for a GSO1 staff job.

In November he managed to arrange for Peggy and their two boys to fly out and join him in his air-conditioned house near Khormaksar. However, they were only able to stay for five months as William became seriously ill and on 30 April he had to be flown back to go to Great Ormond Street Hospital in London. William's illness remained undiagnosed, but in late May he made a sudden and unexplained recovery.

In November 1961 the APL was renamed the Federal Regular Army, but the role remained the same as battalions were deployed as necessary in shows of force which, at that time, were sufficient to keep the peace. In December Brigadier James Lunt took command. Woodhouse, who considered Lunt a far more able commander than Wormald, got on very well with him. It seems to be the way of things that the paths of SAS warriors constantly cross. In mid-1962 Captain Peter de la Billière was seconded as GSO3 (Int) FRA. He was well-known to Woodhouse from his days as a competent troop commander in Malaya, and Woodhouse, who also liked and respected de la Billière, was able to help him settle into life in Aden. Unknown to either of them at that time was how their paths were to intertwine in the years to come. By that time his next appointment – that of CO 22 SAS Regiment in December 1962 – had been confirmed. The annual report written by Lunt was excellent:

He is a man of strong character who shows to best advantage when things are difficult. During the past four months he has had to endure more than his share of domestic problems but he has never allowed this to affect his work or determination to give of his best. I greatly admire him for the way he has managed to keep his private worries apart from his public duties. He is an officer of great loyalty, complete personal integrity and is absolutely reliable.... Neither by temperament nor by training is he a staff officer.... His characteristics clearly mark him out for command and yet he has managed to overcome his lack of staff training by the application of hard work and common sense... I am confident that he will make a competent GSO1 on the completion of his period in command and I would gladly accept him in that capacity.

The 'domestic problems' mentioned referred to William's illness.

Woodhouse was given a few days' leave in May which allowed him and Peggy to visit William in hospital, after which they went to stay with his father at Melcombe. At that time his mother was visiting her brother, John Fairlie, in South Africa. Woodhouse moved back to Aden to prepare for his handover, but sadly on 9 June 1962 his father died and he returned to attend the funeral. His feet had hardly touched the ground again in Aden when he was told that his command of 22 SAS Regiment had been brought forward to 1 July. On the flight back he reflected on his time in the Middle East. He had not particularly enjoyed his year as a GSO2 staff officer; however, he had learned not only staff duties but a great deal about the military and political situation in the Aden Protectorate. Little did he know at that time how useful that knowledge was to be in both the Middle and Far East theatres in the not-too-distant future.

On 27 June, James Lunt wrote a personal letter to John Woodhouse:

My Dear John,

I cannot let you leave Aden without writing to thank you for all your loyal support and cheerful companionship during the past seven months. I was very overwhelmed when I first arrived in Aden, partly I suppose because being a Brigadier is a more complicated business than being a Lieutenant Colonel! And partly because Brigadier Wormald seemed to have everything at his fingertips – particularly his eye for country which has never been my strong point! I felt that I would never make up the ground.

My morale and self-confidence owed a great deal to your calm and steadfast support and I am most grateful to you for it.

Although delighted for you that command has come earlier I shall miss you a great deal. You know that you can always call on me for help or advice at any time – should you ever need it – and – I hope you will continue to carve out for yourself the career in the army which your character and talents abundantly justify.

Our love to Peggy and the children, and many thanks for everything.

Yours ever, James

# Chapter 19

# The 'Keystone' is in Place

Lieutenant Colonel John Woodhouse took command of 22 SAS Regiment from Lieutenant Colonel Dare Wilson on 1 July 1962. In his own words:

I found it to be in good order. I had only been away for one year but much had improved in that short time. Dare had got a total grip on the administration and that aspect of regimental life was running very smoothly. All the specialist troops were now well equipped to meet their roles and in particular some sporting members of the Free Fall Troop, mainly due to Dare's personal interest in parachuting and a few dedicated addicts, were performing successfully on a national scale.

After many detailed discussions with Dare Wilson (now a total believer in the SAS and in close contact with his namesake, Dare Newell) we found that we had one imminent concern which was to dominate my thinking for a while. Fourteen years after its formation 22 SAS had some very experienced WOs, SNCOs and Troopers who actually represented the workaday engine room of the Regiment. They were faced with the fact that the officers taking command of their troops were very, very inexperienced. I made one immediate decision. After an officer passed selection he would face another three months of probation.

Woodhouse made some basic plans to improve the status and efficiency of the officers and he designed a number of tactical exercises to be carried out under his personal scrutiny. On his instructions new officers were briefed that they would be subordinate to their troop sergeants for the first few weeks of their command. SNCOs were also brought into discussions and given advice on how to treat their new officers, nurture and encourage them. Some found this hard. He did not have a great deal of time initially to spend on those matters as, within what seemed like only a few days, he was instructed to take half of his regiment to the USA for Exercise 'Eagle's Nest' which would consist of three months of exercises and cross-training with the US Special Forces Group based in Fort Bragg, North Carolina. Since 1960 the SAS and the US Special Forces had been taking part in an exchange programme whereby an officer and an SNCO from each unit would spend a year with their counterparts. The first Americans to have a tour with the SAS were Captain Elliot 'Bud' Sydnor and MSG Richard 'Dick' Meadows. Those two stalwarts had already impressed the members of 22 SAS with their wide-ranging expertise. In particular Meadows, with his knowledge of survival skills, had been especially helpful in designing the first Army Combat Survival course which Woodhouse had overseen as second-in-command to the regiment. Both Sydnor and Meadows were later to achieve fame for their exploits in Vietnam and particularly for their courage and leadership during the attempted rescue of PoWs from Son Tay.[1]

The role of the US Special Forces was quite different from that of the SAS. While the latter took part in either reconnaissance or direct strike action, the former worked on the business of training indigenous guerrillas to do the fighting. They were expert in that role and Dare Wilson, John Woodhouse and Dare Newell had lobbied the War Office for the chance to study the USSF role at close hand. They were quite certain that this could well become a requirement for the SAS in years to come. Already they had read good reports from the two SAS men currently carrying out the exchange at Fort Bragg; both Captain Roger Woodiwiss and Sergeant 'Mo' Copeman were enthusiastic about the USSF role and the high level of individual skills held by the American soldiers. Their exchange had started during the tenure of Lieutenant Colonel Deane Drummond as CO of 22 SAS Regiment. Intelligence, Psyops, explosives, medical, heavy and light weapons and communications skills were taught by soldiers who were well-practised in instructional techniques. Each

---

1. The raid to rescue American PoWs from the Son Tay prison close to the Vietnamese capital city, Hanoi, is a classic in the annals of USSF history. Both Sydnor and Meadows played vital roles and were awarded the DSC for their courage and leadership.

operational team would also include men who spoke the language of the guerrillas they may eventually be called upon to train. Now the chance had come to examine their training methods and Woodhouse looked forward to it immensely.

In early August 1962 the SAS contingent departed the UK via RAF Lyneham on a journey that has passed into SAS history. It became known as 'Five Breakfasts to Bragg'. The unit was driven to RAF Lyneham after breakfast in Bradbury Lines; the RAF provided a further breakfast; on board the waiting Comet aircraft they were given a packed breakfast; on arrival at Gander airport in Newfoundland they were given another breakfast; and this was followed by a packed meal to be consumed as they flew down the Eastern Seaboard of the USA to the Seymour Air Force Base in North Carolina.

The British soldiers were dressed in khaki drill: cotton uniforms that were issued for wear in the Middle East. It was not a uniform designed to win any sartorial awards. After twenty hours of cramped travelling, the once nicely-starched clothing was sweat-stained, odorous and wrinkled. On getting off the buses that had transported them from Seymour AFB to Fort Bragg, the men were looking forward to a shower and clean-up before meeting their American hosts. Not so! The road to their accommodation was lined on each side by Special Forces soldiers dressed in their best Class A uniforms and standing at attention! The commanding general was preparing to take the salute. The RSM, Ken Phillipson, quickly formed the SAS contingent into three ranks and they managed to make a reasonable job of marching along between the ranks of their impeccably-dressed hosts. Somehow Lieutenant Colonel John Woodhouse (not known as a snappy dresser) managed to look quite military as he marched up to return the salute. Eventually the band stopped playing and General Yarborough, no doubt recognizing the discomfort of his guests, made a very short welcoming speech. The men were then informed that tea was available. The Americans got their first taste of soldiers' English when the British squaddies found that it was actually iced tea and not the hot brew to which they were so looking forward. As a consolation prize they discovered what became known as the 'tin tits': these were huge containers fitted with taps that were full of cold fresh milk; they were drained far quicker than the iced tea urns.

The American training facilities were far and away better than those available to the SAS in the UK. The demolitions training went well beyond the creation of LZs and laying small defensive booby-traps in the jungle. Formulae for calculating accurate explosive quantities and placement for sophisticated sabotage were taught and practised. For the USSF, language training was carried out in well-equipped laboratories and classrooms in Monterey. Medical training included actual surgery on anaesthetized dogs in preparation for the need to treat battle wounds. That and the high level of diagnostic teaching were far in excess of the SAS medics who, with a few exceptions, at that time were not much more than good first-aiders. Those being trained as weapons instructors had access to an amazing range of 'foreign' firearms. Only in the field of communications was the SAS ahead of the Americans; their hosts had nothing that could match the performance of the British lightweight (11lb including battery) RS128 with a range in excess of 250 miles. Also the British lightweight dehydrated ration packs were of special interest. In training for their wartime role the USSF had access to Logistics Corps personnel to act as their guerrillas; this had an incidental advantage as those loan soldiers actually benefited greatly from the training.

The US Army Special Forces had two Psychological Warfare Battalions well-equipped to produce leaflets and broadcasts, show films, and monitor and twist enemy broadcasts for use against him. The staff of those battalions were keen to talk to the British troops who had the 'Hearts and Minds' experience of Malaya behind them.

A series of well-organized exercises involving US Airborne troops with good helicopter support took place. In this aspect the SAS fieldcraft was far superior to that of the Americans. On one occasion an exercise was held in the Everglades swamps and the American troops acting as the enemy who had laid ambushes on all the tracks likely to be used could not understand why they failed. When they were told that the British soldiers had not used any tracks they shook their heads in disbelief!

Woodhouse had done some hard thinking as to how his regiment could benefit in the longer term from this US/UK liaison and he had been in constant contact with Dare Newell and Hugh Gillies at SAS HQ in London. He wanted to pass on his thoughts to give them as much ammunition as possible in their dealings with the War Office. At that point 22 SAS Regiment was still not written into the British Army of the Rhine War Plans and that was essential to long-term development. Exercises in Norway, Denmark and Germany were at the planning stages.

Though Woodhouse was impressed by the USSF, he seriously thought that they should extend their role from just instructing guerrillas to carrying out offensive action themselves. It is highly probable that this statement made to General Yarborough actually sowed the seeds that would result in the US Delta Force. Certainly when the founder of Delta, Colonel 'Charging' Charlie Beckwith, made his pitch to the Pentagon he found that a degree of basic study had already been made some years earlier into the possibility of raising an SAS equivalent. Certainly during the Vietnam War, Special Forces soldiers on many occasions were on the front line and often well over it. It was not widely known outside the US Special Forces that teams had already been using free-fall as a method of entry behind enemy lines.

In the meantime he thought that the SAS should immediately begin to look at:

1. Improvements to the standard of medical training
2. Increasing the linguistic ability
3. Begin to study both guerrilla and insurgency trends on an international basis
4. Prepare to be committed to guerrilla training operations
5. Begin to collect as many foreign weapons as possible
6. Get as much training time with helicopters as possible
7. Follow up on the requests for specialist pay
8. Continue to lobby for a permanent cadre

These preparatory notes were well timed as in September that year Exercise 'Eagle's Nest' had an important visitor, General Sir Charles Richardson, the Director of Military Training at the War Office. Yarborough and Woodhouse made sure that Richardson saw every aspect of the work that had gone on. The general was impressed and said that Woodhouse should make sure that he got a personal copy of the after-exercise report that he would be writing as soon as possible.

There was little doubt that the SAS and Woodhouse in particular had made yet another powerful friend in Whitehall. Richardson's report, written shortly after his return to the UK, showed his interest in the future of the SAS. In his final paragraph he wrote:

22.FOLLOW UP
I will be following up these points on my return from Pakistan in mid-October:

(a) Doctrine on the scale and use of helicopters for anti-guerrilla operations.
(b) Helicopter communications.
(c) More joint training with US Forces.
(d) SAS training.
(e) Language training, particularly for SAS.
(f) Film and tape playlets for leadership training.
(g) The UK system of control of unit and formation exercises and scheduling of aircraft for exercises.
(h) Training in civic action.
(i) Reserve training.

Hence the value of Richardson's support becomes obvious as the SAS above all other units was to benefit the most from his evaluation and follow-up intentions. On the return of the regiment to the UK, all of Woodhouse's requests for further special training were granted. An increase to the training budget was secured and very quickly Mountain Troop soldiers were attached to the German Army Mountain Division in Bavaria; vacancies were found on Arabic courses at the Army School of Languages at Beaconsfield; private Thai language courses were organized in London (with follow-up visits to Thailand); some medics were sent back to Fort Bragg to be trained alongside the USSF medics; and attachments to A&E departments at NHS hospitals in the UK were initiated. The exchanges of officers and SNCOs was planned to continue, though this quickly dwindled to SNCO exchanges only as it was not always feasible to lose an officer for a whole year of his three-year tour with the regiment. The argument for making jungle training a part of final selection was also won. For cost reasons the jungle training would be part of the selection course proper, but it would take place annually with the successful members of two selection courses making up the students. To fail the jungle training was to fail selection. The RSM of 22 SAS would be in charge and during John Woodhouse's tour of command this training took place in Malaya. The basis for the inclusion of this was that the jungle, as a particularly demanding venue, posed more challenging individual tests to the soldiers than any other theatre of operations: it improved the standard of navigation; it produced a need for excellent fieldcraft, self-reliance and self-imposed battle discipline. Also it was a fact that the pleas for specialist pay and the establishment of a permanent cadre, though still being met with some resistance, were no longer falling on totally deaf ears and the inclusion of yet another 'special' aspect to SAS training was all grist to the mill.

Soon after the return to the UK in October 1962 the regiment, now together again, moved into a period of hard training concentrating on their troop specialist skills. During this the question of a memorial clock tower was raised again. It had initially been the idea of Dare Wilson and it was proposed that it should be a memorial to Corporal Keith Norry who had died in a free-fall accident in January 1962. The Wilson suggestion further proposed that the funding should be raised locally and should include a voluntary levy of one day's pay from all ranks. Woodhouse disputed this. Though he was agreed that an internal memorial would be a good idea, he did not think that it should be dedicated to one man. Twenty-two SAS men had been killed in action in recent years and a memorial should reflect that and also cater for deaths yet to come. That idea gelled with the regiment and funding (which did include donations from local Hereford businesses and individual soldiers) was eventually completed. SAS humour is dry and it can be a little wicked. At the time of the clock project there was a family TV show called *Sunday Night at the London Palladium* hosted by Bruce Forsyth and featuring the 'Beat the Clock' game imported from America and it was Corporal 'Spud' Murphy of the Signals Troop who applied the phrase to SAS soldiering: to survive the rigours of regimental life one had to 'Beat the Clock'. Sadly Spud did not 'Beat the Clock': along with two other key members of the regiment he died in a helicopter crash in Borneo. The Clock Tower at the regimental base now bears more than 100 names.

Now well into troop specialist and individual skills training, the soldiers of 22 SAS Regiment were in general ignorance of significant developments in the Far East where the misguided egoist, Soekarno, President of Indonesia, had a grand plan to unite Indonesia, Borneo, Malaya and the Philippines into an Asian powerhouse. Already this had led to a rebellion in Brunei followed by Indonesian army incursions into Sarawak leading to the deployment of British troops, initially from Malaya. The Brunei rebellion was quickly quelled by the Royal Marines but the threat to Borneo remained. The British force was ordered to remain in situ and Major General Walter Walker was appointed as Director of Borneo Operations (DOBOPS).

# Chapter 20

# The Far East Beckons Again

In Hereford John Woodhouse impatiently awaited the call to deploy the SAS to Borneo, a call that never came. With the help of Dare Newell and Hugh Gillies he managed to get a meeting with the Director of Military Operations at the War Office. General Sir Charles Richardson, mentioned earlier, was of paramount assistance in arranging the meeting. It came as no surprise to Woodhouse to learn that the SAS was not even included on the list of troops available that had been sent to Walker. His forceful arguments that centred on the deep jungle experience of 22 SAS Regiment were rewarded by having one squadron added to the list of available reinforcements. Yet what did Walker know about the SAS? That situation had to be remedied.

In early January 1963 Woodhouse left the snow and ice of one of the UK's harshest winters and headed off to the Far East and a meeting with Walker in Brunei; he was determined that the SAS should be committed as soon as possible. Though Walker and Woodhouse hit it off immediately as 'fighting' soldiers, the meeting was not an easy one and it took time to convince Walker that he could benefit from an SAS deployment. It was the argument that 'A' Squadron had the ability to operate in deep jungle in four-man patrols each with a radio and Malay speaker. Furthermore they could sustain such operations for at least four months at a time. They could act, together with the native tribes of the interior (as they had done in Malaya), as the eyes and ears of Walker's forces to give early warning of Indonesian incursions; their communications equipment was excellent. Once Walker was convinced, his support for the SAS was constant and forceful.

Prior to 'A' Squadron's deployment, Woodhouse made an important decision regarding security. During his tenure as CO his wife, Peggy, further showed her mettle by her involvement with the Regimental Wives' Club. Though this role was not in any way official, it was generally expected that the CO's wife would take an active part in regimental welfare. Peggy's charm, warmth and wit as well as her experience in the nursing profession made her an extremely well-liked and respected patron. She was remarkably easy to talk to and those ladies with problems could be sure of not only a sympathetic ear but sound advice. This was an extremely important factor in a regiment where separation was so frequent and most of the wives did not know why or where their husbands had gone and why they could not receive letters from their spouses. Constant separation with no information on which to base loyal support could lead to bitterness and increasingly difficult relationships and the majority of wives were as difficult as their husbands when it came to admitting to having concerns. Peggy had an instinct for spotting potential problems and helping to head them off. Her informal task was made much easier when, on 9 January 1963, John Woodhouse made a decision (helped no doubt by Peggy's concerns) and wrote a letter to be read by all the wives:

> I am writing this note personally so that it can be passed on to you explaining insofar as I can what is going on.
>
> 22 SAS Regiment, as I am sure you know, is trained for special operations and is always at short notice to move anywhere in the world to uphold British national interests and those of our Allies.
>
> It can help us in our task to arrive unknown to our enemies, and for this reason sometimes we may have to move without the publicity that is usually given to troop movements. Moves in secret can only be carried out in peacetime by two methods. The first is to pretend to you that we are going on an exercise, the second is to tell you the truth relying on you to tell no–one else. I have chosen to trust you with the truth believing that you will tell no–one else.
>
> In the next two days a considerable part of the Regiment will fly overseas to carry out an operation. I have not told the men of the Regiment where this will be yet. I know you may feel some concern, as indeed my wife will, about our safety. I can assure you that this operation is certainly no more dangerous, in my opinion, than the operations we carried out in Malaya.

Our address will be:

Number Rank Name

Force 45,

BRITISH FORCES POST OFFICE 608

<u>On no account write 22 SAS or the Squadron on the envelope.</u>

Do NOT post letters before Saturday, 12th January as no facilities to receive them will be ready until then.

Men can write home through the Field Post Office on arrival. Cards will be sent fortnightly to next of kin for those on operations who are unable to write letters themselves as was done in Malaya in 1951–1959.

You will wish to know when the news of this SAS operation will be made public. I do not know exactly when that will be but I think it will be this month. In any case I promise that you will be informed before long.

> Yours sincerely, John Woodhouse Lt. Col.

The result of the meeting with General Walker was that 'A' Squadron was on the ground in Borneo in mid-January and fielding twenty-one four-man patrols scattered within the border kampongs (villages). The squadron was under the command of Major Peter de la Billière (a troop commander in Malaya and Oman). Enormous amounts of information about the various tribes, their loyalties and customs were gained from Tom Harrisson, the Protector of the Tribes. He had known them from the time of the Japanese occupation of 1942–45, during which period he had lived with them in their remote longhouses. As the threat from Indonesia increased, the SAS patrols moved out of the villages into deep jungle while still maintaining contact with the natives. The squadron quickly gained the confidence of the indigenous tribes who were predominately Land Dyaks (Bidayuh) or Sea Dyaks (Iban), though smaller tribes like the nomadic Punan, Murut and Kelabit also roamed the jungle. The good relationship that quickly developed with the indigenous tribes was helped in no small way by the SAS patrols making basic medical aid available and having the ability and willingness to sit and chat with them. Some of the dealings with the Dyaks required a different form of stamina from the

SAS. In the longhouses of the villages there were regular *jogits* or parties to celebrate anything from a death, a birth, a wedding, the sighting of a rare bird or animal or anything that took the *pengulu's* (headman's) fancy. At such celebrations one of the local alcoholic home brews called *tapai* or *tuak* would be brought out. *Tapai* was a crude concoction made from roots and it would probably equate to a rough 'scrumpy', while *tuak* was a more palatable brew of rice wine. Sadly it was the 'scrumpy' that was usually offered. The brew was contained in large, free-standing, narrow-topped earthenware urns of considerable capacity and it was drunk by sipping through slender hollow bamboo tubes. Down the centre of the pot was a bamboo stick with notches carved along its length. If the headman started the drinking, the next person to partake had to lower the level of the liquid to below the notch of his predecessor. It was a powerful brew and with the urn initially getting wider as the level of the liquid subsided, successive drinkers were required to imbibe larger quantities! Often accompanying this brew would be bamboo platters of foul-smelling rotten meat known as *jarat* (often monkey or tree rat, a delicacy to the natives). The meat would be stuffed into sections of bamboo and then buried to speed up the decomposition. This was viewed as a special gift to be offered to visitors. The SAS trick was to take a minimal mouthful of the stinking mess and get to the *tapai* as quickly as possible to cleanse the palate and hope that stomachs and bowels would remain under control at least until they left the longhouse. A somewhat macabre reminder of days gone by was that a number of the longhouses still quite proudly displayed shrunken yellow heads as mementoes of the unwanted Japanese occupation.

Assistance to the natives was not confined to giving medical aid. Some of the SAS soldiers mastered the local dialects and also it was possible to get by with Malay as the *lingua franca* (common language). 'Gypsy' Smith, a sergeant and veteran of Malaya, was a good craftsman and he puzzled the quartermaster in the RHQ with requests for bicycle dynamos, bulbs, bulb-holders, belts and a variety of tools. With these items Gypsy was able to construct 'paddle wheels' that were powered by water piped from the rivers; in turn a belt linking the hub of the wheel to the dynamo rotated it, thus giving life to the small bulbs sited in the headman's part of the longhouse. A weak light, but a 'magical' light to the natives.

(After Gypsy retired he went into 'hermit mode'. That was not because he wished to be alone but in order to avoid the close scrutiny of the Inland Revenue officers. In a very well-equipped workshop, which from the outside looked like a dilapidated garden shed, he began to develop his talents by producing 'antiques'. His speciality was the construction of very ornate carriage lamps from old tin cans. It has been said that the Duke of Edinburgh, a great carriage-driving enthusiast, on admiring an apparently very old pair of lamps on a carriage at a show, enquired of the owner where he had bought them. This supposedly resulted in a set of Gypsy's lamps being affixed to the duke's competition carriage. It is not known whether Gypsy applied for 'By Royal Appointment' status.)

During that first three-and-a-half-month tour 'A' Squadron had a quiet time but they became armed with so much knowledge that the handover to 'D' Squadron went very smoothly. At this point Woodhouse made a proposal to the Director of Borneo Operations that the SAS should take on the task of forming the Border Scouts, a force to be raised from the loyal tribes. He envisaged the Gurkhas doing the majority of the training under the supervision and administrative support of the SAS. Their main purpose would be to report on Indonesian incursions to the nearest SAS patrol. By 1964 more than 1,000 Border Scouts were trained. The regiment had also become more involved in training special squads of Border Scouts to operate independently on both sides of the border.

Woodhouse, now back in the UK, was facing serious problems. As things stood, 'A' Squadron would have to take over from 'D' in a few months' time and with other commitments there would simply not be enough manpower. Recruitment had to be given a major boost somehow. With the help of Dare Newell and a slowly growing number of allies in the War Office, Woodhouse managed to get a meeting with both the Director of Military Operations and the Vice Chief of General Staff; quite a coup for a mere commanding officer! General Walker's very favourable reports on 'A' Squadron's activities in Borneo served to ensure that Woodhouse got powerful backing for most of what he wanted in terms of recruitment to and the growth of the SAS. During the period from early 1960 the volunteering age for the SAS had been reduced first from 22 to 20 and then down to 18. During the same period direct enlistment into 22 SAS became a reality for members of 21 and 23 SAS regiments. This was a great success. Of the first recruits, two of them were eventually commissioned and one made a major contribution into regimental efforts at psychological warfare in Oman.

Woodhouse was now very stretched. The regiment suffered a major blow in May 1963 when a Belvedere helicopter crashed in Borneo, killing all hands including the SAS second-in-command Major Ron Norman, a squadron commander, Major Harry Thompson, and Corporal Philip 'Spud' Murphy, an experienced signaller. This increased the personal pressure on him as the next second-in-command who was to be Major Mike Wingate Gray,[1] who had no prior service with the SAS, would not be free to take up the post for another seven months!

Compounding the stress on Woodhouse was an added plea from David Stirling to 'borrow' some soldiers from 22 SAS to assist in assessing the situation in the kingdom of Yemen. In late 1962 a *coup d'état* took place and the ruling imam was driven out of the capital Sana'a into the high mountains. Behind the revolution was Gamal Abdel Nasser, President of Egypt, who was being strongly supported by the Soviet Union. Nasser's aim was complete control of the Arabian Peninsula. He was cocking a snook at British Imperialism: control of Yemen would include the port of Aden which had been a British colony since the mid-nineteenth century. Royalist resistance to the Egyptian army was spirited but fragmented. They were outgunned by the Egyptian artillery and air force but so far they had kept the enemy confined to the plain that surrounded the capital Sana'a. Woodhouse was swayed by Stirling's earnest entreaties and agreed, knowing full well that if it became known he would, without doubt, face a court martial. One of the soldiers, Sergeant 'Geordie' Doran, an SAS veteran and an expert mortar man, later said:

In May 1963, I was in my bunk in the Sergeants' Mess. My Squadron, 'A', was on leave after the first Borneo operation. I had a call from the CO to report to his office as soon as possible. I was a bit bewildered but I hurried over the square to Regimental HQ. Also waiting outside

---

1. Brigadier Mike Wingate Gray OBE MC*, ex-Black Watch, had a brilliant mind and was to become a great asset to 22 SAS Regiment. With John Woodhouse and Dare Newell, he complemented an already impressive team. He was a most excellent successor to Woodhouse and continued to build on the foundations of the regiment.

the CO's office were Corporals Taff Chidgey and Jimmy Catterall. I knocked on the door and the CO called us inside. John Woodhouse was sitting at his desk and we saluted and waited to know what he was about. He was cool, calm and collected and definitely in charge. In my opinion he was a good officer and a gentleman.

And I was keen to know what he wanted us for. He looked at us one at a time and then, in a calm voice, said, 'I've called you three here to ask you if you would be willing to go on a secret mission. It could be very dangerous and your chances of survival are just 50:50. It will, though, be for the good of our country.' All three of us just stared back at him for a few seconds. I looked at John and knew he was giving it to us straight. I looked at Taff and Jimmy, then turned to the CO and told him that I'd go. The other two immediately agreed with me.

'Good,' said the CO. 'This afternoon, Johnny Cooper, who is also involved, will meet you outside camp and give you the gen.' There followed a secret, unofficial operation in the Yemen which is told in detail in a book by Johnny Cooper entitled *One of the Originals*. We three, Taff, Jimmy and I, did not hesitate to volunteer when asked by John Woodhouse. We liked, respected and trusted him. We (and he) kept the secret for many years.[2]

It is not difficult to imagine the potential wrath of the War Office and Parliament if it became known that the CO of 22 SAS had released three[3] serving soldiers 'on leave' to take a very active part in an undeclared war against the Egyptian forces that were invading Yemen. There would have been particular disapproval as the SAS was already committed to operations and seeking an increase in manpower. Woodhouse would

---

2. Woodhouse was to become further involved in the Yemen enterprise after he left the army. The full story is told in the books *The War That Never Was* by Duff Hart-Davis, *Britain and the Yemen Civil War, 1962–1965* by Clive Jones, and *Looking for Trouble*, the autobiography of General Sir Peter de la Billière.
3. There was in fact a fourth regular soldier involved in the enterprise, the then Corporal Bill Condie, one of the best Arabic speakers in the regiment, who was working closely with the imam. He rose to the rank of major and was awarded the DCM for his actions during the Dhofar War.

have been thrown to the wolves and the reputation of the regiment would probably have suffered, but the power of persuasion wielded by David Stirling was reinforced by Woodhouse's own distaste of Nasser's actions. The incident also demonstrated that the SAS could keep secrets when they had to but, of course, there was no way that this fact could be broadcast to the wider military world. In this respect a constant worry to Woodhouse during the absence of the three soldiers was the well-known unreliability of David Stirling in keeping secrets! The soldiers returned some three or four weeks later, having confirmed that the Egyptian army was using poison gas. They had also assisted the Royalist forces in inflicting many casualties on the Egyptians. Through Stirling they conveyed the information that the Egyptians were certainly not in control and that an effective resistance to them by the Royalists could be cost-efficient and easily organized. Stirling had a meeting with Sir Alec Douglas-Home (then Secretary of State for Foreign Affairs), Julian Amery (then Minister of Aviation) and Lieutenant Colonel Neil 'Billy' McLean (then Member of Parliament for Inverness) and others, as a result of which the UK refused to recognize the Yemeni Arab Republican government backed by the Egyptians. The very few men who knew about the 'loan' soldiers were extremely influential and their trust in the SAS was to be critical in later dealings with the Yemeni Royalists. Under the initial control of an ex-CO of 21 SAS Regiment, Lieutenant Colonel Jim Johnson, an operation got under way to support the Royalist cause. Stirling's involvement is covered in the book *David Stirling: Creator of the SAS*, also by this author.

The years 1963 and 1964 must have been among the busiest and most stressful ones of John Woodhouse's military life. He had no second-in-command and officers were in short supply. One of the two sabre squadrons was in Borneo for the whole of the year; 'A' Squadron trained the Land Rover Troop in desert driving and astral navigation in Libya in October and July; a target of 50 per cent of all soldiers became able to operate radios using the Morse code; and language training achieved twenty in Malay, four in Arabic, two in Thai and four in German. By November 1963, Woodhouse's training schedule for new officers was reduced to one forty-eight-hour map exercise. The long periods of separation were taking their toll on the rank and file. Nine soldiers purchased their

discharge compared to none in the previous year and a half. The strength
of the regiment on 1 January 1964 was 21 officers and 280 soldiers; 7
officers and 32 soldiers under strength. Woodhouse's recent service with
the Parachute Regiment became a great help in winning that regiment's
backing to encourage soldiers to volunteer for the SAS. Recruiting teams
were authorized to visit units in the UK and BAOR; not popular with
commanding officers, these visits were not particularly successful. Out of
225 volunteers in 1964, 52 passed the initial selection and 4 of those fell
by the wayside during continuation training.

Woodhouse had been trying another tack by advocating that both
the Australian and New Zealand SAS regiments should be deployed to
Borneo and in July 1963 he had made a visit to Perth to brief the Australian
SAS on the activities of 22 SAS. He discussed the 'Hearts and Minds'
campaign along with the border surveillance patrols and the raising of
the indigenous Border Scouts. His overtures to both General Walker
and visiting British government ministers included the desirability of
obtaining help from the Australian SAS. This ploy did eventually pay
dividends as the British C-in-C FARELF told the Australian chiefs of
staff that it would be a great help if Australia and New Zealand could
provide an SAS squadron. This plea was later formalized when the Prime
Minister, Sir Alec Douglas-Home, made the request to the Australian
Prime Minister, Sir Robert Menzies.

In January 1964 Woodhouse wrote to Major Alf Garland who was
commanding the Australian SAS company:

Your Brig Frank Hassett was here on an 'unofficial' visit yesterday
and spent an hour with us. There is plenty of room for you as well
as us, and the Kiwis for that matter! I have the impression that he
thinks your SAS should become independent of the infantry, and I
said that we found this worked best. The most valuable preparatory
training in the event you come here would be Malay language and
medical training.

Things are getting hot here but the bastards have so far not come
through areas where we have patrols deployed – another good reason
to get more SAS here. We should have the third British Squadron
operational by 1 August 1964... we are as keen to see you here as I
know you are to come.

To get the Australians committed took a direct request from the Malaysian government which included the notification that the SAS would be permitted to operate across the Indonesian border. However, it was not until 13 February 1965 that the advance party left Perth; it was followed by the main party on 26 February.

Woodhouse spent Christmas 1963 with the SAS HQ in the 'Haunted House' in Brunei. This quite small complex was a former HQ of the Japanese Secret Police and reputedly visited by the ghosts of those dark days. Situated a mile from the city, it was really too small for the purpose so there was no room for the ghosts of those tortured souls executed by the Japanese. It did serve, however, to keep nosy people away from the area. What also helped was the stark notice fitted to the gates and fences: 'Unauthorised persons will be shot'.

In Borneo operations carried on in the same style and as far as can be determined from available records the SAS detected at least seven incursions by Indonesian troops that led to successful interceptions by British or Gurkha infantry. Two SAS men were killed during the first six months of 1964.

Woodhouse's attitude to SAS soldiering was clear, unconditional and mostly uncompromising but he certainly did not lack humanity: there was an occasion when he learned that all was not well between a troop commander and his men. His letter to the officer demonstrated succinctly what he thought of the situation:

> I understand that relations between you and some of your troop have been strained. I assume that you are still heart-and-mind dedicated to making a success of your SAS career. On that assumption, and my conviction that you have the intelligence and imagination and basic knowledge necessary to command SAS troops, I am going to give you advice which, if you can follow it, will lead to your success.
>
> My personal knowledge of you is based on the short time we spent together in Malaya. I will use an example from that to begin my advice. At the end of a not very tiring day we stopped on a ridge some distance from water. You sent two soldiers to get it. In the SAS as an officer, particularly in your first year or two, you have got to prove your enthusiasm, your superiority in physical endurance, and your SAS skills, to your men.

If you had gone for the water, this enthusiasm to take on more than your share of the burdens would not have passed unnoticed by the soldiers. It was, I think, George Washington, then a General, who seeing some American soldiers struggling to push a gun through mud while officers stood by giving advice, put his shoulder to the wheel with appropriate remarks to the bystanding officers. In the SAS you will never get the devoted support of your troops until you have proved to them by your personal example that you will never spare yourself physically or in any other way. It is true that this could end up with you doing all the work while they do none, but it won't, not least because once you have proved totally unselfish in the literal sense of that word they wouldn't let you.

Next, it is your duty (which should also be your natural wish) to do the best possible for your men. I expect Tp Comds to do their utmost at all times to do their best for their men. You will never succeed unless you like soldiers. If you find that soldiers in general irritate you, then frankly you are in the wrong regiment, for in none will you be in closer and more frequent contact with them.

Lastly you must subdue any embarrassment and swallow your pride and tell your troop that you recognise that things are not as they should be, and tell them briefly that you accept there can only be one person at fault if this is the case – yourself. If you can do this, and do as I advise you, you will not find them unresponsive.

There is only one test I apply to officers and NCOs: are they efficient on operations and a credit to the Regiment when not on ops but in the public eye? With officers you are not efficient in the SAS unless you can win the soldiers' hearts as well as see they carry out their orders. This is a rare ability but I believe you can acquire it if you are determined to do so.

My last word of advice was given to me when I was 19 by my soldier godfather shortly before I went to command a platoon in a strange Regiment in action for the first time. He said to me when soldiers are tired, dispirited, frightened – never forget the value of a smile. There have never been good troop commanders in the SAS who have not been cheerful with their soldiers. I am very keen for you to succeed.

Discussing this letter many years later, Woodhouse contended that in the SAS there were bound to be genuine clashes of personality among such an intelligent and dedicated group of men. Both officers and men could be guilty of letting things slide, but in matters of character differences it was essential to be able to look clearly at the overall picture. In this case he felt that it was not a matter of indifference on the part of the officer, rather a matter of ignorance, and it was sensible to give advice that could easily sort out the situation if it were taken. That was much better than bidding an early farewell to a young officer with good potential.

John Woodhouse was very good at keeping his troops well-informed. In a letter addressed to all ranks, 'D' Squadron, written on 10 March 1964 while the squadron was on a Borneo tour, he wrote:

> There was a Regimental dance on 6th March. It made the usual profit of £50 or so. The RSM organised it and by the lack of heating (it was freezing) I assumed it was some sort of endurance test. Spirits sales were well up.
>
> I have had a beer mat sent to me asking for 'Dynamite' to be sent out – it was signed 'Frustrated'. She says if I can get her an 'indulgence' passage she would love to take on a patrol at a time!

('Dynamite' was a lusty Hereford maiden of large proportions topped by a not so pretty face. She was renowned for her willingness to service all and sundry of the male population of the city, but she did have a preference for SAS soldiers and she could often be spotted lurking in the shadows outside those popular hostelries, the Three Crowns, the Ulu Bar or the Bunch of Grapes. It was rumoured that she gave the City Arms and the Green Dragon a wide berth because those were officers' pubs and they were very bad tippers.)

# Chapter 21

# The Red Wolves of the Radfan and a Peep into East Africa

W hile 'D' Squadron was spending its extended six-month tour in Borneo, 'A' Squadron was not exactly idle. In April the squadron left Hereford for Aden at twenty-four hours' notice and was soon deployed into the Radfan Mountains of Yemen. A number of clashes with the so-called 'Red Wolves of the Radfan' followed with minor casualties on both sides. A more serious conflict (on 30 April) left Captain Robin Edwards (OC of 3 Troop) and Trooper Nick Warburton dead with Bill Hamilton and Paddy Baker wounded after a day-long confrontation with 100+ enemy tribesmen. Their survival for the whole of that day was undoubtedly down to the skilled RAF support with Hunter fighter aircraft. As dusk approached, the troop broke out with a burst of fire from each member; sadly Nick Warburton was killed a short time before the break-out and Robin Edwards was killed as he stood to join the outward charge. The break-out was successful. During that escape Corporal Paddy Baker and Trooper Bill Hamilton fought a rear-guard action by laying a series of ambushes in which they killed a number of the enemy who were determined to follow up. For his actions Baker was awarded the Military Medal.

In an unprecedented situation, the news that the bodies of the two deceased soldiers had been decapitated with their heads displayed on poles in the Yemen capital of Sana'a reached the UK newspapers and the next of kin before the official notification.

The mission of 3 Troop had been to move into a wide wadi (Wadi Taym) to secure and mark a drop zone for men of the Parachute Regiment who were scheduled to jump in to make an assault on a nearby enemy position. When 3 Troop was compromised and unable to complete the mission, it was passed on to two patrols of 1 Troop under command of Captain Ray England and Sergeant 'Gypsy' Smith to insert into the wadi by helicopter, establish communications, mark the drop zone and await the Paras. The two helicopters took heavy ground fire which ruptured the fuel tank of the lead aircraft and both were forced to turn around. It so happened that ''Mahu Mahu' and 'Spike' in the rear seats of the lead helicopter opened fire on the rebels with a rifle and a Bren gun. On getting out of the helicopter it was noted that a bullet hole was only a matter of inches from where the third occupant, Stan Jenks, had been sitting. This unconventional act of firing from the chopper possibly paved the way for Scout helicopters to be fitted out with GPMGs; a process closely followed by Ray England who later transferred to the Army Air Corps!

Paddy Finn (ex-22 SAS) wrote to the author:

When I was 'claimed back' by my parent regiment we became the first Infantry unit to move into the base for the Radfan operations. Eventually we were joined by 'A' Squadron, 22 SAS Regiment who had been on their way home for inter-tour leave from Borneo. John Woodhouse and the Operations Officer presented themselves for cookhouse duties because the Brigade Commander insisted that the regiment provide two bodies daily for dixie cleaning. (The SAS lads were, in fact, self-sufficient.)

Later I was caught in an explosion of Avgas and badly burned. John W, who at the time was passing over on high in a recce helicopter, dropped down to earth and handed over his heli to casevac me to hospital in Aden. I was there for some weeks with Paddy Baker.

When young Captain Edwards and his troop were pinned down up-country I was in charge of the patrol sent to try and relieve them. Halfway there I was told to get quickly up the side of the wadi and take cover as the lads had broken out and were taking no prisoners!

Therefore I met Alfie (Geordie) Tasker, Paddy Baker, Taffy Bendle, Bill Hamilton and the others by making jungle monkey calls. It was as though I'd never left the regiment.

Also in 1964 Woodhouse, at the urging of David Stirling, produced a paper making recommendations to the Chief of General Staff at the MOD for the raising and training of a corps d'elite to resolve the internal security problems being faced by Kenya. Stirling, as a result of his work with the Capricorn Africa Society,[1] had access to a wide range of high-ranking African politicians that included the presidents of Kenya and Zambia. This paper, written in February 1964, found favour with the CGS (General Sir Richard Hull), but it was not to be a smooth path. In May 1964 David Stirling wrote to Sir Richard Hull:

My Dear General,

I was glad in our discussion on Wednesday to find that you were in general agreement with and prepared to back the proposals submitted in our paper regarding the establishing of a Special Force in Kenya – although I regret that you may not be able to endorse some of the more sophisticated aspects of this Force's requirements, particularly in respect of the air support component. I know that the affirmative aspect of your decision will be very well received by the SAS. I have written a confidential letter to Lt. Col. Woodhouse telling him of our discussion. Obviously the one really vital thing is that the Force should be trained by the SAS rather than through the normal training facilities already available in Kenya.

In the light of our conversation I was surprised to receive a letter today from a Cabinet Minister in Kenya stating that General Freeland [GOC East Africa Command and later GOC British Troops in Kenya] was opposed to the proposition that the Special Force should be trained by the SAS. To counteract the depressing effect that this has had on the minister and his colleagues I have immediately written out, in confidence, telling him of our discussion. In my letter I restressed the unassailable fact that to consider training the Special Force through the normal training facilities already available in Kenya would be quite impractical and that nobody was more aware of this than yourself.

I gather from the Minister concerned that the Corps d'elite proposal had been supported by Duncan Sandys and his advisers in principle. I have hastened, therefore, to assure him in my letter that

---

1. Stirling's Capricorn Africa Society was an attempt to create an African Federation of the East African countries to forge an international amalgamation of those countries that would become a potent trading organization. The story is told in the author's previous book *David Stirling: The Authorised Biography of the Creator of the SAS*.

there is no change of attitude by HMG regarding their support for the project. I was fortunately able to be particularly emphatic in this matter since I had so recently discussed the project with you.

I agree with you that the Corps d'elite may indeed turn out to be predominantly Kikuyu but I do not see that this should cause us too great a degree of anxiety. The fact of supreme importance is that those selected for service in this unit should be 100% reliable and loyal, otherwise protecting of the 'Government in leaguer' role, as well as many other functions envisaged for the Special Force, could not be effectively carried out.

As I discussed the Kenya Special Force with the Duke of Devonshire I have taken the liberty of sending him a copy of this letter to you so that he will know that we have had a talk and that the proposals are now being, in the main, implemented – apart from the presumably temporary hiatus unwittingly caused by General Freeland.

Again thank you very much for seeing me and explaining the situation. I am sure that the SAS will carry out their task of training the Force efficiently. Although I am very much out of the picture these days, what I have seen of their personnel is most impressive.

Yours sincerely,

David Stirling

PS. it was clear from the Minister's letter that their relationship with General Freeland was exceedingly good and that the only point of issue seemed to be this all-important question of SAS training.

All of the above led to Woodhouse being invited to meet the Colonial Secretary (the Duke of Devonshire) in London to discuss his concerns about events in Kenya. He told Woodhouse that the Soviet Union was definitely involved in training Kenyan dissidents in Moscow. He was asked to go to Kenya to advise on the security measures that the government should immediately take to thwart a *coup d'état*.

On 1 July he met the High Commissioner (G. de Freitas), the Inspector General of Police (Sir Richard Catling) and the army commander. He was able to give advice for short-term measures and stressed the importance of being able to protect government functions; maintaining control of radio communications; monitoring the sale of material that could be used to improvise explosive devices and stressed the impact that would result if the SAS were to train Kenya's para-military police, the General Service Unit (GSU). This led to a further meeting and in December 1964 a formal proposal was made. He must have done a first–class sales job because some time later a composite team was tasked to train President Jomo Kenyatta's personal protection unit and this was followed by an 'A' Squadron training team that concentrated on the GSU. In the case of the GSU it was ostensibly to be deployed along the Northern Frontier to contain border infiltrations by the Shifta (terrorists, looters and poachers). It has been postulated that the two training operations carried out in Kenya did actually prevent a coup by the Communist-supported Luo tribesmen. It may have been a different story if the War Office had not absorbed the recommendations that followed the deployment in North Carolina with the USSF.

Important to all SAS dealings in Kenya in those days were the absolute support and high-quality advice tendered by South African-born Mr Bruce McKenzie, the Minister of Agriculture and Animal Husbandry. He had served in the South African Air Force and been seconded to the RAF during the Second World War with which he served in North Africa, the Mediterranean and Europe, gaining the DSO and DFC. He was the only white person on the president's staff and some in Kenya (and other African countries) suspected him of being an 'intelligence agent' acting against Kenyan interests. This was far from true; his service to that country proved him to be a real patriot. In June 1976 he persuaded President Kenyatta to permit Mossad agents to participate during Operation ENTEBBE. It is a sobering fact that he was assassinated on 24 May 1978. When flying back from Uganda after a visit to President Idi Amin, a bomb exploded in his aircraft as it flew over the Ngong Hills in Kenya on the way to Wilson Airfield. It transpired that the bomb was contained in a carved wooden lion's head given to him by Idi Amin.

*Chapter 22*

# '... a man to compare with Ho Chi Minh'

Meantime operations in Borneo continued and the regiment was indeed stretched. It seemed that any political or senior military visitor to Borneo would eventually arrive at SAS HQ. Woodhouse welcomed this and was quick to press his case for an urgent increase in SAS manpower. Often he was pre-briefed by Dare Newell of particular points to make with the different visitors. On the occasion of a visit by Peter Thorneycroft (the Defence Minister) and Denis Healey (the Labour Shadow Defence Minister) on 8 June 1964, he was helped by General Walker who arranged that, at a formal dinner, he should sit between Healey and the commander-in-chief. Woodhouse was impressed by Healey's mastery of his brief and the amount of homework he must have done on the detailed situation in Borneo. Healey must have been equally impressed because in his autobiography, *The Time of my Life*, he made mention of Woodhouse:

The helicopter was king; a battalion with six helicopters was worth a brigade with none. But most useful of all were units of the Special Air Service and its marine equivalent, the Special Boat Service. It was on that visit to Borneo that I first came to appreciate the extraordinary qualities of these elite forces.

Walter Walker took me to the group of huts which served as headquarters to 22 SAS. I was met by its commander. Lieutenant Colonel John Woodhouse, a diffident, unmilitary figure, in rumpled khaki, who might have been a botanist. He was, by common consent among the few who knew his record, the greatest guerrilla warrior yet produced by the West – a man to compare with Ho Chi Minh. When his job in Borneo was over, the British army marked its appreciation of his unique qualities by putting him in charge of rifle ranges in Germany!

The SAS in Borneo worked in sixteen patrols of four men each, carrying medical supplies, sophisticated signals equipment, explosives and a variety of other weapons. Both officers and NCOs could speak Malay, Thai and Arabic. They had been attached to casualty wards in British hospitals to learn how to treat all types of injury, and made a point of treating the local people as well as themselves. The key to their success was good relations with the tribes on the frontier, who provided intelligence and scouts for the British forces; the SAS lived in the tribesmen's huts and ate the same, often revolting food.

The respect that Denis Healey took away from Borneo was to stand 22 SAS in good stead for some years to come. On 9 June 1964 John Woodhouse wrote to Mike Wingate Gray with his own feelings on the meeting with Healey; the letter shows a shrewd appreciation of the possible values of the meeting:

Dear Mike,

This is mainly to let you know what I learned from Denis Healey who spent a disproportionate time talking with me at a dinner party last night. Before going on to that can you check on a letter 10/309 dated 2 May 64 which I sent to MOD (L/AW) and apparently copies to HQ Southern Command and RHQ SAS Regiment?

It should be followed up since it deals with SAS operations in MID-EAST and proposed roles. I wrote the gist of it to you when I left ADEN on 30 April. I doubt HG (Hugh Gillies) will have done anything except, perhaps, read it.

Healey had heard a little about the SAS before he got here and was already 'in sympathy'. Talking to politicians (particularly ones in opposition with no power at the moment) I believe in exciting their interest rather than satisfying their curiosity! I gave Healey, therefore, a rather patchy briefing emphasising a few particular points rather than giving a balanced view of the whole. I emphasised the value of SAS presence for recce, intelligence, and psywar <u>before</u> operations began. The value of medical and language training, the problem of getting the right men were emphasised.

We have in him more than a supporter, we have an ardent advocate. General Walker told me that when Healey asked him for his views on the SAS he told him how useful we were but tried also to give him the opposition to SAS views. He said 'of course they do tend to take the best men from the Infantry'. Healey replied 'And why not, they make the best use of them'!

Healey believes that VIETNAM long term is lost and that we should <u>now</u> be preparing to hold THAILAND. If we get ready now he thinks we can do it. SAS are included in his ideas and he was interested to hear if operations permit we have asked to 'exercise' there in late 1969.

He also supports a strong Gurkha element in the Army and said he has never been able to get to the bottom of the real reasons for opposition to their expansion. He thinks the BAOR commitment must be reduced appreciably but believes this must follow a new negotiated agreement with our Allies, or at least we must attempt this. Only in this way will the Army be strong enough to meet its commitments. He pointed out that the HONG KONG garrison was considerably stronger than our total strength in the MIDDLE EAST before RADFAN and implied a possible cut there. The C-in-C obviously did not agree, but could not give his reasons at a dinner party or to Mr. Healey which has made me curious to know what they are!

Healey goes to ADEN shortly and will I hope hear favourable comments on us there. He is sharper than Thorneycroft but one has to take into account the relative complacency of all in office to those in opposition. A very intelligent man and obviously a clear thinker. I was impressed. Of course you may feel this is just bias knowing that my politics incline towards Labour anyway!

The generals told him the Government, while publicly agreeing to 15,000 Gurkhas, privately have stopped them recruiting for that figure by saying that they must avoid redundancy when BORNEO operations end and Gurkha strength is reduced. I fancy Thorneycroft is going to hear more of that one in the House! Of course after all this we shall probably find Healey is made Minister of Agriculture or something equally remote from Defence!

I remembered – at the last minute – to get PR to take photos and will send back so that 'Soldier' can get on with our operations. Have you got photos of ARABIA for them? They could do something good on the Regiment now. Did they get what they wanted on Selection?

Bexton's body flown out last night, SSM Turnbull escorted it across to LABUAN today. The SAS in Nee Soon will meet and SAS and Guards Para attend the funeral.

John Woodhouse

In 1967 Denis Healey, in a break from protocol, accepted an invitation to be guest of honour at the SAS Regimental Dinner at the Hyde Park Hotel. It was, he said, 'An unusual step in my position.'

Woodhouse was quite happy to send long and detailed letters often containing information that should be graded 'Secret' through the BFPO postal system as he reckoned it was as secure as any other form of transmission.

Soon his thoughts turned again to Yemen when a letter from Peter de la Billière, written on 3 June 1964, offered some sound advice:

Condie has arrived back from Yemen with glowing reports from everyone including the Imam for whom he was working. Col Jim has asked if he can go out there again, and he has asked me to thank you very much indeed for allowing him to come in the first place. There is no doubt that he has proved most useful. There have been two airdrops over the last month and this has not only impressed the Arabs but also our own political contacts who now consider the set-up to be most professional. I think that there is every hope that a permanent organisation will come out of it all. Col David is currently in America so have not been able to see him but you may feel it would be worth giving him some form of suggestion as to how it might run when next you see him.

With regard to replacing him I am not sure that we are getting sufficient return for the risk you are running and feel that it would be best left for the time being. If it is decided to send anyone else they must be medically trained as that is the number one priority after language. The only other Arabist I have is Jenks and he is not medically trained. I feel that medical training and language training should as far as possible go hand-in-hand before any other skills being paired with language. Condie is on leave and I have shelved the whole idea of replacement until Jim returns from his leave on 15th June when I shall see him before I depart.

At that point in 1964 the value of the SAS in current operations in both Arabia and Borneo was such that the War Office was being strongly urged to raise more squadrons. Authority to re-form 'B' Squadron was granted and this was done under command of Major Johnny Watts, an ex-troop commander in Malaya and squadron commander in Oman who would eventually become Director SAS before taking up the post of chief of the defence staff of the Sultan of Oman's armed forces. The squadron became operational in November 1964. The Gurkha Parachute Squadron was adapted to an SAS role specific to Borneo operations and the Guards Independent Parachute Company began to be trained by the SAS for Borneo operations. The latter is interesting because the Brigade of Guards had produced very few volunteers for SAS selection up to that point; it later transpired that many of the soldiers who had volunteered for the selection course had been dissuaded (sometimes with accusations of disloyalty). The now high 'credit rating' of the SAS was to bring about a change in the Guards policy and led to the formation of 'G' Squadron 22 SAS, initially made up of volunteers from the Guards and Household Cavalry, and for the first time there were officers within those volunteers. Those officers included Captain Charles Guthrie who commanded a troop in 'G' Squadron and later returned as squadron commander. Guthrie would later become a field marshal.

There were some most impressive parties held in Borneo when squadrons came out of the jungle at the end of their four-month tour. Somewhere in the annals of the Malayan Scouts' history there must lie an explanation for a strange habit. It was quite customary during the hard drinking festivities for a person to sneak up behind another, grip the bottom of the back of his shirt and rip it all the way up to the collar. The attacked person would either pretend not to notice or try to rip the other's shirt in the same manner. At one particular 'A' Squadron farewell party that was attended by both British and New Zealand soldiers, John

Woodhouse, as CO, brought along a senior military officer to meet the squadron. He was observed whispering to his guest and then they both took off their shirts and the CO hid them in a fold of canvas in the wall of the marquee. When the time came for them to depart they were quite disappointed to find their shirts had been very neatly torn from tail to collar. 'One up to 'A' Squadron,' came a shout from an unidentified source.

On his visits to Borneo Woodhouse tried to get in to see as many of the patrols as he could and on one occasion, accompanied by the operations room sergeant, he met up with 1 Troop, 'A' Squadron at a disused but passable airstrip at Long Semado. The patrol base was quite close to the airstrip but well set up. The CO and his escort were given their stand-to spots and as dusk approached everyone moved into position. The CO told the troop that he personally would give the order to stand down and it would be signalled by him scratching his webbing belt. He duly gave the signal and the troop quietly resumed their places by their bashas and began to prepare their evening meals. No escort! A member of the troop rose to go to and fetch but was told by the CO to leave him to it. There were only two members of the troop who had seen service in the Far East, Thomas 'Sam' Oddy and Sandy Powell. Sam was a born storyteller and began to relate hair-raising (but humorous) tales of derring-do in the jungles and bars of Malaya with Sandy occasionally interjecting with his own amusing comments. The CO's shoulders could be seen trembling with suppressed laughter at times as Sam continued his monologue. This was only interrupted by the crestfallen appearance of the escort who had finally got the message, no doubt from the smell of curry, that stand to was over.

Sam Oddy was one of the famous 'characters' in the regiment. He was slightly rotund with a somewhat chubby face and clear blue eyes. An excellent medic, he was well-spoken (if he wished to be) and had an earnest expression. He is well-remembered for a brief moment of fame during the handover of Tony Deane Drummond to Dare Wilson when he infiltrated the officers' mess during the festivities and buttonholed Wilson, explaining that he was the local curate and that he hoped that Wilson would be a little more persuasive than Deane Drummond had been in exhorting members of the regiment to support the local church by attending Sunday services. Woodhouse, who was present at the time, allowed the farce to continue for a while before gently escorting Sam out of the mess. As far as is known he never betrayed Sam's identity!

After 'D' Squadron took over from 'A', veteran SAS soldier Roy Lemon recalled how the CO had visited his patrol at Sematan in Borneo. When it was time to leave, Lemon escorted him from their base to the nearby airstrip. The single-engine Pioneer was awaiting them, but the engine was not turning over. On investigation the RAF pilot informed them that all the ignition cartridges had been used and that they would have to wait for an engineer to fly in and fix the problem. The CO was not best pleased as they were in a very exposed position.

Under questioning the pilot then admitted that he had spare cartridges but he did not know how to fit them and in any case he had no tools. Lemon had a look at the engine and decided that the job was doable. He stripped down his Remington pump gun to use one of its parts to extract the used starter cartridges and then he was able to fit a new one. Meantime he saw that the CO had found a suitable position to lie down and cover them with his SLR rifle. The engine successfully fired up and Woodhouse departed, no doubt delighted that SAS ingenuity had saved the day once more. Pity the poor pilot on his return to base!

There was a memorable occasion in 1960 when 'D' Squadron was awaiting an airlift back to the UK from Ibri in Oman after exercising in the desert and paying a nostalgic visit to the Jebel Akhdar. The airplane landed and the crew enjoyed a somewhat gritty sandwich and cup of tea as the plane was prepared for the return journey. The time came and the troops poured aboard and settled into the uncomfortable canvas-bottomed seats. Time and time again the pilot tried to start the engines but to no avail and the batteries faded. The only solution, they said, was to call upon support from an RAF station in Bahrain to fly in fully-charged batteries. That, the only option, could take up to five days. The troops disembarked with some good-natured chuntering.

A tall figure emerged from the waiting troops and asked to speak to the captain. A long discourse took place, with the captain gesticulating wildly and obviously saying 'No' to whatever was being proposed. The squadron sat around this enjoyable vista with no real thoughts of the situation changing; however, it was a diversion, wasn't it? At a point of high drama the captain appeared to acquiesce to Trooper Charlie Surridge's proposal. He was a self-trained and very competent engineer who had proved his expertise many times with 'D' Squadron's Mobility Troop. Under Charlie's directions a number of the fully-charged batteries were collected from the Land Rovers and connected to boost the power of the aircraft batteries. Charlie, getting maximum pleasure from his display of engineering competence, stood in front of the aircraft and played to perfection the role of handler as he gave the hand signals to prepare to start engines. He later got a letter of commendation from the RAF. After his discharge from the army, Charlie joined the AA!

Such characters abounded in those days and they were well-beloved. In Kenya when 'D' Squadron was celebrating the end of a couple of months' hard training, the Tusker beer was flowing freely. A troop commander (ex-Parachute Regiment, Captain Glyn Williams) was flexing his muscles and boasting of his prowess as a boxer. Never, he said, had he even been knocked down in all of his bouts in the ring. The assembled audience listened without too much interest, but eventually got a bit fed up with his monologue. A large, quite senior-looking man with a huge handlebar moustache stood up and walked towards Williams who looked at him with undisguised aggression. 'Slosh' Searles administered one punch to the jaw, caught the KO'd Williams as he fell and placed him carefully on a chair before retiring to his own seat. Williams turned out to be a very good SAS officer and often told the story against himself.

Then there was 'Drag' Rowbotham! Drag, who retired after some twenty years or so of SAS service, got a job on the administrative staff at the base where, in the late '70s onwards, the regiment was training men to operate in covert situations. Part of the selection for the students was, of course, fitness. On one occasion they were paraded in PT gear at the HQ building waiting for the briefing for the day's run. The permanent staff instructor said that he was sorry but he had an appointment that he could not miss, so one of his administrative staff would lead the run. He blew his whistle and out of the nearby telephone kiosk came a man in a scraggy ill-fitting Superman suit. He was skinny, almost bald, stoop-shouldered and wearing Wellington boots. The assembled students found it difficult to contain their sniggers as they set off at a gentle pace. However, the sniggers faltered as 'Superman' steadily increased the pace and turned to gasps after a few miles as he really turned on the heat and lengthened his stride. Only two or three of the students were in sight of him as 'Drag', long-distance runner, Cumbrian fell runner and marathon finalist, sauntered home hardly out of breath.

During the latter part of his tour as CO, Woodhouse brought in a number of innovations. He instituted for the first time a JNCOs' cadre. This was initially run by the late Captain David Gilbert Smith who had the strength of character to persuade the somewhat bolshie JNCOs that this was something from which they could benefit. During the course there would be lectures from the CO on the importance of the necessity for SNCOs to 'educate' young officers by sharing their experience and enthusiasm; that, of course, was dependent on the men on the course ever reaching SNCO status. The RSM Bill 'Lofty' Ross would then spend an hour telling the 'pupils' just how ignorant they were and how much they still had to learn. All of these events smacked of normal life in a normal regiment and, as such, young soldiers were slightly fearful of them and it was good to get back to operations again.

Soon after 'A' Squadron returned from that Borneo tour, John Woodhouse took great personal pleasure in publishing the following:

REGIMENTAL PART I ORDERS
BY
LT-COL JM WOODHOUSE MBE MC
COMMANDING 22 SAS REGIMENT

SERIAL 175                                           12 OCT 1964

PERMANENT CADRE – SPECIAL AIR SERVICE REGT
The CO is very pleased to inform all SAS soldiers that a permanent regular cadre of the Special Air Service of approx. 77 men was finally approved by the Army Council on 9 Oct 1964 – six years after our first efforts to secure this major advance in our status. A number of SAS soldiers, mostly WOs and senior NCOs will be invited to transfer to the permanent cadre SAS before the end of this year after the CO has consulted senior ranks in RHQ, the RSM and all squadrons and referred recommendations to RHQ SAS.

This statement, though recognized by most soldiers as a major breakthrough, caused quite a number of young JNCOs and troopers to worry. If they were omitted from the cadre, and it seemed that their current rank decided this, would their parent regiments, now aware of the new system, recall them before any promotion on to the cadre became a possibility? They need not have been concerned. When the analysis was made of those on whose shoulders would fall the happy burden of the establishment of a newly-formalized regiment, it was found that there simply were not enough WO and SNCO veterans of the right age and calibre. 'Jungle' sergeants were not necessarily appropriate to fit the wider needs of the roles being forecast for the SAS. Also it was a fact that a number of SNCOs were approaching the last few years of their army careers and it would have been folly to use up a cadre vacancy when neither the incumbent nor the regiment would benefit. Equally there were a few potential members who had continued to be promoted within their parent units and who opted to return for a more settled existence; a number of those were under pressure from their wives. Nonetheless, the establishment of seventy-seven men had to be filled and there began a process of examination of junior NCOs who looked to have a bright future. Borneo so far had brought to the attention of the CO that there was a real pool of talent at lance corporal and corporal level that had to be secured. The establishment was filled and it turned out to be an excellent balance of experience and individual potential. It was a good start to solidifying 22 SAS's position firmly into the British army Order of Battle. Interestingly the figure of seventy-seven tallies very closely with the number of men that Stirling was initially allowed to recruit in North Africa (sixty-six men and six officers).

There was a further problem in that some of the very experienced SNCOs could not be given their substantive ranks or further promoted because they had not been able to comply with the regulations that required a man to hold the Army Certificate of Education First Class before becoming a substantive sergeant. During active service in Malaya nobody wanted to take time out to go back to school to gain a qualification that seemed unimportant at the time. This should, of course, have been spotted at RHQ level, but it is perhaps understandable in that it seemed that on cessation of hostilities in Malaya the SAS would probably be disbanded once more. It now became obvious that some of the well-respected veterans would not be able to make the grade; this could lead to some disgruntlement as younger men began to overtake them. In an attempt to resolve this problem an Education Corps SNCO was drafted into 22 SAS and regular classes began. The Education Sergeant, 'Schoolie' Thompson, recognizing that in a number of cases the veteran SNCOs would struggle in vain to make the grade, actively encouraged some of the younger NCOs, out of respect for their peers, to masquerade under false names and turn up on test days to take the examinations for them. It is known that John Woodhouse was aware of this because as a lance corporal the author (who had briefly been Woodhouse's signaller) was willingly sitting the exams for one of the Malay veterans when the CO strolled in to chat to 'Schoolie' Thompson who was invigilating. He then wandered around the room, paused by the author's desk, looked him in the eye, and with the merest hint of a smile said 'Good morning, Sergeant X. I hope it is going well.'

Woodhouse was continually thinking about the past, present and future of his regiment and when reminiscing at one point he said:

> One decision I made in Borneo came back to haunt me and to this day I still occasionally think about it. I introduced into SOPs the tactic 'Shoot and Scoot'. In jungle, contacts with the enemy which are unplanned tend to happen at very close quarters with neither side knowing the strength of the opposition. The tactic was intended to save lives by not taking cover to fight for a useless piece of ground or to prevent annihilation in an ambush. On contact whoever had an immediate target would open fire and then the whole patrol would fire a couple of rounds towards the enemy and then scatter and meet up later at their emergency RV.

This went badly wrong on one occasion. The leading scout, 'Chalky' White, rounded a bend in the track and came face to face with the enemy. He opened fire and two of the patrol squeezed off a couple of shots and bolted as the patrol commander shouted 'Get out' in accordance with the 'Shoot and Scoot' instructions. Attached to the patrol was an Australian SAS soldier Geoff Skardon who dumped his rucksack and dropped to the ground in order to cover White's withdrawal. White was then hit by the heavy fire from the Indonesian group. He tried to pull White to some cover and had to discard his belt when it snagged in the undergrowth. White was clearly dead and Skardon had to crawl into a small river in order to evade the enemy who seemed to be rapidly closing in on him. He managed to get out of the area of contact and now without map or compass decided to make his way back to the infiltration LZ. He got there on the following day.

When neither White nor Skardon turned up at the emergency RV, the two remaining members of the patrol cautiously returned to the scene of the contact only to find White dead from the loss of blood from a femoral artery severed by a bullet. It is highly probable that even if the patrol had stood its ground and fired at the enemy the result would have been the same, if not worse, but it always stayed in Woodhouse's mind.

The circumstances surrounding the death of White and the 'Shoot and Scoot' policy did, of course, become the subject of many informal debates among the squadron and there was no fully acceptable tactic to replace it. On the one hand it could be said that if the patrol had all fired a couple of shots in the direction of the enemy and then scattered there may not have been any casualties. On the other hand Woodhouse understood the complexity of the situation:

> I believe troops will welcome, and morale demands, an order that if a man is known to have fallen the patrol will remain in the close vicinity until either they see for certain that he is dead or they recover him alive. I think we should expect to fight to the death for this.

It has been written that he dreamed up the tactic especially for SAS operations in Borneo, but according to his wartime notes and diaries 'Shoot and Scoot' is a term he used when commanding the East Surrey's Battle Patrol in Italy. During those days he also used the system of an emergency RV which constantly changed as his patrol moved forward. He would indicate an easily recognized feature – for example, an oddly-shaped tree, a river or track junction – and indicate to his patrol to study it from all angles as that was where they would meet up if separated.

Reaction to that SOP was varied. Many thought that to scoot without the chance of killing some of the enemy was wrong. There is little doubt that if a patrol saw one of their men downed they would fight to the last. That may have been wrong but it would have been very human.

A significant change in strategy in Borneo took place, mainly as a result of Woodhouse urging General Walker to get permission to allow the SAS to take the war to the enemy by patrolling across the border. If the Indonesians could cross into Sarawak without political kickbacks, then why couldn't the SAS cross the other way? The conundrum facing Britain was that it was not actually at war with Indonesia, but it would be an undeniable act of war if Indonesia were to be invaded. General Walker succeeded in getting permission for cross-border operations (code-named CLARET) with the intention of making the Indonesians feel insecure about mounting offensive operations themselves. The decision was not made easily as both political and military risks were considerable. Key to the positive decision was Defence Secretary Denis Healey whose support was very much based on his earlier visit to Borneo and the subsequent meetings with Woodhouse and Walker. A further meeting with Newell and Woodhouse strengthened his belief in the feasibility of the strategy. He thought that there was a clear chance that it could be a mechanism for shortening the confrontation with minimum casualties to British forces. The permission to begin Operation CLARET came with the caveat that it must remain absolutely secret. Remarkably, and probably because no journalist ever gained access to operational areas in Borneo, the secret was kept for at least a dozen years.

Initially the patrols would be limited to penetration only up to 3,000 yards but this was later increased to 10,000 yards. CLARET operations which began as reconnaissance and observation patrols quickly grew to be full troop operations, multi-troop operations and then evolved into close co-operation with the Gurkhas. An SAS patrol may conduct a close reconnaissance on an enemy position and then, on extraction to the LZ, the patrol commander would immediately turn around and lead the Gurkhas in to the target. This was quite a good way to operate. The contrast between tip-toeing around an enemy camp and then sneaking out of range only to return with a company of Gurkhas who certainly did not tip-toe was very pleasing and, what is more, the Gurkhas carried all the ammunition!

Although most of the squadron commanders were able to either lead or accompany a CLARET operation, John Woodhouse was ordered directly that there was no way in which he, as CO, would ever be allowed to accompany his troops. He had never proposed that he should take part, but his superiors knew him too well and were not about to give him an excuse to tack onto a planned patrol. Though he was thoroughly disappointed, he did fully understand the reasoning. That, he had already accepted, was the difference between the SAS and the Paras; a fact that he had dwelled upon when making his earlier decision to return to the SAS.

In 1964 General Carver, GOC 3rd Division, made his first visit to 22 SAS Regiment to carry out the Annual Administrative Inspection in Bradbury Lines, Hereford. The then Captain Tony Harnett remembered the rehearsal for the inspection of the equipment layout:

During the rehearsal John Woodhouse stopped in front of one of my troopers, looked down at the contents of his rucksack and asked 'Have you been invited out to dinner?' 'No, sir' replied the soldier. 'What have you got a fork for then – you've already got a spoon and a clasp knife.'

There was also the occasion when the whole regiment was summoned for some words of advice from the CO. He duly appeared, resplendent in Service Dress (a form of dress not worn over-much in those days). Among other things, we were spoken to rather sharply about our poor standard of turn-out. The surprised silence that followed was broken by an audible 'tinkle'. The bottom button of the CO's tunic had fallen to the floor!

Now, in July 1964 and conscious that his command of 22 SAS Regiment was due to end on 31 December, John Woodhouse had to think long and hard about his future. Though the SAS very much wanted him to take over the job of SAS Colonel from Hugh Gillies, the War Office decided that he was too junior and chose Colonel John Waddy for the job. SAS Colonel was the forerunner of the post of Director HQDSAS & SAS Group which carried the rank of brigadier. Colonel John Waddy OBE was an experienced and highly-respected Parachute Regiment officer, an

Arnhem veteran who had also seen active service in Palestine and Malaya. He had no previous SAS experience and within the regiment there was some disquiet as it was believed that this may be the first step in the SAS being taken over by the Parachute Regiment, a rumour that had been doing the rounds for some time.

(It is interesting to note that in an interview with the author in 1990 the late Colonel David Smiley said that he had been offered command of all three SAS regiments but he had turned this down because he was set on retirement in 1961. Smiley was an excellent and highly-decorated officer and very experienced in unconventional warfare. He was heavily involved with David Stirling and his ex-comrades-in-arms Neil 'Billy' Maclean and Julian Amery in extensive mercenary operations in the Yemen Republic.)

Actually there was a somewhat quirky SAS connection with John Waddy. Back during the North Africa campaign of the Second World War the consignment of eighty-five parachutes that had arrived at an ordnance depot in Cairo were commandeered by Jock Lewes and David Stirling for 'L' Detachment. The parachutes were actually on their way to India for the training of 1, 2 and 3 Parachute battalions in which Waddy was involved. 'L' Detachment used and lost sixty of the 'chutes on the first abortive operation, leaving the Paras to train as best they could with the dozen or so 'chutes brought in as hand baggage by the army and RAF instructors. They became very patched from being dragged along the sand and gravel as the training progressed.

There were suspicions among the SAS senior ranks that it was the influence of General Napier Crookenden that eased John Woodhouse out of the running for the post of Colonel SAS. The author could find no hard evidence of that, but it has to be remembered that Crookenden had been a GSO1 on General Templar's staff in Malaya for the period 1952–54, a period when the reputation of the SAS was perhaps at its lowest. He was a gallant Airborne Forces officer (having dropped at Arnhem) and he commanded 16 Para Brigade in 1960/61 before becoming the Director of Land/Air Warfare in 1964. He had often stated that the Parachute Regiment could easily do whatever the SAS could do and was in conflict many times with the views held by the SAS in terms of their future roles. He was known at SAS HQ as 'Nap the Crook'.

It was true that some of the Parachute Regiment hierarchy were of a mind that the job of the SAS could be done equally well by their own troops with a little specialized training. There was no truth in the rumoured takeover; that possibility had been negated some time before Waddy's appointment. Though he was very disappointed not to be offered the job, Woodhouse offered Waddy his full support, both verbally and in his letter dated 9 July 1964:

Dear John,

I hope if you are free to do so you will visit 22 SAS in Hereford. I and Mike Wingate Gray will be here between about 25 July and 10 August and will both do our best to put you in the SAS picture as and when you can come here then or later. Stay the night if you wish to.

You are aware of the rather unfortunate background of controversy to your appointment but I can assure that I shall do all I can to see you are well informed on 22 SAS policy, operations and personalities. I am quite sure you will find 22 SAS will reciprocate your loyalty to SAS in full and you will find it an intensely interesting tour. For my part I have no hard feelings, and indeed in December wrote to Hugh Gillies and told him I wished to retire and did not want the job, but allowed myself to be overruled!

I saw DMO and DSD yesterday who have asked my views in writing on the long-term strength and recruiting of SAS and what training on SAS lines should be carried out in the Parachute Regiment.

By the time you take over I am confident with their support that we shall probably have four squadrons approved, direct recruiting from civilian life, and so end our embarrassing dependency on other Arms.

I hope and expect you will thoroughly enjoy your tour and know you have taken an interest in the SAS long before it became 'fashionable' to do so! Anyway I shall do all in my power to help and wish you good luck and success when you join the SAS.

Yours very sincerely, John Woodhouse

In December 1964 the last Annual Administrative Inspection report of 22 SAS Regiment while it was still under the command of John Woodhouse was excellent. A relevant extract from the report is as follows:

<u>General Remarks</u>: The training and administration of this unit is of a very high standard in all departments, and this is particularly creditable against its background of operational moves and commitments throughout the year. The whole atmosphere and tone of the unit, as might be expected, is outstanding.

While their accommodation on the whole is satisfactory there are some glaring exceptions which ought to be put right immediately. The officers' and sergeants' single accommodation is deplorable, particularly in view of the number of foreign visitors, some quite senior, who use it. The Junior Ranks Club is large and uninviting, and well below standard. The unit has done its best with the accommodation, and outside help is necessary if it is to be put right.

<u>General Comments on Training</u>: More than 50% of the unit has, at any one time during the year, been deployed overseas for operations and/or training in operational theatres. The unique selection procedure and the fact that each squadron in turn has the prospect of an operational tour, automatically creates the target for a very high standard of training. The training is allowed to proceed unhindered due to the large civilian back-up in the unit and has been further helped by continuation cadres at regimental level, recently introduced.

The unit does not observe the normal rules for individual training but conforms to regimental standards which are laid down according to the peculiar needs of the unit. I am satisfied that the results achieved are of a very high standard and bear directly on the operational tasks of the unit.

Prior to the Administrative Inspection, Woodhouse asked the Selection Troop for a breakdown of recruits for the year (1964):

| Source | Volunteers | Passed | Approx % |
|---|---|---|---|
| Infantry | 55 | 13 | 24% |
| Parachute Regiment | 15 | 11 | 74% |
| Royal Artillery | 38 | 7 | 9% |
| Royal Engineers | 26 | 3 | 11% |
| Royal Electrical & Mechanical Engineers | 22 | 7 | 31% |
| Royal Signals | 10 | 3 | 30% |
| Royal Armoured Corps | 12 | 2 | 18% |
| Royal Army Service Corps | 26 | 1 | 4% |
| Royal Army Ordnance Corps | 12 | 3 | 25% |
| Misc | 9 | 2 | 18% |
| Totals | 225 | 52 | |

At his final interview as CO of 22 SAS Regiment John Woodhouse was informed by General Carver of the fact that he was considered too junior for the appointment to Colonel SAS and was instead offered the job of commandant of the NATO Training Centre at Sennelager in Germany with promotion to colonel. As he put it in later life: 'Too junior to be an SAS Colonel but senior enough to be promoted as a bloody range warden.'

It beggars belief that the undoubted and proven most expert exponent of guerrilla warfare in the British army at that time should be insulted in such a fashion. It was obvious even in those early days that the necessity for counter-guerrilla operations would reappear and that terrorism was set to become a continuing problem. The word 'insulted' is carefully chosen. Many letters of support (and condolence) were sent to Woodhouse and one that particularly moved him was from the SAS founder David Stirling, written on 20 May 1964:

My Dear John,
I feel wretchedly bad about the adverse decision regarding your SAS appointment. I had a meeting with Bob Laycock[1] last week at which time he had practically decided to resign altogether from his

---

1. Major General Sir Robert Laycock, commander of Layforce (the Commando unit) in the Second World War. Colonel Commandant of the SAS.

position in SAS. I did my best to dissuade him – at least until all of us had met on my return from Hong Kong in early July. I can assure you that Laycock took every conceivable step including seeing the CIGS and feels very badly let down – as do all of us.

As you know, I do not think that there has ever been an officer in the SAS who has commanded such universal confidence and respect as you and, therefore, it is a rebuff for one and all of us. I am afraid that decision is an ominous one as it may well presage a determination by certain narrow-minded staff officers in the War Office to squeeze the SAS into a sort of mould which would destroy its status and significance as a modern fighting force with its highly specialised role. This threat we must regard as a challenge and one which between us I am quite certain we can defeat, but to do so means a concerted effort.

I enclose a copy of my last letter to Hull[2] on the Kenya project. I would be immensely grateful if you could keep an eye on this to make sure that the proper priority is given to it when the appeal for training facilities comes through in due course. Although I suspect Hull was trying to block the 'Corps d'Elite' for Kenya being trained by the SAS I hope that my letter and the other action taken in Kenya will defeat his effort to frustrate our intentions.

Again I can only express deep regret that you did not get the appointment. Please write to me in confidence about your plans for the future.

I cannot end without congratulating you and the 22nd SAS on the superb performance that you put up in Aden. I have heard the most astounding accounts of the resource and gallantry shown by the Regiment.

Yours ever, David

PS. I have sent a copy of this letter only to Brian Franks for him to discuss at his discretion with you and Laycock.

---

2. General Sir Richard Hull, the Chief of General Staff who was, at that time, supporting the efforts of John Woodhouse to get an SAS training team into Kenya.

Woodhouse did not dismiss the Sennelager offer out of hand; there were numerous important considerations. He guessed that if he stayed in the army his promotion ceiling would be brigadier at the very best. He had many very good annual reports but he lacked a balanced career, having spent so much of his time with the SAS. His father's death in 1962 had caused some of the family assets at Higher Melcombe to be let and he was keen to take up residence there and run the estate. That would have been difficult but possible had he been offered a post in the UK. He had had frequent dealings with the FCO when with 22 SAS. His relationship went back to the early 1950s. He had lectured at one of their schools and he knew that he was highly regarded. By the end of August he confirmed his decision to leave the military. In his last interview with Major General Carver, then General Officer Commanding 3 Division (he later became a field marshal), he was advised that he should reconsider his decision to leave the service; Carver told him that he may find it quite difficult to get a job in civilian life. Woodhouse retorted that it would be much easier for him to find employment than it would be for General Carver!

Before the offer of the job in Germany was made, his two final annual reports were written:

I have a close personal knowledge of Lt-Col Woodhouse. His regiment, for which I have a very high regard, has contributed squadrons to Borneo since January 1963. Lt-Col Woodhouse has been in command throughout that time. I consider him to be an expert in the specialised field of counter guerrilla operations, in which he is an acknowledged spokesman. He is perceptive, shrewd, imaginative and level-headed. The advice he offers is invariably well presented, balanced, and to the point. In detail this also extends to training matters in respect of such other units as are operating from time to time in the SAS role, and indigenous irregulars. His first-hand knowledge of the feelings, hopes and aspirations of the Borneo peoples has proved invaluable. In this respect, as in others, his finger is on the pulse. By nature he is quiet, reserved, unassuming, and perhaps a trifle shy. This façade has first to be penetrated to appreciate his work.

His squadrons speak of him with pride. They admire, as I do, the way in which he has devoted himself to raising the regiment to its present high standard of efficiency.

By the special nature of his command, Lt-Col Woodhouse has often found himself in the role of advisor on the employment of Special Forces. In consequence I have also seen him in the role of a staff officer. I have no hesitation in saying that I would gladly accept him on my staff as GSO1 (Intelligence).

To summarise, Woodhouse enjoys a unique unchallenged reputation as an expert on counter guerrilla warfare. In operational command of his regiment he has done outstandingly well. I grade him above the standard required of his rank and service and consider him fit for promotion now.

Signed by Major General Walter Walker

A further report, from Major General R.M.P. Carver (GOC 3 Division), reads as follows:

I have seen very little of Lt-Col Woodhouse since my last report on him owing to my absence in Cyprus and his prolonged visits to Borneo and Aden. My annual inspection of his regiment showed an all-round improvement since the previous year due to the considerable personal effort he had made in the face of many difficulties, caused by the overseas operational commitments of his regiment. He is an excellent trainer and an inspiring leader, in spite of his very quiet, almost diffident manner.

He is a master of his specialty – training and operation of Special Forces, and gathering intelligence. He would make a good GSO1 (Int). Outside this specialised field he would move with less assurance and might find himself handicapped. He thinks clearly and puts over his ideas and orders verbally with precision, clarity and economy of effort. He has won the confidence and respect of all the operational commanders he has served and advised.

After such a good report which clearly defines Carver's appreciation of his strengths, it is strange that he was totally unsupportive of Woodhouse when he was strongly and energetically recommended for the DSO! Not until after he left the service was Woodhouse told that Walter Walker had recommended him for the DSO but had subsequently been told that he was not authorized to do so. An excerpt from a letter to Lieutenant Colonel David Sutherland written on 28 March 1990 shows Walker's frustration:

> This is not the first time that John Woodhouse has taken the initiative in coming to my assistance. As I said publicly at the time, a squadron of SAS in the Borneo campaign proved that they were worth one thousand infantry to me, and John Woodhouse was my wise and trusted right-hand man, confidante and adviser, who never put a foot wrong. When Lord Mountbatten, on his arrival in Borneo, congratulated me on a second bar to my DSO, I said: 'John Woodhouse should be the recipient of this medal, not me.' Try as I did, I could not persuade the 'powers that be' to bend the rules about who the initiator had to be. Fantastic and almost unbelievable.

Also, in a letter to Woodhouse, General Walker wrote:

> I wrote to Colonel Sutherland on 28 March, and thanked him and the Trustees for their magnificent generosity. [The SAS Association funded the purchase of a mobility scooter for him after a botched back operation left him unable to walk more than a few paces.] I took the opportunity of mentioning in my letter how shabbily you had been treated over the question of honours and awards, and that my efforts to ensure that you were awarded the DSO were rejected by the Whitehall bureaucrats on the grounds that I could not be the initiator. I know that the then Colonel of your Regiment tried so hard again and again.
>
> Anyway, you have the satisfaction of knowing that all those of us who can be called 'proper fighting soldiers' thought that you should have been top of the list.

General Walker made a comment in the Preface to his personal memoirs, *Fighting On* (prepared by Tom Pocock), that may throw further light on Carver's resistance to the Woodhouse DSO recommendation. Carver had been incensed by the fact that Pocock's first book about Walter Walker, entitled *Fighting General: The Public and Private Campaigns of General Sir Walter Walker* (published on 1 May 1973) was, for the first time, going to bring into the public eye full and accurate details of the CLARET operations in Borneo. The then Field Marshal Carver summoned Walker and instructed him to read the proof copy of the book and ensure that all references to the CLARET operations were to be expunged. At a meeting with Walker the publishers, William Collins, expressed outrage at Carver's instructions and agreed that they would publish and thereafter would not reveal Pocock's sources. On reading his advance copy of the book, Walker was delighted to see the CLARET operations revealed in full.

It has been conjectured but never proven that Carver suspected one of three people – General George Lea, General Walker or Lieutenant Colonel John Woodhouse – of having been Pocock's source and for that reason the DSO application by Walker on behalf of Woodhouse was obstructed. This accusation would be highly improbable as by the time the recommendation had been made Carver would have handed over command of 3 Division to General Cecil 'Monkey' Blacker who would have had to support the recommendation. Though he may not have been a likeable character, it is improbable that the highly professional Carver, with his already expressed regard for Woodhouse, would have stooped to such conduct. There is a further clue in the extract from the letter to David Sutherland: '... I could not persuade the "powers that be" to bend the rules as to who the initiator had to be...'

Woodhouse had never set much store by medals; he thought that having the respect of his regiment was reward enough. When pressed, he did acknowledge that the award of the DSO would have pleased him mostly because that medal would have reflected very well on 22 SAS as, in his opinion, it would not be possible for a commander to be given that particular honour unless his soldiers had actually earned it for him. (In an interview with Alastair MacKenzie, SAS veteran and author of the thought-provoking book *Special Force*, he did somewhat coyly admit that at the age of 20 he had been very proud of the award of the Military Cross and he confessed to having stood in front of a mirror enjoying the medal ribbon on his chest.) He also thought that he had not paid enough attention to making recommendations for medals, especially during the

Malayan Emergency. When medals were awarded for actions on the Jebel Akhdar operations, it undeniably resulted in an increase in the number of officers applying for the selection course: this was not a case of 'gong-hunting' but a realization that this rather mysterious regiment must be engaged in some serious soldiering somewhere.

However, there was another award of which John Woodhouse was extremely proud. The members of the Warrant Officers' and Sergeants' Mess of 22 SAS Regiment dined him out in Hereford and at the end of his speech the RSM, Lawrence Smith, presented his CO with a farewell present. It is said that it actually brought a tear to John Woodhouse's eyes. It was a genuine sardine tin that had been emptied, cleaned and then, in its open position with the lid peeled back, had a small additional 'shelf' added to take a cigarette. The whole thing had then been inscribed and silver-plated by Garrards of London. Certainly it was a unique and fitting gift.

On 21 December 1964 John Woodhouse formally retired from the army, thus ending a twenty-four-year career. On being asked how he felt at that time, he said:

> I had been lucky to survive the war. Lucky to enter the world of military intelligence by learning Russian. I was lucky above all to volunteer for the Malayan Scouts and thus the SAS Regiment when it re-formed in Malaya in 1950. For ten of the next fourteen years I was closely involved in developing the post-war SAS. I found from my war service days onwards that I had somewhat of a gift for leadership. I liked soldiers and I liked their company. I overcame an early tendency to be overindulgent. I became determined to get the best out of my soldiers. My shyness was an affliction I never really overcame. I like to think that I gave of my best and got the best in return.

That same month John, Peggy and the boys moved into Higher Melcombe where he found that the first necessity was to earn some money. John Woodhouse's welcoming letter to John Waddy was heartfelt but he was not a man to shirk from speaking his mind, as is displayed in this letter to Waddy written after his retirement and dated 16 January 1965. It was in response to him receiving a copy of a draft policy document written by Waddy in his position as Colonel SAS and addressed to CO 22 SAS Regiment. John Woodhouse's full and far-reaching comments are on record and his covering letter was quite blunt:

COPY OF LETTER TO WADDY FROM WOODHOUSE

Thank you for sending your draft paper to me. As it is almost entirely concerned with 22 SAS Regiment I do not feel that my opinions should be sent to you without reference to Mike W-G.

So far as Hugh Gillies and I were concerned 22 SAS in the person of myself put forward policy through him, as you will have seen from the files. Frankly I think CO 22 SAS is in the best position to do so and that Colonel SAS should advise but confine his policy-making to matters affecting all Regiments, not the regular one alone. I shall send some comments on it – I have quite a large number – to Mike.

I would like to call and see you and I do not want you to feel that I am being obstructive over this issue. However, I am afraid that if I was CO of 22 SAS I would not be at all happy if Colonel SAS referred to my predecessor and then possibly put forward policies for 22 SAS which CO 22 SAS did not approve. Had that ever happened to me when I was CO, I should have asked to hand over command.

It may well be that I misunderstand your position, and that you intend to continue supporting and advising 22 SAS rather than commanding and directing policy – if so I apologise for my mistake. It is very nice to be asked my opinion and I hope you will understand my viewpoint even if you do not agree with it. I am particularly anxious not to interfere in 22 SAS matters unless Mike W-G asks me for advice. (The only useful advice in my view that I might have will be either where past history and action is involved or where my new job can be useful to the SAS.) We saw eye to eye on almost everything so it is probably not necessary.

J.M.W. 16 Jan 65.

*Chapter 23*

# Mr Woodhouse Goes to War

John Woodhouse's connections to the FCO went back to the 1950s when he was the second-in-command of 21 SAS Regiment. On his retirement he was taken on strength without a formal contract and paid at a rate just a little higher than a lieutenant colonel but only when he was actually working. His overt position was as a consultant on counter-coup, counter-insurgency and guerrilla warfare to the Foreign Office. In that same year, as will be seen later, he became a vice president of the SAS Association.

In June 1965 Woodhouse was asked by David Stirling, who was in close collaboration with Prince Abdullah of Saudi Arabia, to lead a team of three men to the Yemen, and in co-operation with Royalist forces attack the Egyptian airfield at Sana'a. In addition he was to assist, organize and supply the Royalists. He was to be paid the princely sum of £750 per month. His team would consist of Mike Gooley, recently retired after a tour as troop commander in 22 SAS (Mike was later to play a leading role in the Yemen operations); ex-trooper Stan Jenks; and David Bailey (not SAS but the designated interpreter). Stirling's company TIE (Television International Enterprises), which had a commercial radio station in Aden, would provide cover for the Yemen base communications. Woodhouse was stimulated by the situation: he would be where he most liked to be, at the forefront of action with men he trusted and in the mountains that he enjoyed. However, he did wonder whether, at the age of 42, it was wise to leave Peggy and the boys on what he suspected may become a quite risky operation.

On 14 July 1965, while preparing to depart for the Yemen, John wrote to his two sons:

Dear Michael and William,
It is as well to write to you now, so that in years to come you will have some word from me that is important when you are old enough

to understand. I am about to leave England to go to Yemen, there to help the 'Royalists' in their struggle to evict the Egyptian Army. I do this because I have been asked to help; and as you may hear, won something of a reputation for guerrilla warfare when I was in the Special Air Service. I believe that it is in the British interests to force the Egyptians out of Yemen. It is the Egyptians who have inspired terrorism in South Arabia.

In April 1964 Robin Edwards and Nick Warburton of 'A' Squadron, 22 SAS Regiment were killed in action in Radfan, South Arabia.

Before this I sent (in 1963) Sergeant Geordie Doran, Lance Corporal Jimmy Catterall and Trooper Taff Chidgey into Yemen without Army knowledge or approval with Johnny Cooper to help establish resistance to the Egyptians. Now I go to do my best in the mountains East of Sana'a to finish the war against the Egyptians.

When we are finished it is my intention to return to work for the FCO where I am an advisor on guerrilla operations. In 1965 after I left the Army and SAS I have been in Malaysia advising on operations against Indonesia by guerrilla forces. Colonel Mike Wingate Gray, present CO of the SAS will tell you what these visits consist of. I also went to New Delhi to advise the Indians on training irregulars on the Tibetan border to defend India against the Chinese.

Our estate will be much reduced by Death Duties if I die now, but I hope the land will remain and that you will find a real interest in looking after it, particularly the trees which your grandfather established in Melcombe Park.

Do your best to be loyal to friends, to do your duty to your country, above all to be unselfish. You must choose a career in what you like to do, not what you think I would like you to do. You have inherited money which neither you nor I did anything to make. Use it wisely and help others less fortunate when you can. What more can I say except that I love you dearly.

I try to be a Christian but it is very hard to be a good one. Look after your mother, she was very loyal to me and it was not easy for her with our disjointed life. Be brave and do your best and fear not. God bless you.

Your loving father, John Woodhouse

During the build-up to the original Cooper reconnaissance in 1963 Peter de la Billière,[1] as GSO3 (Int) with the FRA, had found himself persuaded (quite willingly) into becoming Watchguard's[2] covert facilitator by organizing the 'Rat Line'. He took care of clandestine visitors and supplies: smoothing their way into Aden, bypassing Customs and Immigration and on into Yemen through the good offices of Sherif Hussein in Beihan. He acted as a secure messenger and received and passed on intelligence. He was recruited into this role by Tony Boyle, an ex-RAF pilot who was the ADC to the governor of Aden, Sir Charles Johnston. He had also been subjected to the charm of David Stirling and admired his plans to support the Royalist forces in Yemen. It was in Aden that Peter de la Billière first met Stirling and very quickly came to understand how his strong personality and powers of argument so easily persuaded people to follow him. At the end of 1963 de la Billière received his orders to return to 22 SAS Regiment to take command of 'A' Squadron. Like John Woodhouse before him, he had risked his military future by his covert involvement in the Yemen affair.

John Woodhouse and his small band of adventurers flew directly from London to Aden. From there they were passed discreetly through immigration and driven to Beihan which is on the edge of the Empty Quarter and close to the frontier with Yemen. The local ruler, Sherif Hussein, was a loyal friend to the United Kingdom and well-known to Stirling. On 22 July they crossed the frontier in trucks piled high with a mixture of their kit, Yemeni kit and Yemeni people. Woodhouse asked himself if perhaps the Yemeni trucks were the most overloaded in the world; not that it mattered, but as a civilian he was experiencing a mild thrill of excitement that probably was one of the main attractions of his past SAS life. They drove across the flat, fiercely hot desert until they reached the foothills and the ancient town of Marib. Once the centre of a great civilization, it showed the signs of recent occupation by the

---

1. Sir Peter de la Billière's autobiography *Looking for Trouble* gives a detailed description of the period.
2. In 1967 ex-members of the SAS formed Watchguard (International) Limited, a commercial company designed to advise governments of friendly countries how to protect themselves from armed rebellion and sabotage. Though that company no longer exists, John Woodhouse travelled widely on its behalf.

Egyptian army that had looted the museum and other buildings. It was during this part of the journey that Woodhouse found that the interpreter, Bailey, was far from fluent and this was of great concern as he suspected that negotiations with the Royalists would be important and demanding.

They were by then a motley-looking crew dressed in sensible khaki *futahs* (wraparound kilts) instead of trousers, sandals or desert boots, mixed belts of ammunition bandoliers and an assortment of weapons. In true Pilgrim style they looked the part of that band of brothers in Flecker's *Golden Journey to Samarkand*: 'But who are ye in rags and rotten shoes, you dirty-bearded, blocking up the way?' To pay their way they carried a mixture of gold sovereigns and Maria Theresa dollars. All of the funding came from Saudi Arabia. They had accepted the assurances given in London that their lives would be safe with the Royalists, being 'on the head of the Saudi King'.

Faced with a journey of 100 miles or so no-one could tell what was going to happen at the end of it; that lay largely in their own hands. Woodhouse mused that this was a salient difference between being a regular soldier who must conform to an almost interminable chain of command and the guerrilla or SAS soldier who has a single responsibility and but one order: win and don't get caught! He felt strangely at home and also at peace with the world. Was this what he had been born for? A war with fewer rules?

They were advised that the next part of the journey should take three days. Their moves were always unpredictable. A 'final' decision to move out at daybreak was not infrequently amended to 'move immediately' in the middle of the night with a good chance of some of the kit being lost in the darkness, or the electrolyte leaking from the radio batteries that had been loaded upside-down eating its way through clothing, camel skins and other equipment. Soon they were climbing steadily along broad plains of volcanic lava, lined on each side by the dark bulk of jagged mountains. They alternately walked and rode. Woodhouse preferred walking to riding on camels but he mastered the difficult art of mounting and dismounting from the oddly-shaped but well-designed beasts of burden. He often had to snap alert as he found himself drifting into a sleep induced by the almost silent shuffling and the soporific backwards-forwards swaying of his mount. When that happened, he would slide off and walk alongside.

His Arabic was limited to greetings and farewells and when there was an explosion of voices from the front of the small camel train it meant nothing to him, but it soon became obvious that there was a need for someone to become the leading scout with a torch and he took on that task himself. A little time later it penetrated his sleepy brain that the well-worn track they were following had probably been mined by the Royalists when the Egyptians held the ground and though his function may be prudent for those behind it was quite the reverse for him.

On the third day they drew closer to a magnificent line of 10,000ft peaks. They passed wrecked Egyptian trucks and other debris of battle; on occasions human limbs, well preserved in the dry hot air, protruded from piles of rocks. Finally the small mud house that had been used by Johnny Cooper three months earlier came into view sitting on a rocky spur opposite the high narrow-walled houses of the village that lay on either side of the green irrigated cornfields. It was high summer and the grapes were everywhere; they were eaten in quantity as they were presented by the villagers. Other food, apart from the ever-available *khubs* (a local unleavened bread) was expensive and dented the hoard of gold and silver they carried.

The party, which had swelled in numbers, was now on a flattish area and that is where they planned to take their first air-drop. John Woodhouse remembered the occasion well:

Soon we prepared to take an air supply drop by night. The Egyptians knew of course that supply drops were being made, and though they had complete command of the air, the secret of how and who by and when was always kept. Suffice it to say that on this summer night, cool at 6,000 feet above sea level we watched anxiously as a haze of cloud obscured the moonlight. Our aids for the drop were not elaborate, and the enemy as well as the mountains were only a few miles away. Yet two minutes early we heard the stillness tremble with the first faint vibration of engine noise, rapidly growing, until like some ghostly Flying Dutchman of the air I saw overhead the outline of the aircraft vague and insubstantial in the misty cloud belt above. Dark shapes appeared swinging below it, and the parachutes smacked hard onto the rocky ground within yards of the drop zone. I had never seen, in more than a hundred drops from Arctic Norway to the jungles of Malaya, a better one. When the excitement of collection was over we prepared to move forward for reconnaissance in the area of the Yemeni capital, Sana'a, where not many years before the heads of my two soldiers, Robin Edwards and Nick Warburton, had been displayed on stakes.

A new base was soon found. It was a wide-mouthed, deep cave with a heavy stone-walled entrance and it lay just under the towering peaks of one of Yemen's highest mountains at about 8,000ft above sea level. On many of the high points there could be seen the ruins of Turkish forts abandoned some fifty years earlier at the end of their occupation of Yemen, which must have been an arduous and unrewarding one. At that altitude the sun still burned strongly but the arid air was never too hot. The Russian MiG17 fighters whined high overhead, symbols of the would-be new masters.

With an escort of three Royalists the British mercenaries went to view the route to their targets. On the way the group got envious but friendly stares as they passed men on foot, donkeys or camels. All were armed with a variety of weapons that were invariably carried on the shoulders butt-first at about chest level, undoubtedly loaded and cocked and many with the safety catches disengaged. The country was rich by Arabian standards with verdant fields with crops ripening on the *wadi* beds that were lined with trees. The village squalor was, however, increased by the rubble remains from Egyptian bombing sorties. All along the way, like that of the Pied Piper of Hamelin, the convoy grew longer and longer.

With great difficulty, as they came into view of an Egyptian position some 5 kilometres further on, they managed to reduce their escort from the fifty or so who had joined in to about a dozen. They planned to climb about 1,000ft to get a better view of the enemy strongholds. Feeling very conspicuous (as indeed they were), they spent some time after the stiff climb sketching the Egyptian positions. Perhaps the enemy was sleeping but there was no response to the recce party's presence only an hour away. They slept for that night in a badly-bombed village, departing before dawn as they reckoned that the enemy, alerted by their agents, would by then be well aware of their activities.

Looking around him at the walls and buildings shattered by the Egyptian Air Force which had dropped bombs, napalm and poison gas without warning, Woodhouse mused on the power of the press. Though the lack of newspaper correspondence would normally have been a blessing to SAS soldiers, it had been a political disaster to the Yemeni Royalist cause, whose case went largely unreported in the early years. If not for the efforts of one man, Colonel Billy McLean, the British government would almost certainly have remained ignorant of the facts and recognized the puppet Republican regime as the official Yemeni government in 1963. Not to worry, he thought, his party was here to reverse the situation.

Pressing on the next morning, they met Gassim Monassir, a young energetic guerrilla leader and a former sergeant in the regular army of the old imam. They had arrived unannounced and at first Gassim did not make them welcome. The sound of machine-gun fire 2 or 3 miles away was the signal for him to use his Russian walkie-talkie radio to contact his forward positions. Shortly afterwards the Watchguard party left, in Gassim's company, to view Sana'a and one of its airfields from the most forward of the Royalist positions. It was a strange procession: they were led by a barefoot very agile old man at a speed that would not have been out of place in a formal walking race. Woodhouse felt the benefits of wearing the skirt-like *futah* which was a boon when taking very high steps while climbing the steep paths. Trousers soaked in sweat would have gripped the legs, allowing only fairly short steps, whereas the Arab dress was totally unrestrictive. The British party was hard-pressed to keep up the fast pace; there was temporary relief every half-hour or so while the old man stopped to announce the approach of Gassim by blowing stirring calls on his bugle. The echoes resounded bravely from the mountain faces that surrounded the column and Woodhouse was reminded of the G.A. Henty stories of the Indian army on the move. They managed to maintain their positions close to Gassim for prestige reasons and his sidelong glances proved to them that they were doing the right thing. Around them the huge escort swarmed with rifles swinging, chattering, laughing and shouting with no apparent cares.

After a fairly exhausting hour they came to a point where the plateau fell away down a precipitous slope for about 1,500ft and to the front stretched the bare plains. In the haze 5 miles from them lay the long landing strips of the airfields, and roughly the same distance to the south was the occupied capital of Sana'a, its walls and streets intermingled, looking small and provincial but still the seat of power, the home of the imam. The Egyptian army had a mere toehold on the foothills of the broad Sana'a valley with which to protect the airfield and capital. It came as some surprise to see how thin their eroded defences had become.

Their relations with Gassim warmed as the day drew on. Having matched his pace, they had passed the first test. They lunched from the communal bowl of a forward platoon; it was a delicious rich meat and egg stew. Morale was obviously sky-high with these Royalists. They laughed and joked and played around in an almost child-like fashion and their respect for Gassim was obvious. Looking at them, Woodhouse felt supremely confident that they could have a marked effect on the situation in those mountains.

The next few days were spent in assembling weapons and munitions and advance deployment of the various Royalist sections. Detailed planning for a raid on the Egyptian positions took place. All this was disappointingly halted when the news came that King Faisal of Saudi Arabia had agreed a cease-fire with Colonel Nasser of Egypt. Having gained all the intelligence that he wanted and having seen the courage and resolve of the Royalist forces, there was no reason, on this occasion, for Woodhouse and his small team to remain in Yemen. His decision to withdraw, however, was constantly thwarted for almost two months with excuses that the camels were sick, the right men for an escort were not available, weather conditions were not suitable, and statements that the cease-fire could end at any moment. There was possibly a reluctance on the part of Gassim to lose contact with these British soldiers who could probably rustle up supplies whenever they were required. Woodhouse was not overly disturbed by the delays in departure; he half hoped that the cease-fire would be broken and give him the excuse to put the earlier attack plans into operation. He spent time going over the plan with Gassim, who was also hoping that the cease-fire would fail.

Finally, at dusk one evening the cave entrance was struck by half-a-dozen rifle bullets that slightly wounded one of the Royalists; they had to have come from their own comrades! Woodhouse was not unduly concerned; if there was a serious attempt to harm them it would have been easy. He conjectured, and it was later confirmed, that the reason for the incident was probably that the men were overdue some pay. Nonetheless, the next morning he told the group leaders that he and his men would leave that day, with or without help. An escort, camels and rations were duly provided at dawn the next day; they were fired on as they left but no real damage was done and Woodhouse regarded it as just a joke in bad taste. They reached Beihan on 26 October.

Back in the United Kingdom Woodhouse wrote detailed reports for his paymasters. He asked Stirling and his parliamentary group not to reveal his name to anyone who did not need to know. That the Egyptian army was extremely vulnerable as well as lacking in any recognizable motivation was obvious and provable. Further evidence of the indiscriminate bombing and use of poison gas was readily available. The Royalists were keen, they knew the ground well and were willing to take tactical advice and material support from the British team. They held the mountains and had a clear tactical advantage over the poorly-situated Egyptian army positions, none of which was able to offer mutual fire support in the event of attack. He was satisfied that an attack on the Sana'a airfields would be perfectly feasible and that penetration of the Egyptian defences would be simple. It would be reminiscent of 'L' Detachment's early airfield raids in North Africa. He did say that British planning and leadership would be both necessary and welcomed, but heavily stressed that the mercenaries should ensure that their advice and support should be strictly confined within a military ambit. It was essential that Saudi Arabia was not offended as it was they who continued to fund the resistance. This was particularly important as he had observed that most of the operatives had no understanding of the subtle political nuances of the situation. Without such understanding, how could they be expected to cope with tribal differences?

In typical Woodhouse fashion, the consummate professional was not going to pull any punches! He took to task the London-based control centre and the lack of properly-thought-out direction given to the men on the ground; in short there was no effective control or leadership. He could find no record of any written directives being given to the mercenaries. An assistant who was primarily concerned with air supply and administration details had no experience of guerrilla operations, which became a cause of friction between the London HQ and the field operatives. He went on to say that in the field the mercenaries did as they pleased. A considerable amount of weapon training took place and both Cooper and Mills had organized successful attacks. Others did little apart from providing medical assistance, radio communications and the supervision of air-drops. He pointed out that because no training was given to the mercenaries, security was always bad. In the conclusion to the report he stated:

> The mercenary organisation in Yemen played a decisive part in defeating the Egyptian occupation because it raised and sustained Royalist morale.
>
> It could have inflicted much more damage on the enemy factions had it been energetically and efficiently directed in the field. Alternatively, if better trained men had been available its effectiveness would have been considerably greater.
>
> Lack of equipment, particularly suitable radios, was a further disadvantage of the 'amateur status' of the organisation, but this weighed more in the minds of the members than it did in its adverse effect on operations.
>
> National resistance movements can be greatly strengthened at a very small cost in men and equipment by teams experienced in special operations.

Watchguard was quick to note the value of the comments and into their operating philosophy went the following:

- Individuals had to be carefully briefed on all aspects of the job in hand including the precise aims, scope of activity, expectations, political niceties and operational and personal security.
- Recruits had to be of the highest order both in terms of experience and strength of character.
- The director of operations had to be just that, a director who directed, was a leader frequently seen at the sharp end and showed that he was as expert as the man on the ground and fully understood their problems.

This had been an interesting and enjoyable experience and, at three times the rate of pay of a lieutenant colonel, a profitable one. That trip marked the end of John Woodhouse's direct involvement with the Yemen operation, though he remained in contact and continued to recommend ex-SAS volunteers for the Saudi-based operation which, under the efficient overall command of Smiley who liaised directly with Saudi Arabia, lasted until November 1967. After that he continued to advise Watchguard on the availability and suitability of soldiers who were leaving the SAS. He had been very pleased to earn £750 per month which was three times the pay of a colonel; it allowed him to pay Rentokil to treat Melcombe House for woodworm!

# Chapter 24

# Super Salesman

John Woodhouse continued to be employed by the FCO for a short time. His first mission, in early 1965, was to go to the Far East and compile a report on the development of special operations against Indonesia. There were some astonished faces among the SAS contingent in Borneo when their former commanding officer, now in civilian clothes, arrived to interview some of the more senior individuals! Given that he had engineered most of the developments of SAS operations in the Far East, it cannot have been an onerous report for him to write and it became yet another document that recorded the successes of SAS tactics.

Back in the UK Woodhouse had little to do initially except make visits to London to attend various meetings. He remembered with some amusement a strange discussion on how a white agent's face and hands could be stained brown to help him to mingle in the Orient. Eventually the research determined that walnut juice would do the trick, a solution Woodhouse remembered reading as a boy in the books of G.A. Henty and Rudyard Kipling.

Veterans of 'A' Squadron, 22 SAS who were on the first deployment to Borneo may well remember being held up in Singapore for acclimatization and jungle training in an area just across the causeway. One of the topics under discussion at HQ FARELF was whether or not there existed a danger to SAS troops created by their white skins. General Sir Nigel Poett, commanding British troops, decided that a certain amount of sunbathing should take place to tan the soldiers' faces so that the Indonesian enemy would not immediately recognize them as British soldiers. Someone then conjectured that if the skins were too brown, there may be a danger of the Gurkhas thinking that they were Indonesian soldiers. So, back into the fringes of the jungle to work up good sweats to lose the tans. One renowned SAS sergeant, Gypsy Smith, was instructed to take a potion to change the colour of his skin. The story goes that it did: he turned green. For a long time after this nonsensical fuss 'Poett Brown' became the substitute word for 'suntan' in 'A' Squadron. It could be that during that discussion in Century House John Woodhouse remembered all this and had a quiet chuckle at such antics.

At that time John was in frequent contact with David Stirling who was using his company, Television International Enterprises (TIE), based at 21 Sloane Street, London to cover his political machinations in East Africa and the Middle East.

In the spring of 1965 Woodhouse, on behalf of the FCO and travelling alone, made a visit to Delhi and then Rhaniket and on to the foothills of the Himalayas where he met the Indian commissioner of police and spent a few days studying the security situation and advising the commissioner on counter-insurgency training and tactics. This was an interesting visit. The situation was real and he was in some of the most beautiful scenery imaginable; moreover, it was a part of the world he had always wanted to visit since reading his old friend Eric Newby's book *A Short Walk in The Hindu Kush*. He was certainly not disappointed. On his return to the United Kingdom he found himself getting less and less personally involved with the Yemen.

The Yemen operation had given David Stirling the idea of what could be achieved by advisers and technicians from the pool of retired Special Forces manpower. He was now *au fait* with the costs of setting up, running and maintaining a mercenary force and he had a good idea of how such a force may be able to produce a political effect. However, the operation must produce a reasonable profit in its own right. His television company, TIE, could not continue to fund the idea. The answer, he decided, would be to form a commercial company that would offer advice and specialist training. He made an appreciation of the situation.

Terrorism was in its infancy in the mid-sixties; the *coup d'état* was the tactic in vogue for crippling or destabilizing second- and third-world countries. The USSR was fast becoming masterly at the technique, particularly in the Middle East and Africa. Definite patterns of events and activities could be analysed as precursors to probable coup attempts. There existed a potential for prophylactic action. The SAS was developing training skills in Special Forces tactics, including those of personal bodyguards. For years they had been involved in all aspects of guerrilla and counter-guerrilla warfare. Many of those involved were the senior citizens of the regiment who were coming up for retirement. Some would be interested in continuing to work in the military sphere. Of course, the target client had to be benignly disposed towards the West, but what better way of getting close to a head of state than by proving that you had the means to prolong his active life? In training those close to a president, one had to engender deep trust. Once that was established it ought to be possible to put advisers into place who were more than military experts. Of course, the whole thing had to be thought out but if it was possible to detect the advent of a *coup d'état*, it had to be possible to thwart it. One would need to become significantly involved in the setting-up of intelligence agencies, and it would not be possible to set them up and train them without gaining access to a lot of information that could be useful to HMG.

By that logic Watchguard International had continued to function with selected politicians and the security services being fully briefed. Stirling had already talked to Woodhouse and Newell in detail about the enterprise and outlined that there would be two categories of potential clients. There would be those countries that Britain could overtly assist and those that it would like to assist but could not be seen to do so. There may also have been a third category in Stirling's mind: those countries that would like to ask Britain for help but were too embarrassed. If those in the first category bought the service, it would be reasonable to expect Britain to look favourably on official SAS Regiment assistance. After all, John Woodhouse's official visit to Kenya in 1964 had resulted in training teams being sent to that country in 1965. It is highly probable that the presence of the training teams removed the threat of a Soviet-backed *coup d'état* by the Luo tribesmen.

Stirling had made his formal approach to Woodhouse in early 1965 before the visit to Yemen. Woodhouse had left the army and become involved with HMG as a part-time adviser on counter-coup measures in some countries of the Commonwealth. In Stirling's opinion Woodhouse had the best brain and was by far the most respected of senior SAS officers who could help him to get the show off the ground. He had, of course, with his deep knowledge of Africa and his respected status on that continent, been of great assistance to Woodhouse during the

Kenya endeavours the year before. Now the nature of Woodhouse's work allowed him to take on other duties as he wished so there was a natural gelling of both commercial and national interests. Stirling fully accepted that Woodhouse's first allegiance would always be to HMG and the good reputation of the SAS. This laid down the first of the ground rules before Woodhouse accepted the post of director of training.

He was to make a number of visits to the Middle East and Africa, concentrating initially on those countries where Stirling was able to make personal introductions, but before that could happen a long time was spent in working out the 'sales pitch'.

In 1966 he visited Kenya to see how the presidential bodyguard training was progressing and then on to Lusaka (Zambia) to meet President Kenneth Kaunda who had been befriended by Stirling while both of them attended Cambridge University and their friendship lasted. A request to meet the president, if it was accompanied by Stirling's name, was usually granted. His brief from HMG was to discourage Kaunda from organizing sabotage in Rhodesia and to support the idea of a bodyguard training operation for himself. Visits to Kenya and Zambia continued for about two years.

In the same year Woodhouse accompanied David Stirling on visits to Beirut, Jeddah and Aden. In Jeddah they met Prince Sultan where they tried to persuade him (as the Saudi Defence Minister) to employ Watchguard to train a Saudi corps d'elite. There was no success in that respect but Woodhouse was surprised at the extent of Saudi hospitality which included the offer of whisky and gin at the prince's house and their host participated with obvious enjoyment.

In March 1967 he visited Malawi with Malcolm M, an ex-SAS officer. He carried a letter of introduction to President Banda from President Kenyatta. He outlined proposals for training a bodyguard which he later learned had been accepted with Malcolm M as the commander. Woodhouse commented that Malawi was not only a beautiful country but remarkably efficient. All meetings were carried out with punctuality and excellent preparation. The external opposition was centred on one communist leader in the Fort Johnston area who was being given clandestine support by Tanzania. Malawi was on close terms with the Portuguese Colonial Government of Mozambique; they exchanged intelligence among other things. It became clear that Watchguard could not continue trying to provide instructors to Tanzania as well as Malawi, so Tanzania was dropped from the programme. The visit was a success and Watchguard gained a contract to train Banda's bodyguard.

May 1967 brought an interesting invitation to Watchguard and specifically John Woodhouse. The invitation, from Israeli Intelligence, had its origins in the co-operation between them and Jim Johnson in the early stages of the Yemen operation, and more recently the visit of Bruce MacKenzie, then the Kenyan Security Minister. Woodhouse flew to Tel Aviv on an Israeli passport. The purpose of the invitation soon became clear. The Israelis, unsurprisingly, wanted to extend their intelligence network. On 5 May Woodhouse met with the head of Israeli Intelligence.

He was given an interesting tour with most of the travel being by helicopter. He saw the kibbutz-based defences and noted the anti-tank guns stored with the tractors and he was struck by the sight of so many deserted Arab villages. There was time off to visit Jerusalem which was then still divided. 'We will get it back,' said his escort, and of course a month later came the 1967 war and they did indeed get it back. He was taken to meet 'Gandhi', the general of Airborne Forces and some of his officers and asked to brief them on SAS matters. They showed scant interest in his highly-sanitized talk; they probably knew just as much about the SAS as he did! He returned to Britain highly impressed by the ruthless efficiency of the Israelis but his sympathy for the dispossessed Palestinians increased. He reported to David Stirling, leaving him to pass on whatever information he deemed necessary.

He formally joined the Hall and Woodhouse Brewery after carrying out the visits to India, Zambia, Malawi and Israel. He did continue to give his services part-time to the FCO and Watchguard. On a trip to Jordan he visited all the palaces, Army HQ, Amman airport, the prime minister's offices and the house of the Crown Prince. The king's security was vested in the 1,200-strong Special Guards Regiment who were also trained to fight as infantry. Woodhouse advised that a close escort of forty-five men from the Special Guards should be trained by Watchguard and that control centres should be set up at Humar Palace and Regimental HQ to co-ordinate the king's escort. He perceived that Jordan had received training from the USA and Formosa; his advice was duly considered but no contract was awarded to Watchguard. The Israelis soon got to hear of the visit and made it clear that they did not want the company involved in Jordan. This was John Woodhouse's cue to return and pay attention to the affairs of the brewery in Blandford Forum and the family estate at Melcombe Park.

# Chapter 25

# The Country Life

On 22 February 1965, as was noted earlier, John received an invitation that he found very pleasing. A letter from Brian Franks, the chairman of the Special Air Service Regimental Association (SASRA) read as follows:

My Dear John,
At the recent meeting of the Association you were unanimously elected a Vice-President with the particular proviso that you should attend our meetings whenever you find it possible. I hope this will please you, I think it is better than your being an ordinary member of the Committee.

Everybody expressed their gratitude for all you had done for the Association and were as determined as I was that you should not sever your connection with it.

Yours,
Brian Franks.

John had been a member of the association for as long as he had been eligible and had been a very useful conduit between the regular regiment and the SASRA Committee. He accepted the invitation with great pleasure.

Over the next two years he slowly began to separate himself from the affiliation to the FCO. A letter dated 17 October 1966 signalled the end of his semi-formal attachment:

FOREIGN OFFICE
Dear John,
I must apologise for the delay in replying to your letter to Myles of the 29th September. It had been due to various people (including myself) being on leave.

As you know only too well, the possible requirements for which we have turned to you for assistance concern several countries and we have now consulted all concerned. None of them have come up with a firm bid for your services in the foreseeable future and as it is patently most unsatisfactory to ask you to live in semi-retirement waiting for something to turn up, we naturally agree to release you from the 'gentlemen's agreement'.

I would like to thank you for all you have done for us. It is hoped that we do not lose contact with you completely and I shall be grateful if you will let me know what you are likely to do next.

Yours sincerely,

'Paddy'

John passed on an outline of his plans: when he did return to Higher Melcombe his initial desire was to set up an outward bound school and at first he felt that perhaps there could be some scope for using part of the family estate, though he soon ruled out that idea. He had been appointed a board director on the death of his father, and now the Hall and Woodhouse chairman, Edward Woodhouse, who had taken over the post when John's father died in 1962, made it clear that he needed him and that left him with no option but to join the team. However, as usual, he had his own terms. Conscious that he had no experience of brewing, he opted to get involved with the soft drinks side of the business. He said that he would work there on the basis of a six-month trial. If he did not make the grade he would resign and then Edward would be spared the embarrassment of sacking him! So he became managing director of the soft drinks division which at that time consisted of Skona and Sunparlour based at the old brewery in Gillingham. Once back in the brewery he became known to all as 'Jock' once more.

Having spent so many years in a strict regimental arena he made a military analysis of that part of the business and soon ascertained that the small soft drinks division, which had nine depots, was so badly run that the losses were in the region of £25,000. This made a poor comparison with the brewery (a smaller business) which was making a pre-tax profit of about a quarter of a million pounds per year! His role was to turn the division into a profit-making concern and his first action was to call in all the outstanding debts owed by retailers, particularly in the West Country. Was it because he had once commanded the SAS that the debtors didn't argue and the money came rolling in? By 1971 the division was showing a profit of £40,000 which inspired the parent company, Hall and Woodhouse, to open a purpose-built soft drinks factory and appoint a specialist sales director (Colin Plain) to develop the business. Based on the success of children's Panda Pops, the company changed its name to Panda Soft Drinks.

An amalgamation of Panda and the brewery led to cash and carries and wholesalers selling Panda products and the canned beers which became instantly popular; Hall and Woodhouse was the first brewery to offer its products in cans. The main depots at Southampton and Taunton became free trade depots selling the full range of canned and bottled ales as well as the soft drinks. As he commented: 'There was a great deal of benefit in the two operations joining forces because it meant that there were less overheads for both sides.' The brewery showed innovation when it introduced fruit machines into its 200+ pubs and began, successfully, to produce Brock Lager which became very popular quite quickly.

He was stunned when he first joined the brewery to note the complete lack of communication and consultation that was passed on by business managements to shop-floor workers compared to the military services where information was given to everyone. He made an early decision to rectify the situation and encourage more consultation with the workforce and he introduced a profit-sharing scheme which was greeted enthusiastically. Like any good commander, he spent time getting to know the entire workforce and their families by spending the maximum amount of time with them. This was appreciated and the workers' attitude to 'Sir Jock' was almost reverential.

He never lost his insistence on punctuality and could show a momentary fierce bout of temper if he was kept waiting for a meeting. The current chairman, Mark Woodhouse, who had occasionally been late for board meetings, had borne the brunt of John's wrath. Amusingly he recollected missing one meeting entirely because of problems not of his own making. When he phoned in to apologize, Jock told him that it was perhaps better to miss a meeting than be late for it!

During all this time he continued to devote as much time as he could to his old regiment and in 1977 he accepted the post of chairman of the SAS Regimental Association. His tenure lasted until April 1997 when he chose to resign. On being thanked by the new chairman and the trustees for his many years of outstanding work for the SAS Association, he responded by saying that the meetings had not always been enjoyable but that the company had!

John retired from Hall and Woodhouse at the end of 1983 but in 1988, on the death of his cousin Edward Woodhouse, the board of directors met:

> The directors met and decided unanimously to invite Colonel Jock Woodhouse to return from retirement to become the Chairman of the Board. He accepted the invitation and later that year in his annual statement to the shareholders was moved to write: 'It is largely thanks to his (Edward's) enterprise, imagination, sound judgement and absolute integrity that the firm expanded in size and in profitability from a profit of £70,000 when he took over in 1956 to nearly £3¼ million when he handed over the managing directorship to David Hart two years ago.'
>
> The word retirement meant very little to Jock and he continued weekly visits to the brewery for so long as his own health permitted. The words 'non-executive' meant nothing either as he was quick to give his opinions at board meetings and strongly argue his case if he felt it necessary.

In April 1993 the chairman announced the setting up of the 'Woodhouse Brewery Trust'. 'A family business meant more,' he said, 'than a business owned by a family. It should be a community in which all the shareholders and employees share an interest and an identity.' The capital had been provided by certain shareholders, the income from which was to provide small–scale financial assistance to employees and ex–employees of the company who through no fault of their own had suffered exceptional hardship.

In an interview by Clive Smith of *The Licensee and Morning Advertiser* printed on 6 July 1995, he said that he had thoroughly enjoyed his time at Hall and Woodhouse but admitted that he was one of the last of the amateur status. He observed:

> I came in from scratch with no knowledge of the industry whatsoever, simply because it was the family business. Today, it is a far more complicated and sophisticated world. People can no longer rely on their family connections to guarantee them a job. They have to prove themselves just like anyone else which is why we have made it clear to all members of the family that before they can join Hall and Woodhouse, they must prove themselves elsewhere in industry.
>
> We have remained independent since 1777 and, with the right leadership and backing of the shareholders, I see no reason why we shouldn't remain independent for generations to come.

It is a fact that Lucinda Woodhouse, one of Jock's grandchildren who had 'proved' herself, now works for the company as a surveyor. She is an eighth-generation member of the Woodhouse family.

John did not confine his activities to the brewery. He took great pleasure in the forestry that his father had so loved and he spent many hours tending personally to the woodland areas of Melcombe Park and continuing to add to the thousands of daffodils planted alongside the approach drive to the house. He supervised the opening of the family home of Higher Melcombe every year for the brewery employees to visit and also to support a number of charities. He was still a trustee of SASRA, vice president of the local branch of the Royal British Legion and chairman of the Ansty Parish Council. He had slowly tapered off his official connection to Watchguard, though he still passed on details of suitable potential recruits for their operations.

In 1974 General Walter Walker made headlines with his organization Unison which was described in the press as a 'strike-breaking force'. He was convinced that the conditions were ripe for another devastating General Strike; on his committee he had George Young and Ross McWhirter, a right-wing Conservative, and between them they sought to formulate a plan to respond to the foreseen strike. David Stirling was invited by Walker to join forces but he declined as he felt that Unison, to be effective, would have to be deployed only on government orders.

Also the press was speculating that Walker appeared to be in contact with senior serving army officers. Stirling would have no part of that as his SAS background would be exploited in the press and possibly bring disrepute to the regiment.

Instead Stirling set up his own response, the Great Britain 1975 (GB75) organization which he invited Woodhouse to join. The response letter was unequivocal:

Dear David,

Many thanks for your letter. My comments are as follows:

You must 'go public' before the election as if you delay and if the Conservatives win it, you will look like being an extension of that political party.

There are too many people doing the same thing independently – the various organisations must merge.

Thirdly ex-officers of the Armed Forces are a liability because they will all too easily be misrepresented.

Finally any support from right-wing extremist parties must be totally excluded.

I would only be interested if the organisation acts only at the call of a parliamentary majority, or in response to an illegal seizure of power by any group whatever its view.

The only satisfactory solution is to get mass national support in a political party which will include extremists – don't ask me how, I am not taking up politics!

I will let you know if I am coming to London in late September, and hope to see you then.

Yours ever,

John

15th August 1974

As it happened, Stirling's GB75 and a slightly later organization, the Better Britain Society, did take a sarcastic hammering from the national press and both Walker and Stirling were portrayed as rather eccentric 'Colonel Blimp' figures. Though Stirling's SAS background was mentioned there was no reflection on the serving SAS regiments and the name of John Woodhouse never featured. Both GB75 and the Better Britain Society are covered in Stirling's biography.

John took his membership of the SASRA Committee very seriously. An SAS man by his very nature tends to be self-reliant and an approach to SASRA for help, financial or otherwise, is often an anathema. John as a respected leader was known and trusted by many serving and retired members of the association and occasionally he would be tipped off, sometimes anonymously, about a problem some SAS veteran was having and this enabled him to make sure that a tactful visit was made to ascertain the problem and help when necessary. In April 1979 he was dealt a bitter blow. One of his ex-'D' Squadron soldiers, the highly-respected Bill 'Lofty' Ross MM, made tentative contact suggesting that he had 'some problems'. Bill was a dour North Country man (ex-Green Howards) and before his retirement he had risen in rank to RSM. At meetings with a number of serving men (including the author) he was reluctant to talk about his problems. Eventually it transpired that a bad business deal had left him bereft of most of his savings. It was a bitter pill to swallow as it was a member of the SAS orderly room staff and the WOs' and Sergeants' Mess who had conned him into thinking that he was investing in a new road haulage business before vanishing into thin air. Most of his remaining money had been spent on a futile diamond-hunting trip to South America with some friends. Now he had only his small army pension to survive on and no home. He was living with his sister and he felt that he was a burden on her.

Bill was too proud to sign on for 'the dole' and the association could only offer him the occasional small loan. John Woodhouse twice offered Bill a job with Panda Soft Drinks but he would not take them. Not having been employed for more than ten years, it appeared that he simply could not work. The word came through that he was in 'dire trouble' but he wouldn't (or couldn't) meet for a chat. All came to an end in early April 1979 when it was reported that he had committed suicide. John Woodhouse, with absolutely no reason to do so, felt very guilty! He felt that he should have recognized the depths of Bill's despair, but this was surely a case of impotence when dealing with a man too proud to talk about his true state of mind.

Indeed, today the association is still frequently alerted to problems by tip-offs from ex-comrades.

*Chapter 26*

# Reminders of Rhodesia

In Rhodesia on 11 November 1965 Ian Smith had made his Unilateral Declaration of Independence. As the years rolled on, the black African political parties of ZANU and ZAPU had amalgamated into the Patriotic Front and, part-funded by the Soviet Union and China, intensified their self-labelled 'guerrilla' war against the Smith regime. The probability of Mozambique and Angola becoming independent resulted in the Rhodesian forces losing the vital military support from South Africa. As the Rhodesian Bush War (as it had become known) escalated, the terrorists continued to commit terrible atrocities against their fellow countrymen and forcibly recruited able-bodied males into their armies. In the UK media coverage of the situation was scant and the intelligence services hungered for accurate information. In late 1973 his old masters asked John Woodhouse if he would make a visit to Salisbury and report on the situation.

Woodhouse agreed with some alacrity, but there were two main problems to surmount. Firstly he was well-known to Rhodesian intelligence as the ex-commander of 22 SAS Regiment so he would require a very good reason to visit the country. Secondly he knew that the only reliable information he could expect to glean would have to come from his old comrades in 'C' Squadron. The first problem was resolved by stating on the now necessary paperwork that he was going to visit his cousin (and godfather) Brigadier L.J. Woodhouse who, with his daughter Susan, was a known opponent of the Smith regime (primarily for religious reasons). Through his cousin Woodhouse thought that it may be possible to meet some senior army officers and hopefully the CO of the Rhodesian Squadron. Assistance from an unsuspected quarter arrived in the mail. A letter from Major B.G. Robinson dated 14 January 1974 read:

Dear Colonel Woodhouse,

You will, no doubt, think it presumptuous receiving a letter from the opposition, but in true SAS tradition Who Dares Wins.

I command 'C' Squadron Rhodesian SAS and spent two months with the Regiment in Hereford prior to UDI in 1965. I have recently become interested in the possibilities of the formation of the equivalent of the Border Scouts. I have been picking the brains of the 'Old and Bold' such as Ken Philipson and Peter Rich on this subject and they suggested that as you and Tom Leask were responsible for the formation of the Scouts, you would be the best person to contact.

The African we are dealing with is in no way anything like the tribesmen found in Borneo or Malaya. In fact generally speaking he is bone idle and wouldn't breathe unless it were absolutely necessary! We have reached a stage in our little 'Guerrilla War' where the terrorists are now bumping off the indigenous. The tribesmen now follow the person who wields the weapon. In my opinion I feel the climate is just about right for an SAS Hearts and Minds Operation which would be linked with the formation of Border Scouts whom the Squadron would arm, train and lead. Once the Scouts had completed their tour of duty they would then form the nucleus of a village civil defence and should be able to protect themselves to a limited extent.

I do realise that you can't possibly be expected to assess the situation having read ten lines on operations in Rhodesia; however, I would be grateful if you could give me a steer on Border Scouts or put me onto the right reading material.

I only wish the Squadron PRI could afford to bring you out to Rhodesia for a few months as I am sure you would be most interested in the situation here.

I trust you will excuse this informal letter but believe it or not we still regard you as 'Mr. SAS' in Rhodesia.

Yours sincerely,
Major B.G. Robinson, MCM.

John Woodhouse responded very quickly by sending a basic paper on the Border Scouts to Robinson (see Appendix). A correspondence quickly developed and with the paper went the news that he would be visiting Rhodesia to see his cousin and it would please him immensely if he could meet up with men of 'C' Squadron. That was just as quickly confirmed.

The situation stirred his memory and his thoughts went back to an incident that took place some ten years earlier. He had been summoned from Hereford to London by a general 'of some importance' who asked how he and his regiment would feel if ordered to Rhodesia in the event of UDI:

> My reply of 'delighted' was not the one he wanted nor perhaps did he fully realise that we should have been meeting our very good friends of the Rhodesian SAS. Perhaps when Denis Healey became Minister of Defence in 1964 I should have suggested that the arrival of the British SAS after UDI would be not only bloodless, but productive of good common sense solutions. Maybe HMG thought that they might lose a Regiment instead of just a Squadron!
>
> Certainly the sentiment of the British SAS was, in 1964, overwhelmingly pro-Rhodesian, but it would never have crossed my mind to refuse an order to act against a *coup d'état* whether in Salisbury or London. Others apparently held the Oath of Allegiance of less account but I was born a romantic, was thrilled as a boy by the words of G.A. Henty, and even now can still feel emotional as the National Anthem resounds over a parade ground and the Sovereign takes the salute. In spite of this, logic and sympathy for the underdog makes me a 'liberal' in politics and I went to Rhodesia convinced that King Canute ruled their land.

He had an eerie sensation that time had been frozen when at the airport the unmistakeable figure of Dudley Coventry stepped out to meet him. Coventry was apparently indestructible and unchanged over the fifteen years or so since they had last met. He was warmly welcomed by every soldier he met, some of whom were known from the Malayan campaign and indeed, some were ex-22 SAS Regiment; all showed the traditional determination to carry on fighting. He was given a grand tour of the country, taking in Kariba and the natural beauty of the grand Zambezi valley. He was impressed by the settled farms of a land once so prosperous and peaceful. It was a very emotional visit for John Woodhouse and he was moved to make a diary note:

> Will no one stand up and say 'Enough of this obstinate folly by politicians, let us get together and build a multi-racial state ruled by those of ability.' There are many here who would like to help and in such a state who would doubt their ability to defeat 'all knavish tricks' now being hatched by our common enemies.

It is interesting to note that not just John Woodhouse had been approached by a 'general of some importance'. In late 2010 Colonel John Waddy recalled in an excerpt from a letter to John Slim, a meeting shortly after the UDI:

> A question for you. Way back in the mid-60s when Dare and I held the fort in the Duke of Yorks, and shortly after Smith declared UDI in Rhodesia.
>
> I was sent for in a hurry by Shan Hackett DCGS (I know him well). I was kept waiting for a half hour, without seeing him, and was then ushered into the CGS's (Cassells) office and the VCGS (Baker – a dull person) was there. Cassells at once asked me 'What would be your reaction if I asked your Regiment to take action against Rhodesia!' I was amazed at my immediate reply: 'Sir, I and all my officers would resign.'
>
> There was silence for about 30 seconds and I thought 'Waddy, you had better leave and hand in your papers.' But, then a slow smile came across Cassells' face, and he said 'Thank you very much' – Baker looked daggers! We talked a bit about the Regiment and especially 'C' Squadron. I believe Cassells had been C-in-C FARELF in the early 50s.
>
> I imagined that Harold Wilson had wanted the Army to take some action against Smith but Denis Healey, then Defence Minister, suggested that the SAS could do it with fewer headlines. Cassells, with Baker and Hackett had obviously been having a discussion, until

Shan suggested that I be sent for. He was then held incommunicado, so that he couldn't brief me.

I was ordered to tell NOBODY of our discussion. My question is (after all that time) did 22 SAS or Dare Newell, in his inimitable way, find out about the conversation? If he did, then he never let on to me. It's all water under the bridge now but I am interested.

Viscount John Slim replied in January 2011 and a relevant extract reads:

Dear John,

My memory is getting worse and worse but I remember the incident reasonably well. To begin with I was in the picture about this but of course had no knowledge of your own visit to the MOD, particularly in front of that rather dreary General who I had crossed swords with about the future of the SAS in a small way earlier on. It was not in the MOD and I have a feeling it was in the In and Out Club when an officer I hardly knew told me he was working in the Directorate of Operations in the MOD. I vaguely knew him but simply cannot remember his name.

He took me aside and said that there was some talk and planning afoot, with the permission of the Prime Minister, to plan for an invasion of Southern Rhodesia of about Brigade Group strength and making a base in Northern Rhodesia. He said that there was discussion that 22 SAS could be used in the role of arriving as friends to shake hands with the Rhodesian SAS and thus as it were entering in a friendly manner with no battle. What did I think of this?

I replied much as you but at perhaps a slightly lower level. I said that did he realise that the Head of the Army in Southern Rhodesia was Peter Walls who had commanded 'C' Squadron for three years in Malaya and after Sandhurst had done 18 months to 2 years with our own Black Watch. He was a thundering good chap and would fight for his country. Secondly I told him that I was sure that he was unaware that the man commanding the then 'C' Squadron was Dudley Coventry, also one of the most renowned and popular SAS officers of the Malayan days. Furthermore there were quite a number of ex-22 SAS, including an ex-RSM, who during a quiet period of 22 SAS had left the British Army and joined the Rhodesian SAS who were having more excitement. If he felt that Dudley Coventry and the Rhodesian SAS would welcome 22 SAS with open arms on the border and in Southern Rhodesia he was quite wrong, Dudley Coventry would arrive with an elephant gun under each arm and they would fight for Southern Rhodesia as hard as they could. I further went on to say that I thought it was a completely crazy idea and 22 SAS would want little or no part of it.

I ended by telling him that off the top of my head if they wanted a role in this mad scheme for 22 SAS then I am sure we would be prepared to look outside Southern Rhodesia at the guerrilla/terrorist camps that were causing trouble from Mozambique and other borders. Thankfully I never heard another word from anybody about this. I of course reported my meeting to MWG who told me to say nothing to anybody (and I never have until your letter arrived) and keep my mouth shut. You asked me if DN knew of this and my belief is that he did. I said nothing and he said nothing and we never discussed it. All I can say is thank you for telling the Generals what the SAS opinion would be.

Yours ever,

John

# Chapter 27

# Envoi

Just as many of David Stirling's wartime contacts helped in the establishment of 22 SAS, so did a good number of officers and men who had served under or with John Woodhouse. They all made significant contributions to the SAS as it progressed through conventional and unconventional warfare with aggressive enemies and passed into the grey world of modern terrorism. Some rose to very high rank where their influence and loyalty was extremely good for the SAS long after John retired from the army. All of those to whom I have spoken held John Woodhouse in high esteem. Two of those eminent gentlemen, Mike Wilkes and Johnny Watts, in interviews with the author regarding other matters went so far as to say that they had in some ways modelled aspects of their command methods on those of John Woodhouse. Consider the following:

- General Sir Peter de la Billière KCB KBE DSO MC* MSC DL, Troop Commander, Squadron Commander, Commanding Officer of 22 SAS, Director.
- General Sir John Watts KBE CB MC, Troop Commander, Squadron Commander, Commanding Officer of 22 SAS, Director.
- General Sir Mike Wilkes KCB CBE, Troop Commander, Commanding Officer of 22 SAS, Director.
- Lieutenant General Sir John Foley KCB CBE MC DL, Troop Commander, Squadron Commander, Director.
- Major General Tony Jeapes CB OBE MC, Troop Commandeer, Squadron Commander, Commanding Officer of 22 SAS.
- Colonel The Viscount John Slim OBE DL, Troop Commander, Squadron Commander, 2i/c 22 SAS, Commanding Officer 22 SAS, Patron SASRA. (Like John Woodhouse, John Slim self-curtailed his own military career through his devotion to the SAS.)

- Colonel Richard Lea DSO MBE, Troop Commander, Squadron Commander, Commanding Officer 21 SAS Regiment.
- Lieutenant Colonel Terry Hardy, Troop Commander, Squadron Commander, Commanding Officer 21 SAS Regiment.

The contributions that John made to the development and stabilization of the SAS were many and varied. There follows a catalogue of the facets that he either directly initiated or heavily influenced over his years of service to the regiments:

- The drafting and constant updating of SOPs and the SAS Rules for War. Most of the SOPs and tactics devised by Woodhouse during the early days in Malaya and beyond were still in use when I left in all three SAS regiments in 1981.
- The construction and development of an effective selection course, the bare bones of which continue to serve the same purpose today.
- His insistence on sound battle discipline which eventually became the norm in the regiment.
- His sheer persistence and fine leadership which established 'D' Squadron as the SAS model during the Malayan campaign.
- The establishment of a viable primary NATO role for 21 & 23 SAS regiments plus developing sensible training for their secondary roles.
- The establishment of the 22 SAS Permanent Cadre which did so much to stabilize the regiment and lead to good career prospects for those soldiers interested in long-term SAS soldiering.
- His efforts and arguments went a long way to assisting in the eventual granting of a Special Forces' pay increase. In fact, just before he left the army he was able to tell the troops that an interim decision had been made in which all troopers would be paid as lance corporals and the number of full corporals would be significantly increased. Proper specialist pay would follow. This was another great career stabilizing factor.
- Beginning and continually supporting the UK/US Special Forces relationship which continues to grow in importance.
- Beginning and supporting the increasingly important SAS/FCO collaboration.

- Successfully turning the initial combat survival course into an army-wide project that lasted for some years and resulted in some first-class recruits for the SAS.
- Laying the foundations for direct recruiting to 22 SAS Regiment from its sister Territorial Army regiments.
- Fighting to increase the strength of 22 SAS which led to the re-formation of 'B' Squadron and the formation of 'G' Squadron.
- Laying the groundwork for improving the multi-skill abilities of individual SAS soldiers by establishing effective in-house training cadres. In the case of the medics the in-house training was followed by attachments to various casualty departments at civilian hospitals. Occasionally it became possible to send one or two SAS trained medics to the USSF for further training.
- The development of instructional training skills as practised by the USSF which became so important during the 1960s and '70s.
- Laying the ground work for the SAS to have its own dedicated RAF flight and helicopter support from the Army Air Corps.
- Paving the way for SAS training teams to be employed in allied countries with the subsequent benefits to the security of those countries and improvements to British political relationships and intelligence acquisition.
- Encouraging the study of potential international terrorist trends and beginning to place emphasis on close-quarter battle with purpose-built training facilities which were later greatly improved under the leadership of John Slim. The training was to prove invaluable as the counter-terrorist threat increased.
- Restoring to the post-war regiments the original ethos of David Stirling's wartime SAS. This stands very high on the list of achievements.

Of course none of those achievements was the work of John Woodhouse alone, but so very often he was the initiator of an idea and an energetic supporter of progress for the SAS. At RHQSAS Major Dare Newell, Colonel Hugh Gillies, Colonel Brian Franks, Major Tom Burt and later Colonel John Waddy all worked tirelessly over the early years lobbying and representing SAS interests to the War Office. Dare had his own 'mole' within the Paras who mostly kept him informed of Para thinking, giving him time to talk to the various COs and prepare viable responses to situations and questions before they were actually asked. David Stirling with his high-level security service, military and political contacts was also a potent SAS weapon on occasions. Also, of course, every commanding officer made, and continues to make, progressive changes or improvements when and where necessary; that is part of the job, but John Woodhouse established an early firm platform for all successive commanders to build upon and remained the officer with on-the-ground experience, foresight, presence and the necessary energy to drive things through at the early critical stages of SAS development, many times through personal example. He truly was the 'keystone' that Newell described.

John was aware that his impact on the development of the SAS was very significant, but he was loth to see it as crucial or memorable. Having gone carefully through the achievements of successive COs of 22 SAS Regiment, I could not find any who had the same combination of the wide spectrum of experience (Second World War and post-war), the clarity of thought regarding the future of Special Forces operations and the sheer persistence and energy of John Woodhouse. Of course all those COs made a significant difference in their own way after taking command; that was part of the job. Nonetheless, I contend that it was mainly the early efforts of John Woodhouse that put the regiment on a firm footing in those formative years. Of course the regiment would probably have survived but the importance of John's input was in the timing, the forcefulness and clarity of argument and the strategic 'aiming' of the SAS needs.

To him it was a true labour of love and it did not stop after his retirement from active service. He was hurt but not resentful that he was not given the job of Colonel SAS. He accepted the reason given that he had not had a 'rounded' career; paradoxically, having spent so much of his service with the SAS, that should have made him even more qualified for the job! He knew in retrospect that he should have diversified but there was nothing available that could possibly compare with the satisfaction of commanding his ever-developing regiment.

It is a fact that throughout the history of the British army many key posts have been filled by unqualified officers who were extremely successful in those jobs. I suggest (without evidence) that Woodhouse may have ruffled too many feathers in his passage through his army service. He was immensely proud that even after his retirement he remained in a position of trust and that he was kept very well briefed on most of the activities of the SAS. On reflecting on his military life he expressed both sadness and anger at one situation that marred the many happy memories of his SAS service.

There will be memories in some of the SAS readers' minds of the days when individuals, troops and even squadrons were deployed in the total ignorance of the rest of the regiment and on their return from 'wherever' no questions were asked because the 'need to know' principle was respected by all. Security, both external and internal, became a healthy habit and much of this habit had been implanted by the teachings of John Woodhouse. An early example of this is when John sanctioned the release of Doran, Chidgey and Catterall (all bachelors) to go to the Yemen. There was a natural curiosity when they returned and when they responded to questions of their whereabouts with 'Oh, I had a bit of overdue leave and I went to see Dad' or some such bland statement, there may have been suspicions but the subject would have been dropped.

Woodhouse was in full agreement with this attitude at the time. Rightly or wrongly (and there are plausible arguments for both sides), John Woodhouse felt strongly about what a proper relationship between the regiment and the media ought to be. There should be no collusion with the media in any form if security was to be paramount. After his retirement he initially remained of that belief.

What changed his perceptions? Was it the general ignorance of the bulk of the army of what the SAS could offer? Was it a desire for some sort of public recognition? Was it a perceived need to assist the growth and permanent stature of the regiment? Was it a subtle way of making the regimental bonding even stronger?

In any event, he began to postulate that the regiment should not hide the stories of its successes, provided that there were no security ramifications. He argued that such an approach would be good for the regiment, assist in refuting some of the trumped-up charges that appeared from time to time making the SAS appear to be a sinister force not under proper control, and it could boost recruiting. During the Malayan campaign John had gained first-hand experience of the articles in the *Straits Times* newspaper and the popular *Soldier* magazine proclaiming the successes of the Malayan Scouts and later the SAS. This had actually worked very much in the regiment's favour and in many ways it followed on into the Borneo Confrontation.[1] It could undoubtedly be good for recruiting just so long as the selection process was capable of weeding out the small number of soldiers who had volunteered for the wrong reasons.

In later years, and after his retirement, he even took part, against advice, in a Radio 4 programme about the origins of the modern SAS and he rarely deviated from his coverage of the rebirth of the regiment in Malaya. There are copies of those broadcasts lodged with his family and regimental archives. He reasoned that the media could become allies in the wider scheme of things if they were given sanitized reports of regimental successes on occasions where security aspects were not being breached. He informed the authorities that he had been invited to take part in the BBC programme and there were, of course, objections.

He thought that the regiment should take some pride in such instances. In looking at a rounded picture of the man it is important to recognize his mindset regarding the matter. Once committed to it, he never deviated from that belief.

John's very personal views on public relations and dealings with the media were shared and largely followed by his good friend General Sir Peter de la Billière. DLB, as he is widely known, is the most highly-decorated soldier from the SAS stable; respected throughout the British, American and other allied armies (in both special and conventional forces) and personally appointed as president of the SAS Regimental Association by its founder, Sir David Stirling. His books are regarded as important reading for military students. An unwise decision to introduce a TV show about which he was badly-informed by the producers led to publicly-cited problems with the MOD and the Special Forces community. John Woodhouse felt very strongly that a distinguished servant of the regiment had been shabbily and unfairly treated and he was never reconciled to that situation. Like DLB himself, John refrained from going public with

---

1. The *Soldier* magazine of May 1966 carried an extensive leading article by feature writer John Saar entitled 'The Wild Men of Borneo' which led to a flurry of new aspirants to the SAS selection course.

his views in the wider interests of the regiment he loved. Those events, since resolved, are a part of the history of the ever-developing and ever-learning Special Forces.

Sadly Parkinson's disease struck and eventually John had to retire to a nursing home at Poundbury, a few hundred yards distant from the site of the wartime hutted barracks into which he had been inducted as No. 5733825 Private J.M. Woodhouse, Dorset Regiment in March 1941. Physical movement was difficult and painful but his intellect was unaffected and he maintained his dignity throughout. On a couple of occasions my wife Janet and I lunched with him at the Fox Inn at Ansty adjacent to the site of the first brewery. The walls of the bar are still a tribute to 'Jock' Woodhouse, adorned as they are with photographs of him and his father in their army days.

I kept him supplied with the sort of books I knew he liked and I am certain that he read them as he would often quiz me gently with questions about the content to make sure that I had also read them; in that respect his memory remained phenomenal. Once, to my great pleasure, I found a stained and tattered book by G.A. Henty, *By Conduct and Courage: A Story of Nelson's Days*, published in 1905. John was delighted and somewhat moved to have a work by his boyhood favourite author that he had not read! Sadly the time came when he could no longer turn the pages of the books but he refused the offers to purchase a machine that could do it for him. My wife has a huge collection of audio book tapes but it was not long before he was unable to manage the controls on the tape-player. He was comforted to a degree by the television and radio through which he rarely missed a cricket match. He took in all the news and current affairs programmes and discussed them very articulately. He had many visitors and he enjoyed reminiscing about his military service. One particularly pleasant surprise he had was a visit from a very attractive and lively Chinese lady: one of the daughters of Ip Kwong Lau. One of my visits coincided with hers and it was amusing to hear her chattering away in high-speed oriental fashion about how her father worshipped 'the SAS Colonel John'.

John was a God-fearing man (to quote his own words) which did not always sit easily with a soldier's duties. He believed in the teachings of Christianity but accepted the widely differing interpretations of religious beliefs which he thought were all based on the acceptance of a single deity and common sense rules for a peaceful co-existence.

The end came quite peacefully on 15 February 2008. The funeral, which took place on 22 February 2008 at St Andrew's church in Bingham's Melcombe, attracted a large crowd of mourners, the majority of whom had to stand outside the church. Later in the year on 24 April a Service of Thanksgiving took place at the church of St Peter's and St Paul's in Blandford Forum. That was attended by even more people from all walks of life. There were men from the East Surreys alongside veterans of the Dorset Regiment; many locals with a large percentage of ex- and current employees of the brewery and an impressive attendance by members of all three SAS regiments. The SAS Regimental Collect which is generally attributed to Walter Evans who served for some years as the army chaplain to 22 SAS Regiment and who was highly thought of by John Woodhouse was read out at both services:

Oh Lord, who didst call on thy disciples to venture all to win all men to thee, grant that we, the chosen members of the Special Air Service Regiment, may by our words and our ways dare all to win all, and in so doing render special service to thee and our fellow men in all the world, through the same Jesus Christ our Lord. Amen.

*Appendix*

# The Border Scouts

The concept of the 'Border Scouts' in Borneo arose from the military/political situation in 1963 that faced Great Britain and Malaysia.

A frontier of 900 miles had to be 'screened' and was almost entirely devoid of road communications. Support for the Indonesians among the indigenous population was confined to towns and villages clear of the frontier areas. Most of the frontier area was either uninhabited or inhabited by tribes whose loyalty was to Great Britain rather than to Malaysia. It became part of our task to persuade the tribesmen to accept the British policy of withdrawal and accept Malaysia as their 'nation'. Attempts by Indonesia to persuade the tribesmen to join against GB/Malaysia were neither well-planned nor sustained.

The initial contact between the SAS and the frontier tribes began in February 1963 when pairs of Malay-speaking SAS radio operators were sent to the frontier. These pairs lived with the tribes, were invited after a time to take part in celebrations, church (in Christian areas), hunting and so on. They maintained for security reasons separate bashas hidden near the tribal villages and entering the village by day.

The value of this initial operation was that it supplied cross-border intelligence (because the tribesmen moved freely across the frontier) and it established over a period of months a very strong friendship between the tribes and the SAS. There were the usual reasons for this: skilled medical advice, practical help (I remember electricity generated by water wheel in one village), but above all the natural tact and diplomacy of the SAS troops, combined with that essential virtue, inexhaustible patience. You may know Dare Newell's advice on sex in such conditions: 'You must not get involved with the women – they may not appreciate your forbearance but the men will!' I can recall no single case in Borneo when trouble was caused through sexual relationships. (I must admit there were exceptions to this monastic rule in the non-Christian areas, where the host invited soldier and girl to sleep together as part of the hospitality, but this was exceptional in spite of what you may have heard in Hereford in 1965!)

In 1963 the build-up of Indonesian strength caused us to propose the formation of the Border Scouts. This should have been a slow process with analysis step-by-step to ensure efficiency and revise the concept in the light of experience. However, the time pressed and we had to form units quickly.

Selection was a matter for the Headman. Not only did he know his own people but it was essential that we did not usurp his authority and so destroy it. Being soldiers we made the mistake of putting them in uniform (even wearing boots in places) and teaching them minor tactics.

Later General Pat Patterson, who was a brilliant soldier and 'trainer', agreed that we would have done better to arm them, train them to shoot, done a few 'contact exercises' and trained them to report accurately on enemy strengths. The Border Scouts were not a sort of native levy with British officers/NCOs. In my view that concept died with the British Empire! We were insistent that they should operate independently at patrol/section level. (There was no higher operating level.) We came by providing long-range radio communications in the form of an SAS patrol in vital areas. This could be contacted by Border Scout 'runners' or of course they could, in some areas, contact an Army post.

Our requirement from the Border Scouts was primarily early intelligence of border crossing. Of course there were other ways of indicating enemy presence than radio. On your frontiers, indigenous forces could no doubt display ground signs conveying information to aircraft on recce, if they are not to have radio communications.

In Borneo military virtues of the tribes were dormant but not dead. As recently disclosed by General Walter Walker in his book *Fighting General* we later crossed the frontier ourselves. Unfortunately I cannot elaborate on the tactical use of Border Scouts in these operations since I presume I would be in breach of the Official Secrets Act, and I expect mail to you may be subject to interference!

In summing up this brief report the essential element is a satisfactory relationship between SAS and Border Scout. We had a mutual respect, and I hope this is possible in Rhodesia.

Obviously there are important political factors, and I suspect you may end up with the sort of 'Home Guard' that we had in Malaya in the 'resettled villages'. In Malaya this was necessary because support for the enemy in the villages was on a sufficient scale to make resettlement essential. In Borneo this was not the case and the tribes were not resettled in the interior.

Perhaps the last point I should make was that we decided at top level that air strikes would never be made if there was a possibility of killing civilians. We remembered the damage to our cause in Malaya when aborigines had inadvertently been killed by bombing in the early fifties. Tactics against Indonesian incursions, if they were too strong for direct attack, were to harass by guerrilla tactics. I have no idea how your enemies operate, but in Borneo in later stages they moved in quite large groups; few were capable of small party operations, which would have been more effective, because they got lost in the jungle! The Indonesians did not go in for 'terror killing'; if they had we were ready to make effective propaganda from it, and rouse the tribes to anger. I think your enemy is very foolish to use terror against you, and I am surprised you cannot make more political capital from it outside Rhodesia. I suppose your political isolation makes problems on this score.

I hope the above may be of interest; it is given to you on the understanding that it will not be made public without my consent.

John Woodhouse
4 March 1974

# Bibliography

Allen, Charles, *The Savage Wars of Peace* (Michael Joseph, 1990)

Almonds-Windmill, Lorna, *Escaping the Ordinary* (E-book, 2018)

Beckwith, Charlie A., *Delta Force* (Arms & Armour Press, 1994)

Billière, Sir Peter de la, *Looking for Trouble* (HarperCollins, 1994)

Connor, Ken, *Ghost Force* (Weidenfeld & Nicolson, 1998)

Cooper, Johnny, *One of the Originals* (Pan Books, 1991)

Dickens, Peter, *SAS: The Jungle Frontier* (Arms & Armour Press, 1983). Republished in paperback as *SAS: Secret War in South-East Asia* (Greenhill Books, 2016)

Doran, Geordie & Morgan, Mike, *Geordie: SAS Fighting Hero* (History Press, 2011)

Durkin, Joseph C., *Malayan Scouts SAS* (Spellmount, 2011)

Evans, Bryn, *With the East Surreys* (Pen & Sword, 2012)

Geraghty, Tony, *Who Dares Wins?* (Revised edition. Little, Brown & Co., 1983)

Hanks, John, *Operation Lock and the War on Rhino Poaching* (Penguin Books, 2015)

Hart-Davis, Duff, *The War That Never Was* (Century, 2011)

Healey, Denis, *The Time of my Life* (Penguin Books, 1990)

Hoe, Alan, *David Stirling* (Little Brown UK, 1992)

Hoe, Alan, *Malaya: Re-enter the SAS* (Leo Cooper, 1994)

Horner, David, *SAS: Phantoms of the Jungle* (Greenhill Books, 1991)

Jones, Clive, *Britain and the Yemen Civil War, 1962–1965* (Sussex Academic Press, 2010)

Jones, Tim, *SAS: The First Secret Wars* (I.B. Tauris)

Kemp, Anthony, *The SAS at War* (John Murray, 1991)

Large, Donald 'Lofty', *One Man's SAS* (MW Books, 1987)

MacKenzie, Alastair, *Special Force* (I.B. Tauris, 2011)

Pocock, Tom, *Fighting General (Biography of Walter Walker)* (Thistle Publications, 2013)

Rooney, David, *Mad Mike* (Leo Cooper, 1997)

Saar, John, 'The Wild Men of Borneo' (*Soldier* magazine, May 1966 issue)

Scholey, Peter, *Joker* (Andre Deutsch, 1999)

Seymour, William, *British Special Forces* (Sidgwick & Jackson, 1985)

Smiley, David, *Arabian Assignment* (Leo Cooper, 1975)

Speakman, Nick & Jary, Christopher, *Devotion to Duty* (The Keep Military Museum, 2016)

Strawson, John, *A History of the SAS* (Guild Publishing, 1985)

Sutherland, David, *He Who Dares* (Leo Cooper, 1998)

Warner, Philip, *The Special Air Service* (William Kimber, 1971)

Wessels, Herman, *A Handful of Hard Men* (Casemate, 2015)

# Index